Revolutionaries and Global Politics

Revolutionaries and Global Politics

War Machines from the Bolsheviks to ISIS

Edited by
Ondrej Ditrych, Jan Daniel
and Jakub Záhora

EDINBURGH
University Press

Edinburgh University Press is one of the leading university presses in the UK. We publish academic books and journals in our selected subject areas across the humanities and social sciences, combining cutting-edge scholarship with high editorial and production values to produce academic works of lasting importance. For more information visit our website: edinburghuniversitypress.com

Edinburgh University Press Ltd
13 Infirmary Street
Edinburgh EH1 1LT

First published in hardback by Edinburgh University Press 2023

Typeset in 10.5/13pt Bembo
by Cheshire Typesetting Ltd, Cuddington, Cheshire

A CIP record for this book is available from the British Library

ISBN 978-1-3995-0555-0 (hardback)
ISBN 978-1-3995-0556-7 (paperback)
ISBN 978-1-3995-0557-4 (webready PDF)
ISBN 978-1-3995-0558-1 (epub)

Contents

Part III. . . . And Not That Exceptional?

Notes on Contributors

M. L. deRaismes Combes is an adjunct professor at the American University and George Washington University. DeRaismes received her PhD in International Relations at AU's School of International Service in 2018 and recently finished a postdoctoral fellowship at the Clements Center for National Security at the University of Texas at Austin. Her research draws on the historical roots of identity and colonialism to analyse contemporary US foreign policy and international security better, with a focus on the Middle East and South Asia. She is currently working on a project tracing the origins of counterinsurgency doctrine to US counterinsurgency efforts in Vietnam, Afghanistan and Iraq. Past scholarship and policy work have covered home-grown terrorism, ISIS, the Arab/Israeli conflict, the Islamic world, ethnic and civil wars, and irregular warfare, as well as the theoretical underpinnings of international relations.

Jan Daniel is Head of the Centre for the Study of Global Regions at the Institute of International Relations Prague. He was a Researcher for the HYDRA project, based at the Institute of Political Studies, Charles University, where he received his PhD in International Relations. He has conducted long-term research visits at the European University Institute, American University of Beirut and Orient Institute Beirut. He has published on the theory of contemporary critical security studies, narratives of security and Islamist political movements, and his research has appeared in *Cooperation and Conflict*, *Political Psychology*, *Journal of Intervention and Statebuilding*, *Global Change, Peace, and Security* and *Czech Journal of International Relations*.

Ondrej Ditrych is the Director of the Institute of International Relations Prague and Associate Professor of Political Science at Charles University, Faculty of Social Sciences. Having read International Relations at Cambridge

University (MPhil) and Charles University (PhD), he became a senior researcher at the Institute of International Relations Prague, Fulbright research fellow at Belfer Center, Harvard Kennedy School, visiting scholar at CERI, SciencesPo, Paris; he worked as an analyst for NATO SHAPE and was a guest lecturer in critical terrorism studies at the University of Copenhagen. He is the author of more than forty academic publications, most of which are focused on critical interrogations of international and (counter)terrorism in particular. The latter publications include a genealogy of international terrorism, *Tracing the Discourse of Terrorism* (Palgrave Macmillan, 2014), and papers in *Conflict and Cooperation*, *Security Dialogue*, *Historical Social Research* and *Critical Studies on Terrorism*. He is a member of the Governing Board of the Oriental Institute, Czech Academy of Sciences.

Jakub Koláček graduated in Arabic philology and historical sociology at the Charles University in Prague and is now a postgraduate student and researcher in the field of Islamic and Middle Eastern studies there. In his work he focuses on contemporary Iranian history, especially in relation to Shiʻi Islamism and political theology, and the environmental history of the Middle East; he is currently finishing a PhD thesis on the Islamic reception of environmentalism and the history of Islamic thought about nature.

Miroslava Kulková holds a PhD in International Relations from Charles University in Prague. Her doctoral thesis examined the dynamic transition of regions from a stage characterised by a lack of cooperation to stages characterised by increased cooperation and integration. She studied at the Rheinische Friedrich-Wilhelms-Universität in Germany and at the University of Toronto in Canada, where she worked with Professor Emanuel Adler as a Graduate Research Trainee. She had an internship at the Peace Research Centre Prague in 2019, where she participated in the creation of the new database on frozen conflicts. She is currently junior research fellow at the VITRI Centre of Excellence in Prague, where she studies the decay of security communities. Kulková's interests cover societal transformations, regional security, the Balkans and North America.

Miriam Müller-Rensch is Professor of Sociology and International Inequality at the University of Applied Sciences in Erfurt, Germany and is Director of the Research Center 'Countering the effects of radicalization and violent conflict in social professions' (RUK). She holds a Joint PhD in Political Science, International Relations and the Middle East from the Free University of Berlin and the University of Victoria, Canada. Her expertise lies in the history, politics and societies of the Middle East and their relations with 'the West' (NATO and the EU), with a special focus on security and development. She is interested in terrorist violence, crime, regime change and migration as effects of war and conflict. Her current research project with the Max-Planck-Institute of Social Anthropology in Halle, Germany, on 'Daesh's (ISIS) alternative mode of governance in Iraq and Syria' combines perspectives of rebel governance and critical terrorism studies with an emphasis on the role of ideologies, religion and identities. Her research includes field work in the region and in Europe in both French and Arabic.

Imogen Richards a lecturer in criminology at Deakin University in Victoria, Australia, and a research fellow at the Alfred Deakin Institute for Citizenship and Globalisation. Imogen researches in the areas of social, news and alternative forms of online media. She also writes on the political economy of counterterrorism and the performance of security in response to social crisis. Her first book, *Neoliberalism and Neo-jihadism: Propaganda and Finance in Al Qaeda and Islamic State*, was published by Manchester University Press in 2020. Her second, *Criminologists in the Media: A Study of Newsmaking*, was co-authored with Mark Wood and Mary Iliadis, and published by Routledge in 2022.

Alexander Ščerbak is a PhD candidate in the field of argumentation theory and ideology at the Charles University in Prague, as well as a researcher and translator in the field of Russian history of the twentieth century and Bolshevism with a focus on propaganda and speech acts. He graduated in Semiotics from Charles University. In his work he explores contemporary argumentation theories and their further application in political discourse, ideology and education. His PhD work is focused on Pragma-dialectics and the applied usage of argumentation.

Martin Švantner is assistant professor at the Faculty of Humanities of the Charles University in Prague (Department of Electronic Culture and Semiotics) and lecturer at the West Bohemian University in Pilsen (Department of Sociology). His general interest is focused on semiotics, cognitive semiotics, social semiotics, history of semiotics, history of rhetoric, social philosophy, theory of argumentation and critical theory. He belongs to the International Association for Semiotic Studies, the Semiotic Society of America and the Central European Pragmatist Forum. He is also a member of the scientific committee of the International Association for Cognitive Semiotics and the editorial board of *The American Journal of Semiotics*. He has published about thirty titles in these fields (in publications such as *Semiotica*, *The American*

Journal of Semiotics, European Journal of Pragmatism and American Philosophy and *Filozofia*). One of his latest works is a co-edited volume on Peirce's Theory of Signs (*How to Make our Signs Clear*, Brill, 2018) and he is preparing a chapter for a compendium of semiotics (Bloomsbury, 2022).

Arran Walshe is a PhD candidate at New York University, in the Middle Eastern and Islamic Studies department. His work examines the intersection of cultural politics, law and bureaucracy in the contemporary Middle East, with a focus on Iraq, and on how these specific and local demands intersect with the politics of broader struggles for social justice, dignity, democracy and power. He is interested in how, and for what projects, we are called to sacrifice in our contemporary world, the histories and narratives of these projects, and how we respond to their demands in our personal, social, political and cultural life.

Jakub Záhora holds a PhD in International Relations from Charles University in Prague, where he also worked as a lecturer and researcher. During his doctoral studies he held the positions of Visiting Researcher at Hebrew University and Ben-Gurion University, as well as Fulbright Fellow at New York University. His PhD thesis, based on long-term field work in Israel/Palestine, investigated the depoliticisation of everyday life in the Israeli settlements in the West Bank through material and visual configurations. Záhora's research interests cover the Israeli–Palestinian conflict, political ethnography, and critical approaches to security.

1

Introduction: Revolution, Hybridity and Global Order

Ondrej Ditrych, Jan Daniel and Jakub Záhora

This is a book about Islamic State in Iraq and al-Shām (ISIS) and other discontents of the global order. It traces ISIS's continuous becoming as a revolutionary movement and its entanglements with the political order it seeks to overturn. It comprehensively compares this becoming to that of present and past revolutionaries operating within the Westphalian time frame that, despite its many tensions, persists as the basic underlying structure of global politics. It does so from the novel vantage point of continental social theory, benefiting in particular from Deleuze and Guattari's concept of the war machine (*machine de guerre*) and dialogical encounters with it.

A number of ontological claims have been made in the endeavour to understand ISIS – an actor that appeared seemingly out of nowhere and enacted a campaign of horrific violence informed by radically different ideological scripts from those upon which the current international order is based. This book treads a different path from most. It conceives of ISIS, and the other discontents examined here, as revolutionaries rather than, for instance, terrorists, insurgents or even *prima facie* (proto-)state builders. All these categories capture some of these movements' activities and have been used – some more than others – to make sense of these movements. To render a picture that is more holistic and dynamic, the book introduces the category of the 'hybrid revolutionary' who seeks to overthrow, rather than capture, the dominant political order by means of transnational revolutionary practices, or at least enact a political utopia radically different from it. Yet, at the same time, this 'hybrid revolutionary' *recodes* rather than rejects the ideas and practices of the constitutive norms of this order – from sovereignty to the neoliberal fundaments of global economy – while also appropriating and repurposing more mundane practices for the everyday management of the revolution.

From the standpoint of the hegemonic discourse of international politics that has a (re)productive power over the system dominated by sovereign states, the performative practices of hybrid revolutionaries that challenge state apparatuses, while effecting authority and belonging outside of the 'trap' of the territorial state, are hardly intelligible or even perceivable. A novel theoretical perspective is therefore warranted for illuminating the operations of these hybrid revolutionaries practising sovereignty unbundled from the territorial state and exercising directional violence driven by certain political utopias on the one hand, and the responses that seek to confront, tame and ultimately eliminate these revolutionaries on the other.

The ambition of this book is to provide such a perspective and, by extension, a novel, theoretically advanced, dialogical and comparative insight into revolutionary agency in global politics across cases as diverse as ISIS, al-Qaʿida in Iraq (AQI), Bolsheviks, Khomeinists and the Palestine Liberation Organisation (PLO). By illuminating the becoming and hybrid operations of these revolutionary movements, the book seeks to advance current theoretical and practical debates on the global order, revolution and violence. It starts from the assumption that the normative order and its discontents are locked in a relationship of mutual constitution and complementarity. Moreover, the concept of the hybrid revolutionary renders visible certain features and intensities of the processes of their entangled becoming. It points to the rhizomatic structure of war machines, their peculiar power of metamorphosis and of forming distinct multiplicities. Yet it also illuminates how these war machines repack and repurpose elements of the political forms dominant to the order they seek to overturn – in particular, the state.

ISIS exemplifies this hybrid constitution. Yet, the purpose of this book is to show that it is no exception. In other words, it is cast only as the latest in a historical series of instances of hybrid revolutionary subjectivity in the modern era. The manner in which ISIS realises certain new possibilities of revolutionary subject formation to become a (hyper)event in current global politics, benefiting from the reconstitution of the great (cyber)steppe that once again integrates separate territorial systems and collapses their spacetimes, is indeed unprecedented. Yet, in its fundamental hybridity and the constitutive interaction with the sociopolitical order it seeks to revolutionise, ISIS resembles the discontents that preceded it and operated in similar structural, *longue durée* conditions of this order.

The insight drawn from the engagement with Deleuze and Guattari's *œuvre*, presenting it not as an arcane form of knowledge but rather as an accessible and effective one, is a bridge, we believe, to a better understanding of the violent pressures, now most associated in the popular imagination with ISIS, to change the global political *status quo*; rendering visible practices that are both disruptive and generative of the normative order in global politics and its apparatuses of control; and opening thinking space for much-needed critical reflection, removed from the quotidian flood of the hypermedia event stream, of contemporary transformative political phenomena.

The book proceeds as follows. The first two theoretical chapters present the conceptual groundwork for the project. Ditrych, Daniel and Záhora's opening chapter provides the main theoretical point of reference for the studies that follow, reviewing the extant literature on revolution to define the space for engaging Deleuze and Guattari's concept of the war machine as a means of interrogation of modern revolutionaries' hybrid subjectivity and as a toolbox for interrogating the constitutive relationship between hybrid revolutionaries and the sociopolitical order. It includes illustrative examples drawn from the case studies that follow. In the following chapter, Švantner proposes a complementary semiotic perspective on hybrid revolutionaries as symmetrically material and symbolic, dynamic, representational and relational *becomings*. Their representation is always a combination of a general *tone* (for example, the feeling of danger), a general *type* (a 'terrorist organisation') and a *concrete token* of that type ('ISIS'). These layers, Švantner argues, are not essential categories, but rather continuous moments in the hybrid process of semiosis.

The next cluster of chapters examines several dynamics that illuminate how ISIS's practices are composed of, and operate in, various registers of the social and the political. The authors show here that while ISIS meticulously distances itself from the dominant order it seeks to revolutionise, many of the elements that underpin its political project are deeply embedded in this order. Daniel, Záhora and Ditrych trace the appropriation of certain practices and political rationalities (including government over territory) as well as *spaces*, such as cyberspace, that have been characteristic of ISIS's becoming and advancing its political utopia of a global caliphate, featuring – ultimately – a single authority and deterritorialisation in the sense of erasing the modern state form and its production of territory as a site and medium of statecraft. Furthermore, they interrogate the 'subject effects' of ISIS's emergence on the international order by dissecting the myriad of programmes that have been devised to tame this revolutionary war machine, from military interventions to governmental projects seeking to create subjects resistant to 'radicalisation' and 'extremism'.

Müller-Rensch follows by proposing that ISIS practices should be situated within larger histories of Jihadi-Islamism, as well as other revolutionary visions. By interrogating the interplay of revolutionary objectives and situations in which the revolutionary subject finds itself, she highlights the constant mutations of its revolutionary practice and proposes that ISIS oscillated in a permanent interstice between the state and war machine modes of political existence. She concludes that, in doing so, the group successfully convinced its potential followers of ISIS's ability to transform its revolutionary, utopian vision of an 'alternative modernity' from idea into reality. From a different angle, Richards investigates ISIS's reflexive relationship with the sovereign, state-based and late capitalist opposition to conclude that the group's political programme is intimately linked to the tenets of the neoliberal condition. She demonstrates that, although ISIS depicted and criticised 'the West' as being in the throes of individualistic, neoliberal ideology, its financial and propagandist operations not only exploited these aspects of the international system but even actively replicated them within its own practices. By unearthing these features, Richards shows that even seemingly radically novel political subjectivities reliant upon the precepts of state and capital serve to reproduce and sustain the existing infrastructures – both physical and ideological – that give rise to them. She then questions the emancipatory potential of the war machine concept.

It is these excesses that constitute ISIS as precisely *exemplary* of the hybrid – dispersed and multifaceted – processes of constitution of revolutionary subjects in the Westphalian epochal time. After exposition of these processes, the attention turns to those 'others', showing how – despite the dominance of the discourse of exception regarding ISIS, claiming radical novelty in terms of a descent into barbarism, an unprecedented global threat, or a particular reappropriation and reassembling of different tactics, strategies and ideologies – the movement is not without historical parallels, and 'hybrid revolutionary' is not a category of one.

The Bolshevik Revolution stands out as a paradigmatic case of an attempted total upheaval of the global order, driven by a political utopia based on a radically different notion of collective emancipation, compared to Wilson's liberal internationalism or exclusionary nationalism, with which it competed after World War I. Ditrych, Kuľková and Ščerbak trace the hybrid constitution of the Bolshevik subject – the party as an *avant-garde* war machine – and how conventional geopolitical thought and strategies also constituted elements of Bolshevik international practice along with non-linear instruments of expansion mobilising transnational class solidarity in the labour movement, while the restoration of centralised territorial governance domestically signalled that territory was never waived as a political technology. They further show the multiplicity of responses of the international community as disciplining in order to tame the nomadic movement, also exploring how they contributed to the movement's sedentarisation.

The centrepiece of the following chapter by Záhora is the problem of sovereignty, focusing on Palestinian organisations and the wide array of their practices oriented towards achieving Palestine's statehood aspirations in the 1960s and 1970s. Záhora makes the case for understanding the political life of Palestinians through the prism of sovereignty as a hybrid constellation. By focusing on – and juxtaposing – the political violence in the form of 'first international terrorism' and Palestinian self-governance in refugee camps in Lebanon and elsewhere, he proposes that these seemingly unrelated actions and practices cohere in terms of the overall project of forming a sovereign body politic dispersed at different sites.

Attention is then shifted to the hybrid nature of the Iranian revolution. In his chapter, Koláček explores the becoming of the Khomeinists as a subject operating within the larger framework of the Iranian state. His chapter nuances our understanding of the relationship between the state and the war machine, showing how the latter is situated in an ambivalent position towards the former, even under the circumstances of an (allegedly) complete revolutionary overhaul. Koláček further shows that in spite of many (mis)representations, the Khomeinists did manifest a clear understanding of the international order and adhered to some of its principles.

Echoing Richards's earlier discussion of the role of neoliberalism in ISIS's conduct and the theme of the war machine and the tension of state apparatus elements in revolutionary assemblages, but focusing on very concrete practice, Walshe shows in his chapter that the extension of market principles to the realm of jihadist practice is far from unique to Islamic State. Zooming in on the phenomenon of martyrdom contracts for jihadist fighters in Iraq following the US invasion in 2003, he proposes that even the predecessors of ISIS like AQI – seemingly in radical opposition to the existing normative order – are informed by bureaucratic regulatory mechanisms and rationalities in order to capture their fighters' desires. Even jihadist martyrdom can thus be embedded in and stabilised by institutionalised bureaucracy.

Finally, in a way continuing the story offered by Koláček, Iranian revolutionary actors are also at the centre of attention of the next chapter by Combes, who focuses on the construction of the hybrid revolutionary as transgressor by the United States as the dominant agent in the *status quo* global order. This construction turns around the foundational norm of sovereignty that in this construction is continuously breached by Iran by conducting what is labelled as proxy warfare and terrorist operations abroad. Nonetheless, Combes shows that this practice of transgression is far from merely negating, but is also reconstructing and reinforcing the norm of sovereignty on the international level through the construction of Iran as a hybrid – *war machine / state* – threat to this order.

The editors' first debt in making this book is to Charles University, which supported the project of which it is a result – HYDRA (PRIMUS/17/ HUM/24), hosted at the Institute of Political Studies, Faculty of Social Sciences – as part of its research excellence scheme. We would also like to thank all our friends and colleagues who graciously commented on segments of this *book / machine*, including but not limited to those who took part in discussing the ideas contained here on the panels of BRISMES and EISA's annual conferences, the Karl W. Deutsch seminar at the Faculty of Social Sciences, Charles University in Prague, the research seminar at the Orient-Institut Beirut, and the Critical Studies Seminar hosted by the Institute of International Relations Prague. Needless to say, all faults are owned by us and our fellow authors.

Part I

Hybrid Revolutionaries and Where to Find Them

2

War Machines, Multiplicity and Rage against the Order: A Theory of the Hybrid Revolutionary

Ondrej Ditrych, Jan Daniel and Jakub Záhora

This chapter introduces a novel theoretical perspective to explore the discontents operating in the Westphalian epochal time frame in their becoming as complex processes and events. The intention is to lay the groundwork for tracing the becoming of revolutionary movements in the contemporary global order while eschewing the essentialisation of and reliance on the rigid categories of contemporary hegemonic discourse to describe phenomena that seem deviant or that have become completely banal (Lawson, 2019, pp. 1–3). To this end, the vehicle we propose – and outline in detail – is a theory of the modern revolutionary approached through a lens of hybridity that is mobilised to destabilise the neat boundaries that often define accounts of revolutionary agency and subjectivity.

This theory takes Gilles Deleuze and Félix Guattari's philosophical project as a fundamental source of inspiration. In particular, it mobilises their notion of 'war machine' (*machine de guerre*) as a means to conceive of the revolutionary subjects' hybridity in a profound manner that complements and advances previous approaches to hybridity in cultural studies and social theory (Acheraïou, 2011; Canclini and Rosaldo, 2005; Latour, 1993; Pieterse, 2001) and bypasses its theoretical flattening, which arguably goes hand in hand with the latter's proliferation in political discourse, notably 'hybrid warfare' (Fridman, 2018; Galeotti, 2019; Hoffman, 2007). The exposition of this theory is intertwined with practical, episodic examples from the cases studied in detail later in this volume.

However, a short introduction and analytical overview of the state of the art of current scholarship are first in order, to situate this theory against the established *epistémé* of (modern) revolution as has been developed for more than 200 years since the first shots were fired at the Bastille. It should be made clear from the beginning, nonetheless, that to theorise revolutionary movements and events as hybrid harbours no intention to '[cast] a net to catch what we call the world' (Popper, 2002: 37). Even more so, it does not try to accomplish this in the service of either revolutionaries seeking to justify or interpret their actions or the state apparatuses engaging in more or less violent counterrevolution. Rather, it seeks to open a space for much-needed critical reflection on a global transformative political phenomenon and to probe its aspects, which remain obscured by a sensationalist flood from the global media.

Revolution: What It Is (and Is Not)

Like most political concepts, the notion of revolution is contested, and *essentially* so (Gallie, 1955). Two great visions, Goldstone (2013) notes, proliferate in the general discourse of revolution. Revolution could be treated as a heroic pursuit of social justice (with variable narratives on the subject; see Selbin, 2010). By contrast, as conservatives would have it – dreams and aspirations of *bien-pensants* notwithstanding – revolution is a foolish endeavour that produces only blood, chaos and the destruction of civilised society. Scholarly attempts have been made to consider revolution as an ahistorical concept featuring timeless core characteristics and basic structures (cf. McCaughrin, 1976). Goldstone's (2013, p. 4) own authoritative definition of revolution as the forcible overthrow of a government through mass mobilisation in the name of social justice to create new political institutions aspires to 'catch' the timeless essence of revolution. Yet, other authors (Farr, 1982; Beissinger, 2013) point out dramatic changes in the meaning of revolution related to the dynamically evolving beliefs and practices of revolutionaries themselves. Over the last two centuries, a general conceptual framework allowing revolutionaries to understand their situation, courses of action and possible outcomes emerged and established itself across a global space (Klaits and Haltzel, 1994; Colburn, 1994; Halliday, 1999; Keshavarzian and Mirsepassi, 2021; Shilliam, 2017). The scholarly reflection on revolution has been a creative process, featuring new interpretations and incorporating new revolutionary experiences into the general framework (Selbin, 2010). As Farr (1982, p. 699) reminds us, revolutionaries – like all political actors – hold theories about themselves and politics in general, which guide their revolutionary practice.

In this book, we conceive and explore revolution as a phenomenon of global politics, one that is temporally situated in the Westphalian epochal time frame of modern states which Ruggie (1986, 1993) contrasts to incremental and conjectural frames of social time. Ruggie's premise is that time varies in duration but also in form. It can be a succession of discrete units; it can be thought in terms of cycles or similar temporal movements; or it can have as a frame of reference some structural arrangement governing the functioning of a system within certain boundary conditions. The last is the epochal time. For heuristic (rather than definitional) purposes – as we recognise revolution as an always transforming and contested political concept – we approach it as *a radical transformation in the normative order and its institutions following a certain political utopia over a relatively short period of time and often by resorting to violence*. Revolution conceived as such does not gesture toward a mere relocation of sovereignty, Machiavelli's *mutazioni del stato*, but rather to something 'altogether new' (Arendt, 2006, p. 36) – even if the 'new' is really a hybrid composite of elements, including the 'old' affixed in new constellations which, however, push systems beyond their boundary conditions. Furthermore, taking a cue from the proposition that there is constant labour invested in enacting and (re)interpreting revolution (even on its protagonists' part), and more broadly embracing a process perspective, we argue that revolution is also not something that is simply *done* – as a momentous passing of a certain threshold – but rather is dynamically *becoming*.

Several points of caution are in order. First, one should beware of the traction of social myths that make us interpret revolutionary action as a confrontation of (pure) totalities. Second, revolution as effecting a radical transformation is indeed a modern invention which departs from the earlier ('astronomical') notion of revolution as restoration and recurrence. That said, the patterns of thought and practice of radical transformation predate European modernity – millenarianism, chiliasm and various related social projects underlined by Western eschatological thought are only a few testimonies, as are the Puritans settling in New England's *voyage to the end of time* (Bercovitch, 1975, p. 91). The recurrence previously associated with the movement of celestial objects was later reinscribed in the *study* of revolutions, which both were always an attempt at a radical break and simultaneously followed certain established patterns, allowing for a ('scientific') generalisation (Geuss, 2004, p. 107). The 'new' may also not just incorporate elements of the old but be choreographed along the lines of a political utopia of a Great Return, even while drawing on other repertoires of modernity. This is clearly the case with ISIS (and its predecessors) in its primeval restorative project of the Caliphate, which was imagined to challenge the dominant temporality of the Westphalian epochal frame. Yet, these are only seeming deviations from the classic examples of modern revolutions, for even the protagonists of the American (1776) and French (1789) Revolutions often spoke and acted, in the beginning, in advocacy of restoring ancient liberties, invoking classical Greek and Roman virtues of government (Rao, 2016, p. 259) and, by extension, creating a modern version of the ancient Republic. Third, in our definition, revolution features both radical change – speeding the wheel of history in a certain (possibly even *backward*) direction – and extralegality. While extralegality is also a constitutive feature of counterrevolutionary practice, whereby (state) sovereignty, which is located outside the realm of law and seeks to contain subjects within this realm (Agamben, 2005), suspends the law, the game of extralegality and sovereignty is more complex. While the sovereign exercises exceptional powers to meet the challenge of the revolutionaries, it should not be forgotten that domestic and international revolutionaries reconfigure the norm and practise sovereignty on their own terms, establishing new forms of legality and extralegality (see Hansen and Stepputat, 2006). With these caveats made, let us now turn to how 'revolution' is conceived as 'international' and a matter of global politics in the scholarship.

International Revolution: State of the Art

The dominant story of classic modern revolutions was the one about revolutionaries seizing control of a particular state. However, many revolutionary processes unfold in local and national spaces, yet also transcend them (Halliday, 1999; Lawson, 2019). This has not been lost on studies exploring the international side of revolution that constantly encounters numerous tensions between different levels of analysis. In general, the scholarship on revolutions is often divided into different theoretical generations according to the dominant focus and method of explanation (Beck, 2020; Lawson, 2016; Goldstone, 1980, 2001; Rao, 2016). This results in a categorisation as imprecise as any other intellectual attempt to pigeonhole different thinkers, yet one that has defined the canon of revolution studies. In brief, successive generations have shifted the dominant focus of enquiry from the natural, historical patterns of revolution within the so-called first generation (Brinton, 1965) to psychological and sociological motivations for collective revolutionary action in the second (Davies, 1962), and structural factors influencing the initiation and course of revolutionary processes in the state-centred third generation (Skocpol, 1979; Goldstone, 1991). The fourth generation (Selbin, 2010; Emirbayer and Goodwin, 1996; Foran, 2005; Ritter, 2015) arguably moved on to an exploration of a more complex set of different structural and symbolic factors, their interplay and the agency of revolutionaries, which together contribute to the onset of a revolution, its course and its outcomes (Abrams, 2019; Lawson, 2016).

Importantly for the present volume, although all four generations acknowledge that a revolution is a phenomenon with causes, processes and consequential impacts which transcend the confines of a nation state, and revolutionary ideologies are often distinctly global in their imaginations of change, the 'international' dimension of revolution has received only scant attention in revolutionary studies (Beck, 2020; Lawson, 2019). Some theorists of revolution have explicitly highlighted the role of international systems in shaping revolutionary processes, pointing to the position of particular states in the international system that make them prone to revolution (Beck, 2014; Foran, 2005; Skocpol, 1979; for overview see Goldstone, 2001). Others have explored how ideas travel between local, national contexts and contribute to the emergence of distinct revolutionary waves (Halliday, 1999; Katz, 1999; Motadel, 2021; Weyland, 2014). Many have also enquired how global orders defined by certain types of norm (Beck, 2015; Bukovansky, 2002; Ritter, 2015), as well as racialised hierarchies (Shilliam, 2008; Gaffield, 2020), inform revolutionary (and counterrevolutionary) practice. Regardless, even as these studies embed revolutionary processes in ideational and material structures of the international and show how revolutions are conditioned by certain forms of the international order – which they have a potential to reshape through normalisation and the recognition of a different form of political rule – they largely retain the inside/outside dichotomy.

Similar tendencies – though admittedly rare – can be traced in studies theorising revolution in the field of International Relations (IR). For instance, Armstrong (1993) identified revolutionary states as a distinct actor in international politics and highlighted their interactions with hegemonic international norms (on this see also Terhalle, 2009; Vu and Van Orden, 2020). Although not advancing a specific theoretical approach, Halliday's (1999) influential book comprehensively outlined numerous ways in which revolutions influence international politics, specifically showing their impact on norms and the shape of the international order, connections between revolutions and foreign policy-making, or distinct forms of war waged by revolutionary movements and states. Finally, Lawson's (2019) more recent study seeks explicitly to incorporate the international dimension of revolution and proposes a synthesis in the form of an intersocial approach to revolutions. In his focus on the embeddedness of revolutionary processes in transnational spaces, Lawson connects IR with the field of global history and postcolonial studies, both of which highlight the often-overlooked role of subaltern resistance in the shaping of the international order and its norms (see also Jabri, 2014). Lawson particularly argues for the embeddedness of a revolution in multiple processes that unfold on different scales from local to transnational. In his account, nearly every revolution is (or at least could be) a transnational event as its causes can be located beyond national borders; a revolution is connected in both its inspiration and its aspirations with ideas that do not reside solely in a national space; finally, and similarly, the material and symbolic consequences of a revolution resonate internationally.

Our approach toward the study of revolution builds on the insights of the scholarship discussed, all of which illustrates how revolutionary subjectivities and practices defy the neat distinctions between a national inside and an international outside. By treating the revolutionary subject as hybrid and transcending these distinctions by default, we seek to go beyond the conceptualisation of the international merely as a force impacting domestic political processes. This line of thinking – which we seek to amplify in this volume – is present in works that, first, emphasise the transnational dimension of revolutionary visions and practices (Halliday, 1999); second, point out the sense-making bricolages concerning revolutionary practices that draw on heterogenous domestic and international narratives and repertoires (Selbin, 2010); or third, highlight how a variety of domestic and international actors come together and are impacted by revolutionary projects (Nepstad, 2011). Similarly, we further attend to the new landscapes of networked societies which arguably not only facilitate the previously unimaginable proliferation of revolutionary ideas and their translation into practice (Chenoweth, 2020; Zivkovic and Hogan, 2008) but also enable the emergence of new global solidarities and exchanges (Perea Ozerin, 2021), as well as activist movements that operate in the new global territory of cyberspace (Kraidy, 2017; Page, 2021). In doing so, we do not propose that revolutionary movements operating in what is often labelled as 'late modernity' are radically different from their predecessors. To the contrary, as chapters in this volume demonstrate, we argue that revolutionary conduct and thinking, at least since the fall of the Bastille, have always (in different intensities and forms) been characterised by various political registers that neither followed territorial boundaries, nor simply subscribed to reproducing formal political structures; the current conditions rather modify and sometimes amplify these dynamics. Thus we seek to address the problem of the analytical straitjacket of the Westphalian time frame, which obscures how revolutionary subjectivity and agency exceed, but also draw on, the dominant sociopolitical order.

We push forward in this direction by advancing theories of revolutionary action that overcome the established structure/agency binary. This strategy is accomplished with a distinct focus on revolutionary performances, the constitution of revolutionary actors' subjectivity, and their entanglement with the international order that they seek to upend following radical political utopias. It therefore engages in a dialogue with existing scholarship to provide a novel perspective, in particular on the formations of revolutionary actors, that accentuates the mutual constitution of the dominant sociopolitical order and its discontents. More precisely, the argument put forth here advances the notion of revolutionary actors in the modern epochal time frame as 'hybrid'. Who are these hybrid revolutionaries and, as many have asked before with regard to the concept of hybridity (for example, Pieterse, 2001), why is it worth considering them as hybrid?

Hybrid Revolutionary as a War Machine

The revolutionaries covered in this volume are discontents of the modern epochal time frame. The revolutionary political utopia that governs and guides their efforts transcends the boundaries of the state. (We do not take an interest in rebels seeking to rule within the state's confines while not making the organs of the new 'revolutionary' state a means to advancing this utopia further.) In varying intensities, it negates the notion of the striated plane of states with reaches of their sovereignty delimited by national boundaries: the idealised, to some even fundamentally hypocritical, notion (Krasner, 1999) that persists as central to contemporary discourse and practice of international relations despite its many tensions and contestations (see, for example, Aalberts, 2016; Bartelson, 2014). These revolutionaries seek to enact political utopias founded on radically alternative visions of the dominant normative order (at least, until the moment they are resocialised into it): that is why they deserve the 'revolutionary' label. They challenge state apparatuses, often by violent means, but they also bring authority and belonging outside of the trap of the territorial state (Agnew, 1994). They revolt against the dominant normative order yet cannot completely disassociate from it, instead maintaining a productive relationship with it. As a result, they do not *reject* sovereignty as a contested yet still constitutive norm of this order – not merely a regulative arrangement (that defines basic parameters of interaction) but betraying a power of ordering so as to create possibilities for political action (Ashley, 1988; Walker, 1993). They *recode* it. The recoding and repurposing of this norm, along with other elements in these new combinations in the process of their (continuous) becoming, is a fundamental feature of these revolutionaries' subjectivity. It is also what makes them fundamentally hybrid.

What is meant by this recoding of sovereignty? The point of departure is understanding sovereignty not as an essential, totalising concept but as a set of historically situated practices (Hansen and Stepputat, 2006; Bartelson, 2014; Weber, 1995). Contravening the myth of the modern state as an arborescent structure where sovereign power (and biopower) is centralised, global politics abounds with uncomfortable, sometimes contradictory relationships to the Westphalian order's lines. These range from cases of states that promote and benefit from the affective belonging of diasporas (Ragazzi, 2009), through the dispersed sovereignty performed by 'petty sovereigns' (Butler, 2004), to exercise of sovereign powers *outside* the states by diverse types of non-state actors (Fassin and Pandolfi, 2010; Arjona et al., 2015) in complex 'sovereignty-scapes', where the performance of sovereign power may be rearticulated by all who engage in it, state administrations included (Stepputat, 2013; Fregonese, 2012). The revolutionary recoding of sovereignty alludes to the latter process in which interacting codes of power (as systems of signification) of the state and the revolutionary are hybridised and become difficult, if not impossible, to distinguish from each other. To put it simply, revolutionaries might want to govern differently and create a novel political utopia; however, parts of their revolutionary practices and administration of newly created polities often rely on familiar scripts of past and present political orders. Several chapters in this volume trace such dynamics, including Ditrych, Kulková and Ščerbak's portrait of Bolsheviks as '(arche)typical troublemakers' or Záhora's study of how various Palestinian groups in the 1960s and 1970s enacted sovereign norms while at the same time criticising the existing global and regional orders.

Yet, there is more to revolutionary practice than simply mimicking and transforming familiar sovereignty scripts. It entails recoding not as mutual modification but as an attempt at a more fundamental, wilful rewriting of the sovereignty code. In this case, the sovereignty claims of the revolutionary subject are unbundled from territory and thus *deterritorialised*, resisting essentialism and totalising structures and knowledges – the arborescent apparatus of representation and signification, as discussed by Švantner in this volume. These performances of sovereignty should thus be conceived rather as a multiplicity, a constant motion of decentred components that transcends the Westphalian 'statescape'.

To make this recoding intelligible, and even *visible*, is difficult within the confines of the dominant reading of global politics, which is an integral part of its dispositif (*agencement*): an arrangement establishing a certain structure of relations in a field that itself needs to be established and visualised for the purpose of government. The dispositif does so by distributing the visible and the invisible according to its particular 'regime of light' (Deleuze, 1992, cf. Foucault, 1977). Reified concepts proliferating in this reading do justice only to selective facets of revolutionary practice at best. At worst, they narrow our field of vision to propagate the image of revolutionaries as an absolute enemy, a *hostis humani generis*, a pest to be destroyed because it cannot be reduced or contained, and one divested of its political character when its subjectivity is rendered in other, particularly moral categories – as has indeed been the case with the 'terrorist' (Ditrych, 2014).

In this book, we seek to illuminate the dynamic, composite and relational becoming of revolutionaries as hybrid, and in doing so to contribute to the broader project of a 'cartography of power' in contemporary politics, which seeks to render visible abstract forces generative of the organisation of social systems (cf. Deleuze, 1975). To accomplish this, we propose to draw inspiration, first and foremost, from Deleuze and Guattari's (1987) war machine (*machine de guerre*). Faithful to their philosophical project, we do not conceive of the war machine as a concept, a notion or a (Platonic) idea that can be realised more or less perfectly but rather a set of intensities that can be *activated*. It is not to serve as a totalising theoretical straitjacket. Indeed, later in the book, it is subjected to dialogical encounters with other means of interpreting the investigated movements' hybrid revolutionary practice. With this caveat in mind, what is this war machine, and what does it do?

The war machine in Deleuze and Guattari's nomadic science is the irreducible element of war and revolutionary change that has resisted, over the course of history, appropriation by the state. It has remained outside the state, occupying a milieu of exteriority ('steppe'), a smooth space of pure existence without enclosures (Patton, 1984). The smooth space is manifestly different from the striated space produced by the interiorisation function of the state that captures, measures, regulates and so makes 'governable' (see Elden, 2013). The original Inner Asia's steppe as the habitat of the nomad (Massumi, 1996), the ocean and now cyberspace each represent such milieus of exteriority. In the modern epochal frame, the striated space of the state(scape) expanded to reach near-totality. Yet, the possibility remains for the emergence, from within this dominant sociopolitical order, of nomadic war machines: revolutionary projects that resist the inside/outside separation and constitute heterotopic pockets of smooth space in the Westphalian statescape (some, indeed, with a totalising ambition)[1] – pockets that can be connected by reaching to the virtual steppe of cyberspace as a new, autonomous plane of existence. As we show later in the volume, this feature is exemplified by ISIS with its online outreach which enables to construe political subjection as a process that transcends national boundaries – while maintaining the putatively same group engaged in highly localised and often mundane activities.

A war machine may be conceived as a *diagram* of the strategy of power (Foucault, 1977) that is in a relationship with another such diagram: the state. The two are radically distinct. Producing two different types of space at the interstice of which war takes place, the state seeks to conserve its organs while the war machine is just that, a *machine* and so a body *without* organs (Deleuze and Guattari, 1986). It seeks dispersal and freedom from the bind of striation. Because of this, the state desires to recapture it, internalising and making

governable the smooth space it produces. The manifest failure of internation-
alisation must be removed, and so too must the discomforting, suppressed
memory that the state, an 'empty form of appropriation', was once also a
war machine that perished by sedentarisation. This is how the war machine
perishes: by becoming a (normal) state, a member of the international society.
Such a development is captured by Ditrych, Kulková and Ščerbak in their
reflection on the Bolshevik party and how its revolutionary project collapsed
after Red October into a bureaucratic and despotic state form. Alternatively,
the war machine is destroyed or appropriated as a state's supplemental organ
– a militia turned military, a hybrid violent entrepreneur, or a cyber hacking
group enrolled in a state's service – with its destructive capacity turned out-
wards.

The war machine and the state apparatus are distinct: two diagrams, or two
heads, of political power (Deleuze and Guattari, 1987, p. 351), two specific
sign regimes, imperial and nomadic. Their relationship, however, is also one
of contingent complementarity. This complementarity, in which the possible
functions of the field are activated, produces contingent *hybrids* rather than
pure forms in a process of 'mutated' semiosis in which material, ideational,
biological, social and technological components are integrated (Deleuze and
Guattari, 1987, p. 119; Švantner, this volume). Therefore, any war machine
is a heterogeneous assemblage characterised by a multiplicity (Deleuze and
Guattari, 1987, p. 43) of co-functioning, strategically linked elements and
entire ontological *orders* that, unlike the body organs, subsist independently.
Importantly, such elements comprise forms borrowed ('appropriated') from
the state that are repurposed and recoded; *vice versa*, forms are appropriated
from the war machine and enrolled in the apparatus of the state. Koláček
demonstrates this in this volume when he shows how, following the 1979
revolution, the Khomeinists continued to challenge the newly formed revolutionary state and the order in which it was embedded, while they were, at
the same time, tamed by restrictions imposed by either. In her take on Iran's
case, Combes then highlights another face of the complementarity relationship, tracing how depictions of Iran as a norm breaker reaffirmed the dominant
norm of the existing order, sovereignty.

'The importance of hybridity is that it problematizes [the] boundaries'
(Pieterse, 2001, p. 220) of seemingly clear-cut categories and identities. A war
machine and state assemblages are, from this perspective, constituted matters
that are fundamentally hybrid – creating strata of different planes (content and
matter, actants and actors). Moreover, they are locked in a constitutive relationship of contestation but also mutually enacted hybridisation. In the case of
ISIS, this hybridisation may entail bureaucratic or tribal forms of governance

– the surprising degree of bureaucratisation for a movement associated with networks as a progressive form of social association that has been suggested to be emulated in counterterrorist apparatuses (cf. Arquilla and Ronfeldt, 2001; Ganor, 2009) was already pointed out in relation to al-Qaʻida (Shapiro, 2013). It may also entail snippets of cultural codes ('popular culture') enmeshed in mobilisation (recruitment) narratives or employing elements of the dominant forms of subjectification, such as making and remaking the neoliberal subject (Chouliaraki and Kissas, 2018; Richards, 2020; Roy, 2017). As Richards proposes in this volume, this inability to escape the dominant neoliberal framework even on the part of the supposedly novel formation of ISIS (manifested in its bureaucratic and financial apparatus) betrays the extent to which revolutionaries are embedded in the existing normative order. Similarly, discussing the martyrdom contracts proliferating in Iraq after the US invasion, Walshe points out the individualising and contractual rationales underpinning the jihadist political project which, on the face of it, is diametrically opposed to them.

The repurposing and recoding functions that make it hybrid are closely related to the revolutionary war machine's power of protean metamorphosis, which can be related to its particular *network* morphogenesis (see Sageman, 2004) – a formative innovation that inspires appropriation by state (for a critical reflection see Stohl and Stohl, 2007) and corporate business apparatuses seeking to tackle complexity and infuse creativity into their inert and comatose forms. The abstract functions of the network are horizontality, simultaneity, constant spontaneous reordering through the elements, the (re)creation of their connections and shock resilience. As it enters new spaces and encounters new matters, the war machine transforms previously existing lines of association into non-organic social relations of the militant assemblage. Furthermore, it engages in a contingent process of constitutive ordering that *repurposes* – creates a despotic state machine, such as a temporarily territorialised 'Leviathan in the Levant', that enacts spectacular horror performances of sovereignty (Jabareen, 2015; Kraidy, 2018) – and *recodes*, such as when ISIS's war machine enacts a translocal, territorially unbundled political community characterised by affective belonging that transcends national borders. In ISIS's case, both these forms have been in tension with the nomadic rationality of the war machine and each other, producing a triangular controversy that, notwithstanding the general line of force that arranges the elements of its assemblage and the singular (alternative and limital) spacetime in which it operates, is a display of its schizophrenia. A furthering of this line of enquiry is provided later in this volume by Müller-Rensch, who argues that ISIS and the success (even if temporary) of its political project need to be seen in the light of its reappropriation and reassembling of practices and programmes of jihadist as well as secular revolutionary movements.

The war machine's assemblage is ever in motion – an event, not an essence, whereby the becoming in which the metamorphosis takes place occurs incessantly, never to be complete (Nail, 2017). Like a rhizome rather than a tree (Evans and Guillaume, 2010), 'it has no beginning or end, only a middle, from where it expands and overspills' (Bleiker, 2015, p. 883), enrolling elements with molecular identities, interests and tactics to follow a general line of force through dispersed (and sometimes incoherent and internally controversial) action. In this motion, concurrently or one after another, both territorialisation and deterritorialisation practices can be traced – the latter, as in the case of ISIS, encompassing both a *hydra*-like nomadic insurgency and a community of belonging that transcends extant formations of sovereignty and seeks to empower those who were rendered on the outside of the totalising subject of 'humankind' by the dominant framing of the body politic. The motion may entail not just shifting spatial but also temporal patterns, both aligned with and challenging the hegemonic temporality. The challenge can occur through the acceleration of an apocalyptic time, documented in the case of ISIS as facilitating transnational political mobilisation and immersion in the millenarian project of the Caliphate (Berger, 2015) with effects on the subject constitution performed at the very end of time.[2] Space and time are not independent terms of reference for events. The hybrid revolutionaries may challenge both the dominant spatial and temporal orders. Where sovereignty as unity imposes temporal synthetisation (Reid, 2010; Walker, 1993), various elements of the revolutionaries' assemblage may abide by different times in their – sometimes internally controversial – multiplicity.

Therein lies the utility of the war machine for the concept of revolutionary as hybrid. It signifies a radically alternative positionality toward the order currently made of state(s): the Westphalian statescape. At the same time, it pierces through the hybridity entailed in the processes of constitution for revolutionary subjectivity as a dynamic becoming and metamorphosis of a multiplicity of forms, including some that are repurposed and recoded from the imperial (state) regime, such as the Westphalian statescape's constitutive norm of sovereignty. It illuminates the generative structures of meaning through which resistance to the dominant order is made intelligible, including to the revolutionaries *themselves*, or the normalisation ('sedentarisation') processes they experience under the order's pressure.[3] No less importantly, the relationship of contingent complementarity suggests exploration not only of their (hybrid) subject *constitution* but also of the *effects* on the dominant order and its apparatuses of control. Like Jabri's (2012, 2014) colonised subjects and as some of the

theorists of revolution outlined above have already recognised, modern revolutionaries shape the dominant order that they challenge by means of *resistance*
but also in their very *presence*, provoking responses that range from exceptional,
violent disciplining at the peripheries, eliminating the 'pest' through a liberal
intervention that stresses the normative core of the order, to the introduction
of new governmental programmes ('counterradicalisation') with problemati-
sations and political technologies of stabilisation and normalisation that are
defined in relation to the 'abnormal' – logically second, yet *existentially* first
(Foucault, 2003; cf. Pasquinelli, 2015). Since their presence is one of complementarity, the elements of a war machine and the state apparatus always find
ways to imprint themselves in each other's concrete expressions.

A fine case can be made that all modern revolutionary movements are
adaptable coalitions of social forces (including more radical and moderate) that
betray dispersed agency and resemble dynamic, often rhizomatic assemblages.
They borrow ('appropriate') from their fellow travellers, past and present. To
introduce the concept of revolutionary as hybrid, it ought to be stressed, is not
to propose a category for which a set of clear criteria could be identified, and
that those who do not meet them should be excluded. To think of revolutionary as hybrid is, rather, a notion intended to illuminate certain intensities in
the construction of revolutionary subjectivity, including the key notion of the
complementarity of the revolutionary to the state apparatus – and the related
practices of recoding and repurposing elements, including the organising concept of sovereignty – and, more broadly, the former's entangled becoming that
the war machine usefully delineates. Deleuze and Guattari's project here provides a bridge to a critical understanding of violent pressures that change the
global political *status quo* from the vantage point that promises to push forward,
if not transcend, the boundaries of the Western *epistémé*. Their adamant refusal
of essentialism, and embracing the becoming perspective – the revolutionary
movement is never final, ever becoming something else than it is now, at
this fleeting moment – serve to open the thinking space to novel perspectives
about modern revolutionary movements that look beyond totalising structures and positivist ontologies, thereby challenging the essential, instrumen-
talised knowledge about ISIS and other discontents of the established political
order formed from the hegemonic point of view. What matters to them is
not essences or 'filiations' that can be captured and mobilised by instrumental
reason but relations, alliances and alloys (Deleuze and Parnet, 1987, p. 69),
those contingent features that are knowable only at a particular point of an
ever-incomplete process. Moreover, Deleuze and Guattari's forceful emphasis
on the complementarity of the war machine and the state is a useful challenge to the hegemonic construction of the revolutionaries that excludes and

subjectifies them as radical *others*, now often amplified by Orientalist tropes – as, indeed, tends to be the case in the mainstream 'terrorology', where revolutionary violence ('terrorism') is cast as total war in which there is 'no room for the Red Cross' (Laqueur, 2004, cf. also Hoffman, 1989).

Conclusion

ISIS exemplifies the hybrid constitution of revolutionary agency. Yet, the purpose of this book is wilfully to de-exceptionalise it – to cast it only as the latest in a historical series of instances of hybrid revolutionary subjectivity in the modern era with a globally, rather than locally, bounded political project. The manner in which it realises certain new possibilities of revolutionary subject formation, benefiting from the reconstitution of the great (cyber)steppe that once again integrates separate territorial systems and collapses their spacetimes, is, indeed, unprecedented. It is our intent in this volume to advance a scholarly understanding of the processes in which these possibilities are realised, and ISIS has become the (hyper-)event in current global politics that, without a doubt, it is.

The central proposition is that investigating the various aspects of the ISIS political project, and juxtaposing these with its antecedents, yields novel insights into thinking about the revolution as a phenomenon of the current world order and its protagonists – it makes it possible to explore the tensions between the revolutionary interior and exterior, the local and the global, and the disruptive and the normative. Deleuze and Guattari's framework is fitting for such an analytical move as it enables us to do away with some rigid distinctions which define much of the thinking about revolution in particular, and features and processes pertaining to the existing order in general.

Conceiving (hybrid) revolutionaries in terms of war machine thus provides space for rethinking revolution in global politics. The nomadic existence, striving to resist the imposition of what Deleuze and Guattari call the state – a set of dispositions, rationalities and practices which make the social and political life tamed, ordered and controlled, manifests itself in a revolutionary practice which aims at overturning the existing power constellations. At the same time, by emphasising how hybrid revolutionaries as war machines appropriate, repack and repurpose elements of the state forms of social and political organisation, this perspective (along with the present volume) highlights how revolutionaries can hardly escape the limitations imposed on them by the dominant frameworks of thought and conduct present in the existing order. Indeed, it is the impossibility of detaching themselves from these straitjackets that makes revolutionaries inherently hybrid subjects, (re)incorporating and (re)adjusting elements of the order they purportedly seek to dismantle. It is also this impossibility which orients the studies in this volume.

Notes

1. 'The worst of world war machines reconstitutes a smooth space to surround and enclose the earth,' as Deleuze and Guattari (1987, p. 423) caution.
2. This limit of time is a period characterised by the near-universal transgression of established norms and customs (Ostransky, 2019) but also one which simultaneously actualises a simplified vision of the politics of redemption that reduces a complex reality to a simple contradiction of *good / evil*.
3. In doing so, the theory of the hybrid revolutionary draws but also expands on the previous mobilisation of the notion of the war machine in the analysis of modern subjectivity and violence in global politics (cf. Virilio, 1989; Reid, 2010; Mbembe, 2003; Rosenow, 2013; Kraidy, 2018; Mabon, 2019).

References

Aalberts, T. 2016. 'Sovereignty'. In Berenskoetter, F. (ed). *Concepts in World Politics*, 183–99. Thousand Oaks, CA: Sage.

Abrams, B. 2019. 'A Fifth Generation of Revolutionary Theory Is Yet to Come'. *Journal of Historical Sociology* 32 (3): 378–86. Available at: <https://doi.org/10.1111/johs.12248> (last accessed 14 June 2022).

Acheraïou, A. 2011. *Questioning Hybridity, Postcolonialism and Globalization*. Houndmills and New York: Palgrave Macmillan.

Agamben, G. 2005. *State of Exception*. Chicago: University of Chicago Press.

Agnew, J. 1994. 'The Territorial Trap: The Geographical Assumptions of International Relations Theory'. *Review of International Political Economy* 1 (1): 53–80.

Arendt, H. 2006. *On Revolution*. New York: Penguin Books.

Arjona, A., Kasfir, N. and Mampilly, Z. 2015. *Rebel Governance in Civil War*. Cambridge: Cambridge University Press.

Armstrong, D. 1993. *Revolution and World Order: The Revolutionary State in International Society*. Oxford: Oxford University Press.

Arquilla, J. and Ronfeldt, D. F. (eds). 2001. *Networks and Netwars: The Future of Terror, Crime, and Militancy*. Santa Monica, CA: RAND Corporation.

Ashley, R. K. 1988. 'Untying the Sovereign State: A Double Reading of the Anarchy Problematique'. *Millennium: Journal of International Studies* 17 (2): 227–62. Available at: <https://doi.org/10.1177/03058298880170020901> (last accessed 14 June 2022).

Bartelson, J. 2014. *Sovereignty as Symbolic Form*. London and New York: Routledge.

Beck, C. J. 2014. 'Reflections on the Revolutionary Wave in 2011'. *Theory and Society* 43 (2): 197–223. Available at: <https://doi.org/10.1007/s11186-014-9213-8> (last accessed 14 June 2022).

Beck, C. J. 2015. *Radicals, Revolutionaries, and Terrorists*. Cambridge: Polity.

Beck, C. J. 2020. 'Revolutions against the State'. In de Leon, C., Martin, I. W., Misra, J. and Janoski, T. (eds). *The New Handbook of Political Sociology*, 564–92. Cambridge: Cambridge University Press.

Beissinger, M. 2013. 'The Semblance of Democratic Revolution: Coalitions in Ukraine's Orange Revolution'. *American Political Science Review* 107 (3): 574–92.

Bercovitch, S. 1975. *The Puritan Origins of the American Self*. New Haven, CT: Yale University Press.

Berger, J. M. 2015. 'The Metronome of Apocalyptic Time'. *Perspectives on Terrorism* 9 (4): 61–71.

Bleiker, R. 2015. 'Pluralist Methods for Visual Global Politics'. *Millennium: Journal of International Studies* 43 (3): 872–90.

Brinton, C. 1965. *The Anatomy of Revolution*. New York: Random House.

Bukovansky, M. 2002. *Legitimacy and Power Politics: The American and French Revolutions in International Political Culture*. Princeton, NJ: Princeton University Press.

Butler, J. 2004. *Precarious Life: The Powers of Mourning and Violence*. London and New York: Verso.

Canclini, N. G. and Rosaldo, R. 2005. *Hybrid Cultures: Strategies for Entering and Leaving Modernity*. Minneapolis: University of Minnesota Press.

Chenoweth, E. 2020. 'The Future of Nonviolent Resistance'. *Journal of Democracy* 31 (3): 69–84. Available at: <https://doi.org/10.1353/jod.2020.0046> (last accessed 14 June 2022).

Chouliaraki, L. and Kissas, A. 2018. 'The Communication of Horrorism: A Typology of ISIS Online Death Videos'. *Critical Studies in Media Communication* 35 (1): 24–39.

Colburn, F. D. 1994. *The Vogue of Revolution in Poor Countries*. Princeton: Princeton University Press.

Davies, J. C. 1962. 'Toward a Theory of Revolution'. *American Sociological Review* 27 (1): 5. Available at: <https://doi.org/10.2307/2089714> (last accessed 14 June 2022).

Deleuze, G. 1975. 'Ecrivain non: un nouveau cartographe'. *Critique* 343: 1207–27.

Deleuze, G. 1992. 'What is a Dispositif?'. In *Michel Foucault: Philosopher*, ed. Timothy Armstrong, 159–68. New York: Harvester Wheatsheaf.

Deleuze, G. and Guattari, F. 1986. *Anti-Oedipus: Capitalism and Schizophrenia*. Minneapolis: University of Minnesota Press.

Deleuze, G. and Guattari, F. 1987. *A Thousand Plateaus: Capitalism and Schizophrenia*. Minneapolis: University of Minnesota Press.

Deleuze, G. and Parnet, C. 1987. *Dialogues*. New York: Columbia University Press.

Ditrych, O. 2014. *Tracing the Discourses of Terrorism: Identity, Genealogy and State*. Basingstoke and New York: Palgrave Macmillan.

Elden, S. 2013. *The Birth of Territory*. Chicago: University of Chicago Press.

Emirbayer, M. and Goodwin, J. 1996. 'Symbols, Positions, Objects: Toward a New Theory of Revolutions and Collective Action'. *History and Theory* 35 (3): 358–74. Available at: <https://doi.org/10.2307/2505454> (last accessed 14 June 2022).

Evans, B. and Guillaume, L. 2010. 'Deleuze and War: Introduction'. *Theory & Event* 13 (3). Available at: <https://doi.org/10.1353/tae.2010.0010> (last accessed 14 June 2022).

Farr, J. 1982. 'Historical Concepts in Political Science: The Case of "Revolution"'. *American Journal of Political Science* 26 (4): 688–708.

Fassin, D. and Pandolfi, M. (eds). 2010. *Contemporary States of Emergency: The Politics of Military and Humanitarian Interventions*. New York and Cambridge, MA: Zone Books.

Foran, J. 2005. *Taking Power: On the Origins of Third World Revolutions*. Cambridge: Cambridge University Press.

Foucault, M. 1977. *Discipline and Punish: The Birth of the Prison*. New York: Pantheon Books.

Foucault, M. 2003. *Society Must Be Defended: Lectures at the Collège de France, 1975–76*. New York: Picador.

Fregonese, S. 2012. 'Beyond the "Weak State": Hybrid Sovereignties in Beirut'. *Environment and Planning D: Society and Space* 30 (4): 655–74. Available at: <https://doi.org/10.1068/d11410> (last accessed 14 June 2022).

Fridman, O. 2018. *Russian 'Hybrid Warfare': Resurgence and Politicisation*. Oxford: Oxford University Press.

Gaffield, J. 2020. 'The Racialization of International Law after the Haitian Revolution: The Holy See and National Sovereignty'. *The American Historical Review* 125 (3): 841–68. Available at: <https://doi.org/10.1093/ahr/rhz1226> (last accessed 14 June 2022).

Galeotti, M. 2019. 'The Mythical "Gerasimov Doctrine" and the Language of Threat'. *Critical Studies on Security* 7 (2): 157–61. Available at: <https://doi.org/10.1080/21624887.2018.1441623> (last accessed 14 June 2022).

Gallie, W. B. 1955. 'Essentially Contested Concepts'. *Proceedings of the Aristotelian Society* 56: 167–98.

Ganor, B. 2009. 'Terrorism Networks: It Takes a Network to Beat a Network'. In Kleindorfer, P. and Wind, Y. (eds). *The Network Challenge.* Upper Saddle River, NJ: Pearson.

Geuss, R. 2004. 'Dialectics and the Revolutionary Impulse'. In Rush, F. (ed). *The Cambridge Companion to Critical Theory,* 103–38. Cambridge: Cambridge University Press.

Goldstone, J. A. 1980. 'Theories of Revolution: The Third Generation'. *World Politics* 32 (3): 425–53.

Goldstone, J. A. 1991. *Revolution and Rebellion in the Early Modern World.* Berkeley: University of California Press.

Goldstone, J. A. 2001. 'Toward a Fourth Generation of Revolutionary Theory'. *Annual Review of Political Science* 4 (1): 139–87. Available at: <https://doi.org/10.1146/annurev.polisci.4.1.139> (last accessed 14 June 2022).

Goldstone, J. A. 2013. *Revolutions: A Very Short Introduction.* Oxford: Oxford University Press.

Halliday, F. 1999. *Revolution and World Politics: The Rise and Fall of the Sixth Great Power.* Basingstoke: Macmillan.

Hansen, T. B. and Stepputat, F. 2006. 'Sovereignty Revisited'. *Annual Review of Anthropology* 35 (1): 295–315. Available at: <https://doi.org/10.1146/annurev.anthro.35.081705.123317> (last accessed 14 June 2022).

Hoffman, B. 1989. 'The Contrasting Ethical Foundations of Terrorism in the 1980s'. *Terrorism and Political Violence* 1 (3): 361–77.

Hoffman Galeotti, M. 2019. 'The Mythical "Gerasimov Doctrine" and the Language of Threat'. *Critical Studies on Security* 7 (2): 157–61. Available at: <https://doi.org/10.1080/21624887.2018.1441623> (last accessed 14 June 2022).popp, F. G. 2007. *Conflict in the 21st Century: The Rise of Hybrid Wars.* Arlington, VA: Potomac Institute for Policy Studies.

Jabareen, Y. 2015. 'The Emerging Islamic State: Terror, Territoriality, and the Agenda of Social Transformation'. *Geoforum* 58: 51–5.

Jabri, V. 2012. *The Postcolonial Subject: Claiming Politics/Governing Others in Late Modernity.* London and New York: Routledge.

Jabri, V. 2014. 'Disarming Norms: Postcolonial Agency and the Constitution of the International'. *International Theory* 6 (2): 372–90. Available at: <https://doi.org/10.1017/S1752971914000177> (last accessed 14 June 2022).

Katz, M. N. 1999. *Revolutions and Revolutionary Waves.* New York: St Martin's Press.

Keshavarzian, A. and Mirsepassi, A. (eds). 2021. *Global 1979: Geographies and Histories of the Iranian Revolution.* Cambridge: Cambridge University Press.

Klaits, J. and Haltzel, M. H. (eds). 1994. *The Global Ramifications of the French Revolution.* Cambridge: Cambridge University Press.

Kraidy, M. 2017. 'The Projectilic Image: Islamic State's Digital Visual Warfare and Global Networked Affect'. *Media, Culture & Society* 39 (8): 1194–209. Available at: <https://doi.org/10.1177/0163443717725575> (last accessed 14 June 2022).

Kraidy, M. 2018. 'Terror, Territoriality, Temporality: Hypermedia Events in the Age of Islamic State'. *Television & New Media* 19 (2): 170–6. Available at: <https://doi.org/10.1177/1527476417697197> (last accessed 14 June 2022).

Krasner, S. D. 1999. *Sovereignty: Organized Hypocrisy.* Princeton: Princeton University Press.

Laqueur, W. 2004. 'The Terrorism to Come'. *Policy Review* 126: 49–65.

Latour, B. 1993. *We Have Never Been Modern.* Cambridge, MA: Harvard University Press.

Lawson, G. 2016. 'Within and Beyond the "Fourth Generation" of Revolutionary Theory'. *Sociological Theory* 34 (2): 106–27. Available at: <https://doi.org/10.1177/0735275116649221> (last accessed 14 June 2022).

Lawson, G. 2019. *Anatomies of Revolution.* Cambridge: Cambridge University Press.

Mabon, S. 2019. 'Sectarian Games: Sovereign Power, War Machines and Regional Order in the Middle East'. *Middle East Law and Governance* 11 (3): 283–318.

McCaughrin, C. 1976. 'An Ahistoric View of Revolution'. *American Journal of Political Science* 20 (4): 637–51.

Massumi, B. 1996. 'Becoming-Deleuzian'. *Environment and Planning D: Society and Space* 14 (4): 395–406.

Mbembe, A. 2003. 'Necropolitics'. *Public Culture* 15 (1): 11–40.

Motadel, D. (ed.). 2021. *Revolutionary World: Global Upheaval in the Modern Age.* Cambridge: Cambridge University Press.

Nail, T. 2017. 'What Is an Assemblage?' *SubStance* 46 (1): 21–37.

Nepstad, S. E. 2011. *Nonviolent Revolutions: Civil Resistance in the Late 20th Century.* Oxford Studies in Culture and Politics. Oxford: Oxford University Press.

Ostransky, B. 2019. *The Jihadist Preachers of the End Times: ISIS Apocalyptic Propaganda.* Edinburgh: Edinburgh University Press.

Page, S. 2021. 'Jeremy Corbyn and the War Machine: Assemblage and Affect in the 2015 UK Labour Party Leadership Contest'. *Environment and Planning C: Politics and Space* 39 (7): 1319–37. Available at: <https://doi.org/10.11 77/2399654419841385> (last accessed 14 June 2022).

Pasquinelli, M. 2015. 'What an Apparatus Is Not: On the Archeology of the Norm in Foucault, Canguilhem, and Goldstein'. *Parrhesia* 22: 79–89.

Patton, P. 1984. 'Conceptual Politics and the War-Machine in "Mille Plateaux"'. *SubStance* 13 (3/4): 61.

Perea Ozerin, I. 2021. 'The Exemplary in Transnational Social Movements: The Legacies of the Alterglobalization Movement'. *International Political Sociology* 15 (2): 232–50. Available at: <https://doi.org/10.1093/ips/ola a025> (last accessed 14 June 2022).

Pieterse, J. N. 2001. 'Hybridity, So What?' *Theory, Culture & Society* 18 (2–3): 219–45.

Popper, K. 2002. *The Logic of Scientific Discovery*. London: Routledge.

Ragazzi, F. 2009. 'Governing Diasporas'. *International Political Sociology* 3 (4): 378–97.

Rao, R. 2016. 'Revolution'. In Berenskoetter, F. (ed). *Concepts in World Politics*, 253–70. London: Sage.

Reid, J. 2010. 'Of Nomadic Unities: Gilles Deleuze on the Nature of Sovereignty'. *Journal of International Relations and Development* 13: 405–28.

Richards, I. 2020. *Neoliberalism and Neo-jihadism: Propaganda and Finance in Al Qaeda and Islamic State*. Manchester: Manchester University Press.

Ritter, D. P. 2015. *The Iron Cage of Liberalism: International Politics and Unarmed Revolutions in the Middle East and North Africa*. Oxford: Oxford University Press.

Rosenow, D. 2013. 'Nomadic Life's Counter-attack: Moving Beyond the Subaltern's Voice'. *Review of International Studies* 39 (2): 415–33.

Roy, O. 2017. *Jihad and Death: The Global Appeal of Islamic State*. London: Hurst & Company.

Ruggie, J. G. 1986. 'Social Time and International Policy'. In Karns, M. (ed). *Persistent Patterns and Emergent Structures in a Waning Century*. New York: Praeger.

Ruggie, J. G. 1993. 'Territoriality and Beyond: Problematizing Modernity in International Relations'. *International Organization* 47 (1): 139–74.

Sageman, M. 2004. *Understanding Terror Networks*. Philadelphia: University of Pennsylvania Press.

Selbin, E. 2010. *Revolution, Rebellion, Resistance: The Power of Story*. London: Zed Books.

Shapiro, J. N. 2013. *The Terrorist's Dilemma: Managing Violent Covert Organizations*. Princeton: Princeton University Press.

Shilliam, Robert. 2008. 'What the Haitian Revolution Might Tell Us about Development, Security, and the Politics of Race'. *Comparative Studies in Society and History* 50 (3): 778–808.

Shilliam, Robert. 2017. 'Race and Revolution at Bwa Kayiman'. *Millennium* 45 (3): 269–92.

Skocpol, T. 1979. *States and Social Revolutions: A Comparative Analysis of France, Russia, and China.* Cambridge: Cambridge University Press.

Stepputat, F. 2013. 'Contemporary Governscapes: Sovereign Practice and Hybrid Orders Beyond the Center'. In Bouziane, M., Harders, C. and Hoffmann, A. (eds). *Local Politics and Contemporary Transformations in the Arab World: Governance Beyond the Center*, 25–42. Houndmills and New York: Palgrave Macmillan.

Stohl, C. and Stohl, M. 2007. 'Networks of Terror: Theoretical Assumptions and Pragmatic Consequences'. *Communication Theory* 17 (2): 93–124. Available at: <https://doi.org/10.1111/j.1468-2885.2007.00289.x> (last accessed 14 June 2022).

Terhalle, M. 2009. 'Revolutionary Power and Socialization: Explaining the Persistence of Revolutionary Zeal in Iran's Foreign Policy'. *Security Studies* 18 (3): 557–86. Available at: <https://doi.org/10.1080/0963641090313 3076> (last accessed 14 June 2022).

Virilio, P. 1989. *War and Cinema: The Logistics of Perception.* London: Verso.

Vu, T. and Van Orden, P. 2020. 'Revolution and World Order: The Case of the Islamic State (ISIS)'. *International Politics* 57 (1): 57–78. Available at: <https://doi.org/10.1057/s41311-019-00176-w> (last accessed 14 June 2022).

Walker, R. B. J. 1993. *Inside/Outside: International Relations as Political Theory.* Cambridge: Cambridge University Press.

Weber, C. 1995. *Simulating Sovereignty: Intervention, the State, and Symbolic Exchange.* Cambridge: Cambridge University Press.

Weyland, K. G. 2014. *Making Waves: Democratic Contention in Europe and Latin America Since the Revolutions of 1848.* Cambridge: Cambridge University Press.

Zivkovic, A. and Hogan, J. 2008. 'Virtual Revolution? Information Communication Technologies, Networks, and Social Transformation'. In Foran, J., Lane, D. S. and Zivkovic, A. (eds). *Revolution in the Making of the Modern World: Social Identities, Globalization, and Modernity*, 182–98. New York: Routledge.

3

The Revolutionary Symbol Has No Power: A Semiotic Reading of Hybridity

Martin Švantner

It is often argued that symbols have 'power' (cf. Wydra, 2012) in revolutionary actorship. Such claims are questionable and can be considered naive for several theoretical and methodological reasons: they understand the specific notion of the conventional 'symbol' as a general concept for all types of representation (that is, a symbol here means the general conception of 'sign'; cf. Bellucci, 2021); they understand 'symbol' quasi-realistically as something parasitic on the real (that is, as a 'mere symbol' that stands in opposition to the 'real'); or, conversely, they understand the symbol idealistically as something truly real. All perspectives are deeply flawed from a semiotic point of view since they perform these ontological cuts not to describe or understand the meaning-making processes better but to reduce and reify them (cf. Wight, 2006, p. 2). This searing semiotic naivety continues when one starts to talk about revolutionary symbols as also having some 'iconic' power or being symptoms (or indices) of something else. The aim of this chapter, then, is to attempt to explain some of the foundations of a semiotic theory suitable for thinking about hybrid revolutionaries. The term 'hybrid' comes from biology but, as is obvious, the concept itself has expanded its semantic scope:

> Hybridism, after its metaphorical cultivation, presumes the existence of at least two initially separate and essentially different entities of which at least one can (but does not necessarily have to) be a (biological) agent. These entities, by intersecting with one another, acquire a novel joint-identity, not directly derivable from the characteristic of either party. The emergence of 'hybrid' marks the birth of a new quality that is not reducible to its initial components. (Mäekivi and Magnus, 2020)

The chapter offers a theoretical reflection on hybrid revolutionaries as semiotic entities or, better stated, semiotic processes. The reason for adopting this perspective is that hybrid revolutionaries are, by definition, communicative processes and associated with meaning formation. However, what exactly is meant by 'communication' and 'meaning-making'? First, the communicative entity is a mixture of pragmatic, semantic and syntactic layers – that is, semiotic regularities. Agencies of hybrid revolutionaries are semiotic processes since they are relational. Second, from the perspective of general semiotics (inspired in this case by the perspective of Charles Sanders Peirce rather than the Paris School), it is possible to abandon the quasi-Cartesian binaries between the material and the ideational, or rather the symbolic and the real (cf. Bueger, 2014, p. 59).

The Representation of Hybrid Revolutionaries and Two Theories of Semiotic Hybridisation

The production and operation of a specific sign – digital multimodal images – are defining features of the contemporary situation and contribute to shaping the conditions of possibility where the political discourse of contemporary hybrid revolutionaries takes place.[1] The global dispersion of images is the main way in which political messages are conveyed from distant places (cf. Todorov, 2010). The re/production and dissemination of signs in the form of photographs, clips and films significantly shape the dynamics and the very understanding of the role of hybrid revolutionary agencies in international politics. This agency – where revolution is a transnational event, which semiotic aspects resonate internationally – is made possible by the 'dromocratic'[2] (Virilio, 1997) networks of political marketing, fast global dissemination and the circulation of 'technical images' (Flusser, 2011; cf. McQuire, 2000). The dissemination of these spectacular visual (de)signs of terrorist violence is unprecedented in terms of quantity and their impact on global audiences (Kraidy, 2017, p. 1197). This 'operational imagery' (Hoel, 2018) mobilises and legitimises the activities of the political apparatus to an unprecedented degree (Friis, 2015, p. 727; cf. Farwell, 2014) and makes visible how revolutionary subjectivities and practices reassemble (cf. DeLanda, 2006, pp. 10–11) established distinctions between a national inside and an international outside.

This fact is now reflected within the discipline of International Relations (IR) (cf. Bleiker, 2014, p. 78), where there has been a significant increase of interest in the visuality/symbolic practices of hybrid revolutionaries and the broader political aspects associated with them in the last two decades. This interest stems from the realisation that how people know, think about and respond to the development of hybrid revolutionaries is deeply connected to how the mediating signs are made representable (cf. Shim and Nabers, 2013, p. 292; Bleiker 2014, p. 80). Hybrid revolutionaries mobilise a range of semiotic resources (cf. Hansson, 2018) that enter into the operative/performative realisations in international politics. These sources are a coexisting combination of various material/ideational qualities, which have the potential to shape meaning based on their past use and inferred sets of affordances.[3] The idea I would like to develop in this chapter is that hybrid revolutionary agencies are semiotic entities (cf. Bleiker 2014, p. 76). Hybrid revolutionaries are symmetrically material and symbolic (cf. Latour, 2005), meaning-making (that is, bricolages concerning revolutionary practices which draw on heterogenous domestic and international narratives), dynamic, representational, composite and relational *Becomings*.

The representation of revolutionary agencies via digital images implies a semiotic hybridity of its own. The heterogeneous nature of the spread symbols – namely, symbolic images – is embedded in the core of any revolutionary agency. The representation of this agency is also carried by structured visual symbolic flows that articulate their own discontinuities, divisions and continuities, implicitly leading to a diverse range of possibilities for the perception, interpretation and different 'modes of imagination' (Flusser, 2011, p. 11; cf. Sassen and Ong 2014, p. 19). These complex signs – the symbols and images – are never only a point in a single causal chain but always a multiplicity (Deleuze and Parnet, 2002, p. 69; cf. Deamer, 2016, pp. 70–4): that is, a complex entity that has no *a priori* unifying centre (cf. Deleuze, 1968, p. 273; 2004, pp. 27–8; 2006, pp. 40–1). Symbolic representations of hybrid revolutionaries do not stand in opposition to some single, true reality that is adequately or inadequately represented but are a scale of multiplicities: that is, a scale of differently complex entities, each of which generates order-differential processes, flows and shocks that co-create the conception of the nature of a systematic interpretation of real.

In the following subsections, I discuss some theoretical possibilities of how this multifaceted relationship between representation and the hybridity of revolutionary actors can be grasped more precisely. I investigate the semiotic nature of hybrid agency with an overview of two important semiotic perspectives: the first is associated with Bruno Latour and his translation of Julien Algirdas Greimas's structural semantics (Greimas, 1983, 1987) – and its notion of actant/actor relationships – to the social sciences. The second perspective is associated with the influence of Charles Sanders Peirce[4] and, in contrast to the first case, does not understand semiotics as connected exclusively with human speech discourse or some sort of social constructivism but more broadly with a general logic of representation. Instead, the sign stands as a modal triadic inferential relation whose basal and most important capacity is to hybridise and aggregate the social and the natural, the human and the non-human agencies. Both of these approaches are important because they are relational[5] and do not dwell in well-established or reified theoretic binaries as does, for example, the structure/agency approach. Therefore, they can be mobilised to destabilise the neat boundaries that define present accounts of revolutionary agency. In brief, semiotic perspectives can be considered – alongside assemblage thinking (Bleiker, 2014) – as a kind of non-reductive transcendency of artificially divided sources of agencies (*natural / social, psychological / sociological*) and can perhaps provide some inspiration for the exploration of a complex set of different structural and symbolic factors and their interplay that is conducted later in this book.

We Have Always Been Hybrid

The first perspective understands the field of semiotics as intrinsically linked to the organisation of discourse. In short, Latour-influenced investigations into the hybridisation of actors understand semiotics as their mode of existence associated with the formation of meaning and as part of the other two pillars involved in the constitution of any entity: the social and the natural. To paraphrase Bruno Latour (1996), three resources have been developed to deal with agencies in general: the first one links them with nature, the second one is to grant them sociality, and the third one is to consider them as a semiotic construction and to relate agency with the building of meaning. The Latourian perspective comes from the impossibility of clearly differentiating these three resources. Hybrid agency of revolutionary actors is at the same time natural, social and discursive. They are real, human and semiotic entities in the same breath.

The concepts of 'actorship' and 'representation' are therefore inextricably linked. To be an actor means to be represented via actantial agency. The social sciences (more or less inspired by Latour) have adopted the following leading idea, which Greimas originally discovered for general linguistics and later extended to the discipline of literature. The actor and its representation are the saturation of structural roles and positions in a certain narrative grammar: the actants. The actor always appears in a certain narrative-differential structure: for example, in a relation of opposition (hero versus villain), complementarity (state apparatus and war machine), solidarity, interdependence and so on. Latour – following Greimas in this matter – moves this perspective away from anthropocentrism to his form of materialism and away from the perspective of a closed structure to the notion of an open, symmetrical network:

> An 'actor' [. . .] is a semiotic definition – an actant –, that is, something that acts or to which activity is granted by others. It implies no special motivation of human individual actors, nor of humans in general. An actant can literally be anything provided it is granted to be the source of an action. Although this point has been made over and over again, the anthropocentrism and sociocentrism is so strong in social sciences [. . .]. The difficulty of grasping [actor-network theory] is that it has been made by the fusion of three hitherto unrelated strands of preoccupations: a semiotic definition of entity building; a methodological framework to record the heterogeneity of such a building; an ontological claim on the 'networky' character of actants themselves. (Latour, 1996, p. 396)

A revolutionary agency is thus, by necessity, an entity that hybridises both what is socially constructed, tied to abstract, discursive, textual actant networks and symmetrically to their material-actant nature (that is, the aforementioned affordances; cf. Srnicek, 2014, p. 44). Actants can be saturated by different actors, and, equally, actors can act as carriers of multiple actantial networks. Thus, in this view, a given ideological narrative is inseparable from the way it is transmitted. By analogy, the agencies of revolutionary agencies cannot be separated from their material and / or ideational actantial networks: they are always re/coded by them.

We Have Always Been Inferred: Pierce-Influenced Semiotics

In the second semiotic perspective discussed here, every agency is hybridised via three fundamental ontological categories that underline any experience or meaning-making agency – *firstness*, *secondness* and *thirdness*. Nevertheless, they are not bound to resources of a 'social', 'natural' or 'semiotic' nature (in the previous sense that Latour mentioned) but to the idea, whereby the general sign-relation itself is something that enables the hybridising of the social, natural and discursive (cf. Deely, 2010). From this perspective, the sign relation can be interpreted ontologically as a potential quality, a concrete relational existence and a regularity.

As such, any meaning-making *agency* (including that which is related to hybrid revolutionaries) is a semiotic activity: 'The world begins to signify before anyone knows what it signifies' (Deleuze and Guattari, 1987, p. 112). This means that there *is* something that *is* represented or *has* the potential to be represented: the object of a sign. Therefore, the object is anything that can be represented in some propositional schema[6]: whether the proposition is a linear, diagrammatic, linguistic expression or is not bound to verbal language (for example, as gestures or digital images). In this way, the object of a sign may be variously substituted by something other than itself (cf. CP 8.335).[7] For this situation, it is appropriate to choose the relational term 'representamen'. The term denotes the relation between an object (anything that is represented) and the way in which it is represented and enacted by an 'interpretant' (but not necessarily a human interpreter). Hybrid revolutionaries can thus be represented in a *general tone* (as a qualitative feeling of danger or incoming instability), as a general *type* (a 'proto-state' or 'terrorist organisation') or as a *token* of a *type* (concrete cases of a terrorist organisation). However, these layers are not simply and neatly distinguishable, essential categories but relational continuous moments (Stjernfelt, 2014, p. 4) in the hybridising processes of semiosis (that is, of actions of signs). It is important to add that from this ('contra-Latourian' and contra-psychologism) perspective, the sign *per se* – that is, not in the sense of *representamen* – is not a dyadic relation between an object and its representation or a dyadic representation between a representamen and its effect. The sign is an irreducible, triadic relation of an object, representamen and interpretant. Interpretant is the effect of the sign that in some way determinessign-interpreting agency – again, not necessarily a human mind. Semiosis is, then, a process that symmetrically perfuses and hybridises the whole universe of human or non-human agencies.

The interpretant can be understood, first, as something that potentially qualifies the propositional schema (in language – for example, a free-standing verb; in logic, an unsaturated proposition; in visual communication, colours and textures; in the case of revolutionary agencies, the various general ideological beliefs; cf. Bell, 2018); second, as a particular assertoric proposition (in logic, this is a judgement; in visual representation, it can be a photograph considered as a document; and in the case of revolutionary agencies as, for instance, the understanding of these beliefs as embodied to the systems of action); and third, as a rule / principle governing or connecting a set of propositional schemata (such as, in logic, a syllogism; in rhetoric, an argument; in the case of an image, any conventional symbol such as a dove for peace; and in the case of revolutionary agencies, the rules under these systems of action are regular and/or justifiable). From this point of view, revolutionary agency is considered as a collective (war) pragmatic machine that hybridises symbolic (conventional) rules toward its users and interpreters; these regularities are built to code specific semantics and actions that are also constructed according to given general syntactic rules (not only verbal or visual but multimodal). Every representation and meaning-making process (such as coding or recoding and action) is spread between these three basic possibilities of meaning-making (*interpretantial*) formations.

The representation of any object cannot – by this definition – be radically random but is part of other representations: a part or a result of different inferential / interpretative chains (CP 5.213–5.263). Peirce understood 'inference' broadly. According to him, it is the elementary process in which one infers based on something which is represented (CP 5.462), and this concerns not only the traditional concept of reasoning but essentially any interpretive activity. An inference is a causal process, which creates or produces belief or its acceptance (CP 2.442–4; 5.109). Peirce explains this with the help of three general forms of reasoning – forms of inferential responses to the represented object – which are: the 'abduction' or hypothesis, 'induction' and 'deduction'. The deduction helps to derive testable consequences from the explanatory hypotheses that abduction has helped us to conceive, and induction finally helps us to reach. In the case of abductive reasoning, one has to guess what proportional or qualifying aspects belong to revolutionary agencies: why can ISIS, for example, be considered as a *proto-state*? In more complex terms, what types of semiotic forms of qualitative aspects known to us (such as analogies or still fuzzy notions) must one consider binding in order to qualify a potentially unknown (or a new) object of the inquiry? The leading principle of inductive reasoning is experimentation and extrapolation. The inductive question is whether the cases (that share common or supposed aspects) are subjected to a general rule and whether they will be subjected to it in the future (or have been subject to it in the past). In the context of this chapter – and this book – the question is, how can revolutionary agencies be interpreted as a set of symptoms (or indexes) under the scope of presupposed general rules?

The point is that the inferential process in which the meaning / representation of a revolutionary agency is formed is not a static entity, but always a hybridisation of various aspects of the cognitive / inferential field. Thus, an object of a sign is never represented simply as 'material' or 'symbolic' but is inferred: it can be seen *iconically* as a vague quality, as a general *tone*. It can be seen, from the Deleuzian perspective, as the object that is not yet stratified, as a compound of 'operations of reterritorialisation constituting the signifiable' (Deleuze and Guattari, 1987, p. 112). The revolutionary agency can be recognised *indexically*: that is, as a token of some type – as the 'the territorial states of things constituting the designatable' (Deleuze and Guattari, 1987, p. 112). Or it can be established *symbolically* as a representation of a general object as a convention, rule or law (cf. CP 1.304). The representation of any revolutionary agency thus can be understood first as preformed in the plane of immanence through affective-images. This is the plane of pure affect, which is close to Peirce's *firstness*, and so it is characterised by the quality of possible sensation (Deleuze, 1986, p. 98). *Secondness* is implicitly seen in this perspective as an action-image: an existential relation (Deleuze 1986, p. 141). Relation-image is, then, an expression of thirdness – that is, it is dependent on a symbolic patterns. Symbolic or relational image depicts a relation as a relation (Deleuze 1986, p. 198) – in Peirce's words, as a general diagram representing a regularity, a rule or a law.

The sign as a triadic relation is thus never a static or isolated entity. Instead, it is always a scaled intensity of representations that hybridises or assembles various planes, orders and registers. The symbolic sign as a conventional rule of interpretation always denotes a class of some cases that share specific qualities with each other, however remote. The notion of sign thus determined leads us to grasp revolutionary agencies not only in a formal analytical sense but also in the sense of inferential action. The process of semiosis is the necessary condition for any systems of inference and therefore is the necessary condition for all meaning-bearing action – in other words, for all habitualisations and de/reterritorialisations. The revolutionary agencies are always a semiotic-relational blending of different inferential universes, material and immaterial realms. This blending goes from vague feelings to the concrete affects and emotions, to sociocultural logics of representations, and back. The sign inherently (re)assembles what is both independent and independent on the cognitive capacities of organisms (Deely, 2010), as well as on how that which is represented enters any cognitive/discursive field.

Following previous assumptions, the meaning of the technical / digital images produced by hybrid revolutionaries is also not a static entity derivable / inferable from a single source. Thus, representations of revolutionaries are dynamically assembled according to certain rules, notions and situations that are woven into processes of cognition and evolution. The systems of signs are also not static but dynamic; they are not isolated but in permanent contact. This very fact is rooted in the process of sign creation and sign growth (or change; cf. Castells, 1996): that is, semiosis. Hybrid revolutionaries evolve out of their *contact* with previously existing signs, and their making contact will result in future signs. The interpretative cultures that produce symbolic patterns are also rooted in (the above sense of) sign-inferential-habitual systems. They are mixtures containing manifold phenomena: they change, and they are in contact. The conviviality of cultures hence means the exchange of images of hybrid revolutionaries in order of fruitful symbolic growth, which may also be colloquially called mutual learning and understanding (Ipsen, 2004) but can also create various forms of atavism (cf. Todorov, 2010).

Hybrid Revolutionaries as Symbolic Representations

The term 'symbol' is often used very vaguely – especially when talking, for example, about 'revolutionary symbolism'. However, as noted above, the symbol is a complex (growing) sign – a rule that denotes a class of cases: that is, it contains specific types of indexical signs. Insofar as these cases are not just purely accidental, they are subsumed under the given (symbolic) rule; therefore, they share some common qualities and are thus characterised by some kind of likeness. Symbols also contain a specifically distributed (and inferred) iconicity within them. Symbolic systems can therefore denote a set of cases that is codified more (such as an alphabet) or less (such as an image of an assault rifle) strongly (cf. Eco, 1986, p. 132).

An illustrative example here can be the '*tawheed* gesture'. A photograph of the gesture of the raised index finger is only possible in the first place because of a number of perceptible, displayable qualities such as colours and textures that coexist in a particular depiction. These qualitative textures coexist in their relations to each other and can be co-localised in propositional schemata that are directed to the recipients. This blending of qualities (or the semiotic resources) in a propositional sign shapes both the visibility of recognisable objects in general and the possibilities of their interpretation. In this case, the *tawheed* gesture simultaneously represents the man in the uniform with the raised index finger, the threatening gesture of a soldier and God as an immanent and transcendent deity.

Choosing a more complicated example to illustrate the theoretical perspectives discussed above – the videos depicting brutal violence, what many authors (such as Farwell, 2014) refer to as an essential part of the struggle of hybrid revolutionary actors like ISIS – leads to the following points. First, these are not simple iconic signs, as is sometimes inaccurately stated (cf. Hansen, 2015), nor only purely affective indices (cf. Kraidy, 2017), but complex symbols. These symbols often both bring a composed spectacular visual design that purposefully 'materialises discourse' through colour and texture and are signs that act as indexical, affective 'projectiles'. The meanings they shape, the affects they spark and the messages they mediate are implicitly related to our bodily / mental / social experience – our habitualisation. The emotional and affective interpretants generated by these images – that we interpret as (socially, ethically and so on) inappropriate or unacceptable – are based on our inferential–semiotic capacity to extend physical experience into knowledge and to symbolically requalify / reterritorialise perceived materials, which is in principle possible precisely because of the (*hybrid-relational-inferential-triadic*) nature of the sign.

The symbol as a complex sign associated with regularity is characterised by the fact that it just denotes what is not seen and what is to be seen. It seals a mode of interpretation, inviting the following of discursive regularities; in other words, it evokes discursive (inferential) expectations. The dynamics of the sign system and its symbolic growth and action sets, expands and qualifies the conditions of possibility for the representation of an revolutionary action – the symbolism can work as a vague indication of moods and emotions, thus stimulating various forms of hypothetical abstraction; vaguely coded representations leave the most room for 'guessing' their meaning. This is evident in both artistic abstractions and various ideological techniques. The representations of hybrid revolutionaries can further work inductively as instructions to replicate specific actions: that is, operating as 'weapons', inciting concrete action such as promoting an increasing irritability and mobilising actors to act. Finally, representations of hybrid revolutionaries bring new 'deductive' rules – new instructions into public discourse about how to interpret familiar or hitherto unproblematically accepted social phenomena.

Violent Signs / Signs of Violence: Semiotic Representation of Hybrid Revolutionaries

Digital images, which are complex symbolic signs used as 'projectiles' that 'present an auspicious opportunity to grasp the growing role of digital images in emerging configurations of global conflict' (Kraidy, 2017, p. 1195), may be an example of the very semiotic nature of hybrid revolutionary agencies. These signs are tokens of the hybridisation of barbaric-transgressive violence (Todorov, 2010) through the multiplying, functional (Farwell, 2014, p. 50; cf. Whiteside, 2016, p. 25), ideological narrative, which is inseparable from the technological affordances that offer the possibility of easy dissemination through global media networks (cf. Mitchell, 2011, pp. 2–3). This actor-material network, a key aspect of which is deprofessionalisation (Farwell, 2014, p. 51) of the control, editing and dissemination of media content, not only allows actors to amplify the dissemination of given ideological content but also forms a 'global networked affect' and is a 'systematically applied policy' (Kraidy, 2017, p. 1195). This global network of widespread affections can be seen as a hybridisation of various actantial networks across the mediascapes: as a hybrid narrative that interconnects, on one hand, ethical features of the spectacular society of consumption and, on the other hand, configurations that involve social / political actors, professional and non-professional[8] technological actants guiding message formation and circulation, work-practice activities and different kinds of audience. The grammar of the blending of these technosocial interactions can be analysed semiotically: image producers work – consciously or unconsciously – with iconic / qualitative potential (sharpness, darkening or lightening), the indexical accentuation / shading of important details, and presentation of the image in relation to the regularities of a genre.[9]

As Kay O'Halloran et al. (2018) have shown, the crucial semiotic aspect of this global, actant–actor network of affects is the multimodal recontextualis-ation of images across different media.[10] This semiotic case study is focused on ISIS's online magazine *Dabiq* and investigates how the images, article types and their combinations change over time, tracing their recontextualisations in different media. In terms of representation, *Dabiq* constructs meaning through the following meaning-making semiotic sources (O'Halloran et al., 2018, p. 185) that can form various organising actantial networks and inferential agencies: (i) the 'far enemy', which is used by jihadist Salafists to denote Western sponsors of Arab regimes (the United States, its Western allies and Israel); (ii) the 'near enemy' (mostly secular Muslim regimes); (iii) 'ISIS heroes' (those alive, mostly *mujahidin*, and the dead, the martyrs); (iv) 'ISIS icons' (ISIS flag, AK 47 assault rifle, *tawheed* gesture); (v) 'historical recreations' (staged photoshopped representations of apocalyptic and historical events); (vi) 'ISIS law enforcement' (documentary shots showing ISIS involvement in Sharia law enforcement); (vii) 'ISIS social welfare'; (viii) 'pledges of allegiance to ISIS'; and (ix) 'scripture' (images of Arabic scripture and depiction of *mujahidin* reading scripture or praying after 'victory'). This basic structure of organisational actants creates the conditions for saturation. It forms a space of representation in which ISIS as a hybrid revolutionary is articulated as symbolic: that is, complex and regular signs that denote propositional states and also point out vague qualities and feelings. The content of the magazine goes from vague iconic signs that are meant to 'inspire' ISIS members – portraying heroes, ideology and social practices as embodied through emblems, logos, flags, rituals and ceremonies – to the 'perception-images' of documentary-like photographs and articulate symbolic instructions and laws. In the case of *Dabiq*, these inferential-symbolic universes are carried through the system of 'instructive' symbols. So are the articles *From/To Our Sisters*, which deal with a range of what ISIS considers to be women's issues, coded in verbal / visual signs – for example, advice to wives of Muslims fighting against ISIS, the role of women in jihad, how many wives a man can have, how widows should behave – but also in purely abstract symbolic rules where 'although women are included as social actors in the linguistic text, all women are visually excluded from the discourse' (O'Halloran et al., 2018, p. 190).

This symbolic representation means a symbol-image (or relational-image), therefore the images that comprise icon-image and index-image or – to put it in

Deleuzian terms – purely-affective-image and perception-image. It represents a range of different-iconic general visual qualities (such as colour, sharpness and so on), is something that is indexically efficacious (for example, a camera angle that directs the gaze of the spectator, can elicit an affective response and so on), and is associated with a range of social-conventional interpretations. This perspective makes it possible to grasp and clarify better the notion of iconicity and inter-iconicity discussed in theories of visuality and political representation (cf. Hansen, 2015). This is especially so in the sense mentioned above – there is no such thing as pure iconicity, indexicality or symbolicity in the representation of revolutionary agencies (and in representation in general). If one specifically speaks, for example, of inter-iconicity, it should also be understood as inter-indexicality and inter-symbolicity that generates and hybridises order-differential processes, flows, shocks and inferential chains that co-create the conception of the nature of a systematic interpretation of reality. Likewise, as far as the affective states that the representation of revolutionary agencies can evoke are concerned, the emotions that the 'image-projectiles' are capable of awakening are a matter of conflicting modes of discursive expectation or, in other words, of different universes of inferences.

Conclusion

The Peircean semiotic prism articulates actantial networks of revolutionary agencies in a plastic way. This plasticity is nothing other than hybridity – hybridity that connects the ontological nature of objects: that is, it tries to describe the modes of how they can be represented at all. In contrast to other semiotic approaches, a Peircean-influenced framework directly works with a certain freedom that is the very nature of the (material or ideational) represented object. Peircean logic of representation describes how the object is represented as such, how the object is causally and existentially potent and active, and how this representation coded, codified and habitualised. In other words, this semiotic blending is a homologous specification of the first plane by another and a third. This inter-signifying inferential specification – that is, semiosis – is the founding condition for the emergence of any actorship.

If one takes the idea of the cartography of power and the articulation of the power diagrams of the war machine as discussed by Deleuze and Guattari as an example, both the state apparatus and the war machine are semiotic mechanisms. These entities mix symbolically contextualised iconic qualities (where the semiosis of the state apparatus consists of, among other things, artificiality, sovereignty and, in the case of the war machine, fierceness and force), which are embodied in concrete relations (in the case of the state, law-governed institutions; in the case of the war machine, the disorderliness of nomadic movement) and finally shape various rules of denunciation. The diagrammatic rules of the state are symbolically exemplified by the *game of chess* (situational and deduction-like qualifying specifications) and the war machine is exemplified by the *game of go* (as an abductive iconic-like situationality). The symbolic representation of revolutionary agencies – in the strict sense of the symbol as a complex sign – is 'materialised' in habitualisation, standing for inferential responses to the represented objects that can generate sets of mutually interpenetrating interpretations – 'emotional' (qualitative-general), 'energetic' (immediate-existential) and 'logical' (argumentative-regular). Likewise, the symbolisation of any action is possible only through abductive and inductive (re)iteration (cf. Kraidy, 2017, pp. 1202–3).

As this chapter showed, one has to be more a bit more cautious when speaking of the simply symbolic representation of revolutionary agencies. The semiotic perspective can provide us with some sort of catalogue of symbols or a mere overview, or can limit us to the banal statement that symbols cause emotions. The rigorous understanding of the sign as an inferential process that connects different modalities of discursive universes can deepen the understanding of an arrangement establishing a certain structure of relations in a field that itself needs to be established and visualised for the purpose of government. The final line is, therefore, that power does not belong only to reified conceptions of symbols. It is always relational and is distributed across a hybrid mixing of various inferential universes, cartographies and experimentations with (ideational / material) diagrams.

Notes

1. The semiotic term 'multimodality', introduced by G. Kress and T. Van Leeuwen, is defined as the mutual and simultaneous interaction of different modes of representation, including the interaction between the image and the written/spoken word (Kress and Van Leeuwen, 2001, p. 20).

2. Virilio used this term (along with 'dromology') to define the growing importance of the role of speed in the socio-economic nature of contemporary politics. He defines the speed of communication in relation to increasing technological advances, and it becomes a key aspect of innovations aimed at continuously exploring the evolution of spatio-temporal relations.

3. The perceptible, physical qualities of objects that, together with the interests and needs of sign-interpreting agencies, define their possible uses (Gibson, 1978).

4. In contrast to the (post)structuralist approach, the Peircean view has not yet received sufficient attention in the field of IR.

5. At least in the sense that any considered element of any considered system has no meaning in isolation.

6. Specific mixtures of sets of integrated qualities constituting objects (that is, semiotic resources, in this sense aspects of the visual such as colour saturation, sharpness, or detail and the whole) and their relation to social-interpretive rules can lead the recipient to perceive / infer the image as more or less 'natural', 'technical' or 'abstract', and therefore also as 'true' or 'false'.

7. To cite Peirce's Collected Papers (Peirce 1931–58), I use the standardised international abbreviations, where the first number indicates the volume and the second the relevant paragraph.

8. A significant change in the semiotic landscape that has had an impact on the dissemination of digital images is the 'democratisation' or 'deterritorialisation' of digital technologies: even non-specialists are able to use semiotic resources that were previously associated with highly specialised fields.

9. Propaganda images of ISIS work, for example, by portraying a fearless warrior in detail, where these images are meant to serve as recruitment and recruitment tools, or depict brutal violence serving as affective indices of intimidation and, last but not least, as depictions of welfare being (Farwell, 2014, p. 50).

10. Her approach is built upon Van Leeuwen's (2008) semiotic model of 'recontextualisation principles', 'which explains how changes in social practices take place recursively through multimodal discourse, and which involves the reconfiguration of social actors, activities, and circumstantial elements across sequences of multimodal activities (or genres), which function to regulate social practices' (cited in O'Halloran et al., 2018, p. 181).

References

Bell, P. 2018. 'The Limits of Semiotics – Epistemology and the Concept of "Race"'. In Zhao, S., Djonov, E., Björkvall, A. and Boeriis, M. (eds). *Advancing Multimodal and Critical Discourse Studies: Interdisciplinary Research Inspired by Theo Van Leeuwen's Social Semiotics*, 51–66. London and New York: Routledge.

Bellucci, F. 2021. 'Peirce on Symbols'. *Archiv für Geschichte der Philosophie* 103 (1): 169–88.

Bleiker, R. 2014. 'Visual Assemblages: From Causality to Conditions of

Possibility'. In Acuto, M. and Curtis, S. (eds). *Reassembling IR Theory: Assemblage Thinking and IR*, 75–81. New York: Palgrave Macmillan.

Bueger, C. 2014. 'Thinking Assemblages Methodologically: Some Rules of Thumb'. In Acuto, M. and Curtis, S. (eds). *Reassembling IR Theory: Assemblage Thinking and IR*, 58–66. New York: Palgrave Macmillan.

Castells, M. 1996. *The Rise of the Network Society*. Oxford: Blackwell.

Deamer, D. 2016. *Deleuze's Cinema Books: Three Introductions to the Taxonomy of Images*. Edinburgh: Edinburgh University Press.

Deely, J. N. 2010. *Semiotic Animal: A Postmodern Definition of 'Human Being' Transcending Patriarchy and Feminism*. South Bend, IN: St Augustine Press.

DeLanda, M. 2006. *A New Philosophy of Society: Assemblage Theory and Social Complexity*. London and New York: Continuum.

Deleuze, G. 1968. *Différence et répétition*. Paris: PUF.

Deleuze, G. 1986. *Cinema I: The Movement-Image*. Minneapolis: University of Minnesota Press.

Deleuze, G. 2004. *Desert Islands and Other Texts (1953–1974)*. New York: Semiotext(e).

Deleuze, G. 2006. *Two Regimes of Madness: Texts and Interviews 1975–1995*. New York: Semiotext(e).

Deleuze, G. and Guattari, F. 1987. *A Thousand Plateaus*. London: Continuum.

Deleuze, G. and Parnet, C. 2002. *Dialogues II*. London: Continuum.

Eco, U. 1986. *Semiotics and the Philosophy of Language*. Bloomington: Indiana University Press.

Farwell, J. 2014. 'The Media Strategy of ISIS'. *Survival* 56 (6): 49–55.

Flusser, V. 2011. *Into the Universe of Technical Images*. Minnesota: University of Minnesota Press.

Friis, S. M. 2015. '"Beyond anything we have ever seen": Beheading Videos and the Visibility of Violence in the War Against ISIS'. *International Affairs* 91: 725–46.

Gibson J. J. 1978. 'The Ecological Approach to the Visual Perception of Pictures'. *Leonardo* 11 (3): 227–35.

Greimas, J. A. 1983. *Structural Semantics: An Attempt at a Method*. Lincoln, NB, and London: University of Nebraska Press.

Greimas, J. A. 1987. *On Meaning: Selected Writings in Semiotic Theory*. Minneapolis: University of Minnesota Press.

Hansen, L. 2015. 'How Images Make World Politics: International Icons and the Case of Abu Ghraib'. *Review of International Studies* 41 (2): 263–88.

Hansson, S. 2018. 'Defensive Semiotic Strategies in Government: A Multimodal Study of Blame Avoidance'. *Social Semiotics* 28 (4): 472–93.

Hoel, A. 2018. 'Operative Images: Inroads to a New Paradigm of Media

Theory'. In Feiersinger, L., Friedrich, K. and Queisner, M. (eds). *Image – Action – Space: Situating the Screen in Visual Practice*, 11–28. Berlin and Boston: De Gruyter.

Ipsen, G. 2004. 'Hybridity and Heterogeneity: The Balance of Interpretation'. *International Studies Perspectives* 14 (3): 289–306.

Kraidy, M. M. 2017. 'The Projectilic Image: Islamic State's Digital Visual Warfare and Global Networked Affect'. *Media, Culture & Society* 39 (8): 1194–209.

Kress, G., and Van Leeuwen, T. 2001. *Multimodal Discourse: The Modes and Media of Contemporary Communication*. London: Arnold.

Latour, B. 1996. 'On Actor-Network Theory: A Few Clarifications'. *Soziale Welt* 47 (4): 369–81.

Latour, B. 2005. *Reassembling the Social: An Introduction to Actor Network-Theory*. Oxford: Oxford University Press.

McQuire, S. 2000. 'Blinded by the (Speed of) Light'. In Armitage, J. (ed.). *Paul Virilio: From Modernism to Hypermodernism and Beyond*, 143–60. London: Sage.

Mäekivi, N. and Magnus, R. 2020. 'Hybrid Natures – Ecosemiotic and Zoosemiotic Perspectives'. *Biosemiotics* 13: 1–7.

Mitchell, W. J. T. 2011. *Cloning Terror: The War of Images, 9/11 to the Present*. Chicago: University of Chicago Press.

O'Halloran, K. L., Tan, S., Wignell, P. and Lange, R. 2018. 'Multimodal Recontextualisations of Images in Violent Extremist Discourse'. In Zhao, S., Djonov, E., Björkvall, A. and Boeriis, M. (eds). *Advancing Multimodal and Critical Discourse Studies: Interdisciplinary Research Inspired by Theo Van Leeuwen's Social Semiotics*, 181–202. London and New York: Routledge.

Peirce, C. S. 1931–58. *Collected Papers of Charles Sanders Peirce*. Cambridge, MA: Harvard University Press.

Sassen, S. and Ong, A. 2014. 'The Carpenter and the Bricoleur: A Conversation with Saskia Sassen and Aihwa Ong'. In Acuto, M. and Curtis, S. (eds). *Reassembling IR Theory: Assemblage Thinking and IR*, 17–24. New York: Palgrave Macmillan.

Shim, D. and Nabers, D. 2013. 'Imaging North Korea: Exploring its Visual Representations in International Politics'. *International Studies Perspectives* 14 (3): 289–306.

Srnicek, N. 2014. 'Cognitive Assemblages and the Production of Knowledge'. In Acuto, M. and Curtis, S. (eds). *Reassembling IR Theory: Assemblage Thinking and IR*, 40–7. New York: Palgrave Macmillan.

Stjernfelt, F. 2014. *Natural Propositions: The Actuality of Peirce's Doctrine of Dicisigns*. Boston: Docent Press.

Todorov, T. 2010. *The Fear of Barbarians: Beyond the Clash of Civilizations*. Chicago: University of Chicago Press.

Virilio, P. 1997. *Open Sky*. London: Verso.

Whiteside, C. 2016. *Lighting the Path: The Evolution of the Islamic State Media Enterprise (2003–2016)*. The Hague: International Center for Counter-Terrorism.

Wight, C. 2006. *Agents, Structures and International Relations: Politics as Ontology*. Cambridge: Cambridge University Press.

Wydra, H. 2012. 'The Power of Symbols – Communism and Beyond'. *International Journal of Politics, Culture, and Society* 25: 49–69.

Part II

The Islamic State: Inside Out

4

ISIS's War Machine Between the Revolution and the International System and Its Adaptation

Jan Daniel, Jakub Záhora and Ondrej Ditrych

The Islamic State in Iraq and al-Shām (ISIS) has often been cast as the nemesis of the contemporary international system – an actor deliberately so extreme and hostile to international (liberal) norms that it stands completely outside the field of their enactment (Dallal, 2017; Mohamedou, 2017). Whereas other contributions focusing on ISIS in this volume problematise this simple opposition by showing how the movement and its predecessors have become embedded in neoliberal conditions – impacting on its hybrid subjectivity (Walshe, Richards, this volume) – or highlight the resemblances and mutual borrowing between different revolutionary visions (Müller-Rensch, this volume), this chapter presents a different take on ISIS's hybridity. Without disputing the many violations of the most basic human rights that it has routinely committed and the numerous cases of extreme violence that it has been involved in, we turn our attention to the embeddedness of ISIS within the international system and its multiple entanglements with it. Using the theoretical lens of hybrid revolutionary agency, we show how the revolutionary aspirations of the movement and the means of their communication are nonetheless still situated within the matrix of the system ISIS seeks to dismantle, as well as how the international system of states has adapted to such a challenge. As such, via illustrative excursions into different registers of ISIS operations and reactions to these, we seek to render visible a series of entanglements of different practices and rationalities, as well as their effects.

This study of ISIS will deploy the framework presented in the theoretical section of the book to stake out a space for a new interpretation of how ISIS has been constituted in the cyberspace and information sphere and what its effects have been in relation to the sociopolitical order which it has sought to revolutionise. The analysis departs from the premise that, with no attempt to impose a false unity on ISIS as a constantly becoming entity, it acts on and, in many ways, against certain organising principles of the contemporary world order. This principle defines a fundamental authority structure and is constitutive of the legitimacy of the process of actors' constitution, as well as their form and operation (Mendelsohn, 2012, p. 593).

The Westphalian organising principle of the state-system entails sovereignty as a property of multiple privileged entities (states) in mutually exclusive jurisdictional domains. Subscribing to a different principle of political authority that prefers authority over bodies and values that together form the global community of believers (see Roy, 2004), authority over a coherent stretch of territory has not necessarily been a key feature of the polity that ISIS sought to form. In other words, ISIS's political utopia has emphasised a single spiritual and political authority combined with political deterritorialisation or, alternatively, territorialisation for the sole purpose of localised administration but potentially *without* the modern state taking part in the international system. Such a peculiar combination of territorialisation and deterritorialisation processes then resulted in agency that was firmly present in certain territories and space(s), yet which also was able to connect with subjects around the globe and constitute itself worldwide (Kadercan, 2019; Kraidy, 2018b).

This interrogation of the ISIS constitution, closely entangled with the structures of the international order, will build on the assumption that it can be conceived as a transient and becoming assemblage: a war machine defying established borders and constituting new ones (see Chapter 2). Such a reading foregrounds the rhizomatic nature of the group that 'grows sideways, has multiple entryways and exits [. . .], no beginning or end, only a middle, from where it expands and overspills' (Bleiker, 2014, p. 79) and the capability of substantial metamorphosis. Focusing on representation of the group in its own media and paying attention specifically to the events in which the ISIS assemblage becomes tangible, the first part of the chapter interrogates the global constitution of ISIS in virtual spaces (see Artrip and Debrix, 2018; Kraidy, 2018b). Consisting of multiple registers and media infrastructures and transcending in their performances the boundaries of national states, these violent acts highlight the fact that while ISIS has formulated a radical vision of an alternative world order based on its vision of the Caliphate as the transnational community of believers, it has – as a fundamentally *hybrid* entity – also adopted many features of the present order in its practices.

The second part of the chapter focuses on the assemblage's effects on the international system. Following a Deleuzian reading of ISIS that treats the group as a war machine whose becoming 'affects sedentaries, just as sedentarisation is a stoppage that settles the nomads' (Deleuze and Guattari, 1987,

p. 430), we trace some of the transformations of the international system in response to ISIS's emergence and operation. Building on an interrogation of the deterritorialisation of ISIS's violence and its reach beyond the boundaries of particular states in the first section, the second section attends less to the military actions of ISIS aimed at recapturing its territorial base in Syria, Iraq or elsewhere, and more to novel responses that have, however, since become an inseparable part of the international institutions that, in turn, have made them globally binding and legitimate (Martini, 2020). Some of these responses took place in the realm of social media, which became designated as a battlespace and distinct area in need of control (Awan, 2017; Ward, 2018; Kraidy, 2018a; Möllers, 2021), while others are visible in the emergence and / or consolidation of (proto-)governmental programmes to counter and prevent violent extremism on the international level (Ucko, 2018; Martini, 2020).

Rethinking ISIS: Beyond Barbarism and Towards the War Machine

ISIS attracted global attention by quickly capturing large swaths of territory in Syria and Iraq. Indeed, at the height of the organisation's military capacities in the Middle East, many observers expressed concern regarding the chances of survival of the Iraqi state. These fears were circulated especially after the surprising takeover of Mosul in June 2014 from the governmental forces which collapsed under ISIS's onslaught. At that point, the advance on Baghdad seemed inevitable (Abdulrazaq and Stansfield, 2016). Although this was ultimately averted, the vision of the Islamic State controlling the territory of the existing states seemed to be a real possibility. Combined with the movement's disdain for borders drawn up by Western colonial powers – visible also in acts of performative erasure of borders drawn by the Sykes–Picot agreement – ISIS's successes brought about anxieties regarding the stability of the postcolonial order in the region more broadly (Hamdan, 2016; Offenhuber, 2018). On the face of it, ISIS's political programme consisted of rejecting the current hegemonic structure of space divided into states – a legacy of Western imperialism – and erecting a novel order subscribing to the vision of the borderless Caliphate. In actual practice, however, it still drew on the familiar codes of the international order as it exercised state-like control over territory: an inherently contradictory mode of political existence (Boyraz, 2021; Hamdan, 2016; Richards, 2020).

Numerous studies have emerged aiming to classify ISIS variably as an insurgent group (Whiteside, 2016), (revolutionary) state (Jacoby, 2021; Vu and Van Orden, 2020) or revolutionary movement (Kadercan, 2018; Mello, 2018). In line with the general scope of this book, we take as a point of departure here those works which provide more nuanced insights into the ideology and practice of the movement (Mohamedou, 2017; Hegghammer, 2017) and which seek to de-essentialise Islamist transformatory political programmes in general (such as Li, 2019). While these works often shy away from proposing clear-cut categories describing what ISIS actually is, they focus on how the use of shocking violence constitutes strategic means and political tools, in many regards indistinguishable from similar practices adopted by a number of state authorities in the past (Mello, 2018). Relatedly, this literature shows that, contrary to its depiction as a nihilist death cult, a close reading of ISIS sources reveals that the movement is animated by an elaborated political thought (Mohamedou, 2017) – though the organisation's appeal cannot be attributed solely, or even dominantly, to its Islamic teaching, and the process of ISIS's recruitment is embedded in other registers of social and political life (Truong, 2018; Roy, 2017; see also Müller-Rensch, this volume). This nuanced reading of ISIS's operation further makes it clear that, despite many statements promoting its radical novelty, the movement draws on a wide, historically established repertoire of thought and practice (Ostřanský, 2019; Dallal, 2017), as well as the founding principles of the contemporary neoliberal order (Richards, this volume).

The complex image of ISIS that emerges from these accounts is thus one of a multifaceted entity which is defined by (re)adopting, (re)combining and (re)formulating political rationalities and modes of conduct extracted from various registers. The notion of hybrid revolutionary coined in this book reflects and advances such complex representations of the discontents of the global order – as rhizomatic, multiplicitous assemblages featuring diverse elements including those borrowed, repackaged and repurposed from the state forms that are the basic building blocks of the world these revolutionaries seek to overturn – to promote their better understanding. As we show in the rest of this chapter, ISIS's becoming features multiple entanglements, from a reliance on existing global infrastructures and message-mixing to a complex composition of its alternative lifeworld construction. The forces of the *status quo* normative order responded to the threat posed by ISIS using the toolbox devised in the counterterrorism *dispositif* enacted after 9/11, but also advanced new means, notably under the countering / preventing violent extremism (C/PVE) heading, featuring governmental interventions to manage society, binding risky populations with the state, and attempts to prevail in cyberspace as a newly constituted space. These new rationalities and technologies, as we conclude, are to be ISIS's lasting 'subject effects' – its lasting legacy.

Think Global, Act Local? The Entanglements of ISIS's Becoming

On 29 June 2014, several days after ISIS captured Mosul from Iraqi forces, Abu Bakr al-Baghdadi proclaimed the establishment of the Caliphate and stated that 'it is incumbent upon all Muslims to pledge allegiance' to himself as the Caliph (Westall, 2014). Pundits of various stripes have dissected different strands of the ISIS ideology, focusing on the Islamic pedigree in general, and the impact of al-Qaʿida and other extremist groups on the formulation of the ISIS political programme in particular (Bunzel, 2015). What is crucial here is that the ISIS imaginary was, at its core, a global one (Halimi et al., 2019): ISIS interpellated the global *umma* and its members, construing the Caliphate as a borderless entity encompassing the globe and ignoring state borders. Simultaneously, its political project was situated within a chiliastic time frame in which the end of times was within reach and towards which ISIS itself sought to contribute (Ostřanský, 2019). As such, the ISIS political programme supposedly constituted a radical – indeed, revolutionary – break with the dominant political, territorial and even temporal order. As suggested by Mohamedou, 'the threatening nature of [ISIS] lies, then, not so much in its violence (terroristic and obvious) but in the nature of the counter-order it is claiming to uphold' (Mohamedou, 2017, p. 22) – a new order released from the spatial straitjacket of the Westphalian state system.

Nonetheless, even if ISIS sought to materialise a particular vision seemingly at odds with the basic tenets of the current global order, its project was deeply rooted in and entangled with structures and features of the very order it sought to dismantle. Among other things, ISIS's rise to power and establishment of its state-like presence in Syria and Iraq must be situated within the political economy of Middle Eastern conflicts and global colonial legacies with their impact on the states in the region and their economies (Matin, 2018; Mabon and Royle, 2017). However, the global ambitions of the ISIS project clearly exceeded the territorial project in place in Iraq and Syria.

Arguably, much of ISIS's rise to prominence on the global scale was related not only to its surprising territorial successes, but also to what has been called its 'propaganda machine' (BBC, 2018). Specifically, ISIS managed to capture the world's attention by its adoption and circulation of spectacular violence, meted out against its enemies, detractors and religious and political opponents. Infamously, ISIS's rise to power and its consolidation were defined by a series of atrocious actions that remain part of the global collective memory – ethnic cleansing, enslavement and systemic rape of the Yazidi community, gruesome public executions, and harsh punishments imposed for even minor transgressions against the prescribed social and religious order shook public opinion.

It was these images and testimonies fleshing out the 'unimaginable cruelty' (BBC, 2020; Friis, 2018) which gave rise to ISIS's notoriety. Nonetheless, what might appear as senseless violence served a strategic purpose recognisable to 'rational' bureaucracies and state apparatuses in different settings, functioning as a means to impose (semi-)domestic political and social order on the governed population, as well as sending a message to its foreign enemies (Mello, 2018; see also Richards, this volume). More importantly, the acts of violence committed by ISIS were entirely up to date with contemporary standards in terms of their curation, distribution and circulation.

Neither the shocking displays of violence nor the appeal of a prosperous life in the Caliphate (see below) would make an imprint on the global public, were it not for ISIS's much-discussed strategic use of cyberspace (Heck, 2017; Milton, 2016). Several authors have noted that the organisation's media output was highly professionally made and curated to achieve widespread dissemination of its violent messages. For example, Kraidy argues that 'although [ISIS's] violence is not exceptional historically, the group's circulation of gory imagery is unprecedented in quantity and reach' (Kraidy, 2017b, p. 1197) and that 'one of the most noteworthy aspects of the Islamic State is its strategic use of multipronged communication campaigns that integrate every possible media modality' (Kraidy, 2017a, p. 168).

So, although these practices ostensibly sought to work towards abolishing the current territorial, political, and even temporal order, they were in fact intimately linked to and reliant on technologies (of various sorts) provided by (hyper)modernity. As such, the revisionist project was closely tied into realities of the order it sought to dismantle. It also manifested a deep entanglement with the (infra)structures of the dominant order in the way it enacted its particular visions, exploiting the realm of the borderless (cyber)space while executing highly localised operations. The media strategies of ISIS thus highlight one important hybrid feature inscribed in ISIS's practices: The apparent 'ancient' brutality was enabled by utilising the modern infrastructure of electronic communication. The 'unprecedented' violence (or its visibility and reach) and the revolutionary goals it sought to propel would not have obtained its political salience and resonance without the modern infrastructure and intimate reliance on the current (technosocial) order. This hybrid combination would find a peculiar imprint in securitisation narratives. Like other terror movements in the past (Ditrych, 2014), what represented – at the level of the general tone (see Švantner, this volume) – the new and unprecedented danger and anxiety regarding ISIS were the compound of moral 'backwardness' (manifested in the transgression of the norms of 'society', including the distribution of legitimate violence) and state-of-the-art technological prowess.

Relatedly, although the violence exercised by ISIS was shocking to its targets, and heavily featured references to the theological–political pedigree that the movement was embedded in, it was still accessible and comprehensible for global audiences. As several authors have argued (Kraidy, 2017b, 2018a; Friis, 2015, 2018), ISIS's multimedia materials resonated so well exactly because they were recognisable for Western audiences and displayed modern features, such as meshing the audio with the visual, repetition and so on. Although its production did in many regards intensify some of the trends of space and time compression (Kraidy, 2017a, 2018b), the point here is that ISIS practices have posed as a strengthening and continuing of established ways of perception and representation rather than as a radical break with them. Those elements which include these technologies of representation or snippets of Western consumer culture media codes have been integrated into ISIS's hybrid assemblage together with the codes appropriated from the modern political Islam repertoire.

It is important to note that the excessive focus on ISIS featuring acts of (political) violence and its mechanical reproduction runs the risk of concealing the nature of the movement's cyberpresence, which is multifaceted and speaks to various aspects of the reformatory political and social vision. In other words, it is not limited to the disturbing images that shook the West. Even before the rise of ISIS, Crone, drawing on her field work among radicalised Islamist youth in Denmark, argued that 'religious violence in Europe today is largely enabled by aesthetic technologies of the self, such as for instance jihad- and martyr-videos' (Crone, 2014, p. 292). Crone talks mainly about videos that operate in the registers of 'jihad, violence and death' (Crone, 2014, p. 302; see also Roy, 2017). Yet she rightly points out that even these interpellations were mediated – and their recipients made subjects – through 'aesthetic technologies' that 'address not only the intellect, but also the senses, the feelings and the bodies of an audience' (Crone, 2014, pp. 301–2).

This analysis can be extended to ISIS media operations in its more comprehensive outlook. Existing research shows that ISIS's efforts to constitute the global politico-religious community via smooth cyberspace did not consist of exclusively, or even dominantly, conveying images of violence. Rather, ISIS utilised the 'smooth desert' (or 'a steppe') in the form of cyberspace in which 'movement between two points can occur in a virtually infinite number of trajectories' (Kraidy, 2018b, p. 171) to construe a comprehensive vision of organising social and political life. In a statement based on a content analysis of ISIS's official media output, Milton claims that 'more than 50 percent [of the releases] focus on themes outside of the battlefield, such as governance, justice, the importance of religious practices, and life in the caliphate' (Milton, 2016,

p. iv). Similarly, Anna Leander argues that a detailed inspection of ISIS materials reveals that 'friendship, play and community are recurring and prominent themes' (Leander, 2017, p. 355) characterising ISIS's media output.

The revolutionary vision of ISIS and the practices intended to bring it about are irreducible to the lure and horror (cf. Debrix, 2016) of revolutionary 'ultra-violence' (Kraidy, 2017b, p. 1200) that sought to distance it from the present world order. Neither can they be reduced, however, to imaginaries of a territorial state and representations of (desired) sovereignty, materialised in artefacts such as visualisations of ISIS's present and future territorial reach, pasted on to familiar map grids (Offenhuber, 2018) – even if these registers are crucial for comprehending the ISIS political project. ISIS sought to construct *whole lifeworld(s)* as a part of its revolutionary project, based on sets of norms and practices which heavily borrowed from and engaged other spheres of the social and the political, including popular culture (Hegghammer, 2017). ISIS thus engaged in representational practices of the 'good life' that worked against the grain of construing ISIS as a purely (even if perhaps instrumentally) violent actor. In this process of subjectivation, ISIS's aesthetic–technological assemblage combined and repurposed elements taken from widely different repertoires – both revolutionary and those of the present international order. It is here, as well as elsewhere, that we can see '[ISIS] fielding a system of continuities and ruptures under a dominant trait of hybridity' (Mohamedou, 2017, p. 12) – hybridity that actually facilitated the global spread of ISIS's messages and global becoming by accommodating various forms of the social and the political. At the same time, ISIS's visual assemblages obtained their salience exactly because they were portrayed and perceived as a part of the supposedly global, transformative and radically different political project.

The media operations of ISIS in cyberspace accompanied its becoming as a global movement that sought to realise its programme in specific, even if dispersed, locales. The rejection by its members of previous political allegiances to nation states and its recoding of the practice of sovereignty found its expression in constructing a loose network of individuals around the globe who subscribed to the group's ideological strivings and, consequently, formed the revolutionary subject. This resulted in the double-headed nature of ISIS's sovereignty and disconnected territoriality. On the one hand, the ISIS project in Iraq and Syria and its offshoots ('provinces' or *wilayat*) elsewhere around the globe (see, for example, Zenn, 2019) took a territorialised form, in some cases adopting various governmental features of a state. On the other, it also took the form of a heterogenous and dispersed web of individuals who pleaded allegiance to the newly established global Caliphate.

In this respect, ISIS relied in its self-actualisation as much on the imaginary of a utopian polity, realised in the conquered physical spaces, as on the deterritorialised script of borderless entity, connected by the cyberspace which united loose networks of fighters and sympathisers in the global *umma* with the physical territories already captured by the group (Kadercan, 2019). This loose network of individuals who subscribed to the idea of the global Caliphate marked the emergence of a diffused revolutionary movement, made coherent not through organisational or operational practice, but rather through shared (albeit nascent) subjectivation processes of becoming protagonists in the revolutionary process. In this respect, 'the threatening nature of [ISIS]', as it was put by Mohamedou (2017, p. 22), was manifested in the articulation of the global *umma* existing beyond the established borders of Westphalian states (Mendelsohn, 2012; Roy, 2004). Even if only a tiny minority of the members of the *umma* became receptive to the ISIS project and reinvented themselves as members of its Caliphate, this process of redefining allegiances and adopting violent means to manifest them – 'radicalisation', as it came to be known – raised fears regarding its political and security fallout among many pundits and state agents, as well as the general public (Awan, 2017; Ward, 2018; Steinbach, 2016; Koerner, 2016).

Subject Effects: Territorialising Risky Subjects and Digital Spaces

These articulations of ISIS as a hybrid actor becoming in both virtual and physical spaces and deeply entangled in various aspects of the international order presented nation states with a challenge of how to react to it. In many ways, such a challenge was nothing new. Partly originating in the longer experience of national and international responses to political violence massively enlarged after the attacks of 9/11, different nation states, as well as international organisations, had already developed a vast repertoire of distinct practices oriented towards countering various violent challengers of the state-system on both the national and the international level, as well as the international institutional *dispositif* dedicated to tackling the problem (Ditrych, 2014; Shirk, 2019).

International organisations, among others especially the United Nations (UN) as the representative of the will of the international community in its entirety, assumed the task of supporting the building and standardisation of state apparatuses' capabilities in legal and penal matters, with the intention of creating a community of states responding to terrorism in a unified manner. The outcasts of the international community were to be clearly identified and collectively repudiated, while the standardisation of state functions was expected to eliminate non-regulated spaces ('failed states', 'rogue states' or 'ungoverned spaces') that could serve as bases for nomadic war machines (Ditrych, 2014;

Martini, 2021). Furthermore, the additional strengthening of border controls and surveillance of potentially risky subjects across the borders were supposed to limit the mobility of these movements. All of these measures were designed by state apparatuses to contain and break up the structures of nascent transnational violent war machines – and they did so with some success. However, they also impacted on the shape and functions of states and their interaction with societies for years to come (Bigo and Tsukala, 2008; Shirk, 2019).

The responses to ISIS followed a similar pattern, with coercive military and policing measures being among the first attempts to stop the rapidly proliferating war machine. In fact, some of these were taken not primarily by states as such, but by a range of more or less territorialised non-state actors, such as the Kurdish forces, Iraqi Shiʻi militias or local Libyan armed factions cooperating with state actors and themselves further adopting some state functions throughout the anti-ISIS campaign. The territorial part of the Caliphate, with its statist institutions and imaginary, collapsed over the course of a few years of pressure enacted by local ground forces and massive Western aerial attacks (Byman, 2019, pp. 203–5). This induced ISIS's metamorphosis from its hybrid *state-war machine* form to a loosely structured insurgency, active in the deserts of Iraq and Syria and other places scattered around the globe, as well as in cyberspace (Kadercan, 2018).

However, the impact of ISIS on the state system and the reactions to the threat it posed from the hegemonic perspective went beyond places where it had established the territorial form of its Caliphate. It was felt across distinct locales, national contexts and the international arena. Following the concerns over ISIS's worldwide reach and ability to connect with different communities of the global *umma* via cyberspace, and subsequently also its global recruitment campaign, international institutions were called to action to support the collective strengthening of the community of states (Kundnani and Hayes, 2018, p. 29; Martini, 2021, p. 134). While most of the specific responses were to be implemented by the states, the UN assumed a coordinating role, singling out the most important issues of common concern and legitimising specific countermeasures (Martini, 2021).

UN Security Council Resolution 2178, adopted in December 2014 and specifically focusing on the threat of foreign terrorist fighters, epitomised this effort and translated it into a set of more specific measures (Martini, 2020, p. 171). Following previous strategies aimed at strengthening the system, Resolution 2178 called for increasing the capacities of weaker states to make them better equipped to face the emerging war machines and to avoid providing these war machines with (primarily territorial) space where they could take refuge and proliferate (Aoláin, 2021, pp. 50–1). However, Resolution

2178 also called for the enhanced control of spaces of global flows (such as international travel or financial flows) in order to prevent the forming and proliferation of transnational war machines (UN SC, 2014, pp. 5–6). Taking a pre-emptive approach, the UN thus called on states to take legislative and policing actions even before particular subjects openly perform an act that would connect them with ISIS's transnational assemblage (Ginsborg, 2021).

At the same time, with its focus on the need to develop ways how to counter violent non-state actors via education and increased outreach to civil society and non-state authorities (UN SC, 2014, pp. 6–7), Resolution 2178 paved the way for broadening the range of spaces for states to secure and subject to technologies of pre-emptive surveillance and control. As sealing off physical territories was deemed insufficient for stopping the expansion and multiplication of ISIS's war machine around the globe and for ensuring the proper defence of the state system, international attention turned to specific groups that were considered to be at risk of finding ISIS's project appealing and thus also at risk of breaking away from their states. At the same time, as war machines utilised 'social media for the global and real-time communication of their ideas and exploits' (UN GA, 2015, p. 1), increased attention was given to cyberspace and information space, as these represent (partially) deterritorialised platforms, existing outside of the territorial grid of the state system, that allow war machines to spread across the globe (Martini, 2021, pp. 153–9).

One of the widely implemented offshoots of these concerns has been the emergence of a global agenda of C/PVE. Taking inspiration from a range of initiatives put forward by Western European states in response to domestic fears over (predominantly Islamist) violent extremist groups (Baker-Beall et al., 2016; de Goede and Simon, 2013) and presenting a 'softer' side of state-led global counterterrorism efforts (Ucko, 2018), the international C/PVE agenda was formally introduced by the UN Secretary-General in 2015 as a response to 'a global and unprecedented threat to international peace and security' (UN SC, 2015, p. 1), presented by the emergence of ISIS. Encompassing a multitude of different programmes and finding its way into different areas of UN activities, the core element of C/PVE has been its focus on developing non-violent ways – not coercive or even disciplining, but rather governmental in the sense of the 'conduct of conduct' (Foucault, 1991) – of dissuading potential recruits from joining non-state violent extremist groups (Ucko, 2018).

C/PVE put forward the idea that it is not enough to strengthen the capacities of states and their physical control of territory, and that the appeal of revolutionary alternatives to the present state system was not necessarily only in the ideological message that hybrid revolutionaries channelled and embodied, but was also to be found in the subjects' alienation from the present structures of authority and social control (UN GA, 2015; UNDP, 2017a). As one of the UN documents outlining the agenda states: '*Recruiters focus their attention on vulnerable alienated groups in society, and manipulate their feelings of frustration and anger*' (UNDP, 2017b, p. 24). Due to ISIS's deterritorialised operation, these groups represent a potential building block of ISIS's transnational assemblage.

In consequence, as important as it was to develop the state's physical capacities to tackle transnational violent war machines, the C/PVE has rather sought to strengthen the state system and counter (or ideally prevent) the proliferation of revolutionary war machines by building and strengthening links that bound the population (or at least its risky parts) with states and thus also with the present international system. The initial focus on ISIS gave the C/PVE agenda its dominant orientation on the (Sunni) Muslim communities, as well as on the youth or communities that have been politically and economically marginalised and could thus harbour grievances against the state (Breidlid, 2021; Martini, 2021, pp. 143–45; Romaniuk and Durner, 2018; Sukarieh and Tannock, 2018). To reconnect these groups back to the governmental authority, a broad range of internationally sponsored programmes sought to increase their trust in the state and its institutions, propounding an ideological affiliation with 'moderate' belief systems that are not hostile to the state (Martini, 2021, pp. 153–9; UN GA, 2015; UNDP, 2017b; Thiessen, 2019).

The focus of the C/PVE agenda on societal space represented one of the reactions of the system to the ISIS war machine. Another was constituted by C/PVE initiatives aimed at cyberspace and the information sphere, which manifested a different logic. The goal here was rather to increase states' presence and control and, by doing so, limit the possibility of war machine formation and proliferation in these spaces. Although the UN again performed a coordinating and legitimising role, while the primary role was played by the states or other international organisations, the digital spaces became ever more monitored and controlled (UN GA, 2015, p. 19; UN SC, 2017; see also Möllers, 2021). As states turned to cyberspace as an area of conflict – with revolutionary war machines, but also among themselves – they started to make this space legible and actionable. This gradual territorialisation of cyberspace (see Lambach, 2020), made more urgent by the encounter with ISIS, allowed states to act against the movement's online sympathisers and bots, and in cooperation with social media companies to break up the war machine gradually and limit its spread (see, for example, Europol, 2018).

The struggle between the war machine and the state apparatus in cyberspace has continued ever since, with ISIS periodically 'amassing territory on Facebook' (Ayad, 2020, p. 7) or on other social media platforms, just to be taken down and deleted once discovered by state agencies (see, for example,

Pearson, 2018). Besides the direct control of cyberspace, the states have also developed a range of offensive and defensive capabilities to be used against the ISIS war machine. Among other means, the rapidly proliferating field of countermessaging was supposed to increase the ability of states to confront the adversary directly in the information field, establish their dominance there, and separate the ideational connections between the war machine and the larger civilian population (Bjola and Pamment, 2019).

Conclusion

ISIS is far from simply a terrorist group, or insurgent actor, or doomsday cult. Rather, it adopts and combines a number of rationalities, modes and practices. This chapter highlights and exemplifies what makes ISIS such a compelling case for study in this book – in spite of simplistic representations, the movement is hard to pin down as a representative of this or that category of political actor, as 'it alternates / combines statism and terrorism' (Kraidy, 2018b, p. 172), among others. The concept of hybridity, as presented in this book, makes it possible to illuminate and grasp the multiplicity at the core of ISIS's wide array of practices with a global imprint: reaching from the formation of a network of individuals who pledged allegiance, publicly or in private, to the idea of the world Caliphate; to the establishment of more conventional structures and practices in place in the Middle East; the attacks on individuals conducted in the name of the cause globally; and the process of 'franchising', in which various groups subscribe to the vision of the global Caliphate, following the diminishing of the capacities of ISIS in Iraq and Syria by the military countercampaign.

This peculiar hybrid constitution of ISIS has also left its mark on the international system and state practices that have sought to counter it. Due to the entanglement of the movement with the very structures of the international order and its ability to reach across the borders of present states, the system has developed new modes of countering and preventing such actors. As this chapter shows, the resulting reactions aimed at strengthening the control of states – not only over their physical territories, but also over certain parts of their population, which have been considered to be insufficiently attached to the states, as well as over cyberspace and the information sphere. By these reactions, the global and deterritorialised elements of ISIS's assemblage were to be contained and its war machine was to be broken up, reducing ISIS as such to a manageable territorial insurgency. These responses notwithstanding, the territorialisation and increased state control of previously autonomous spaces, which the encounters with the ISIS war machine have initiated, continue to exist. As such, the legacy of ISIS and its nomadic charge on the present state system will continue to live on in the present state system. So will the newly developed capacities of states in new spaces that have been colonised into states' territories and made objects of their responsibility.

References

Abdulrazaq, T. and Stansfield, S. 2016. 'The Enemy Within: ISIS and the Conquest of Mosul'. *The Middle East Journal* 70 (4): 525–42.

Aoláin, F. N. 2021. 'The Ever-expanding Legislative Supremacy of the Security Council in Counterterrorism'. In Vedaschi, A. and Scheppele, K. L. (eds). *9/11 and the Rise of Global Anti-Terrorism Law: How the UN Security Council Rules the World*, 34–55. Cambridge: Cambridge University Press.

Artrip, R. E. and Debrix, F. 2018. 'The Viral Mediation of Terror: ISIS, Image, Implosion'. *Critical Studies in Media Communication* 35 (1): 74–88. Available at: <https://doi.org/10.1080/15295036.2017.1393099> (last accessed 14 June 2022).

Awan, I. 2017. 'Cyber-extremism: Isis and the Power of Social Media'. *Society* 54 (2): 138–49. Available at: <https://doi.org/10.1007/s12115-017-0114 -0> (last accessed 14 June 2022).

Ayad, M. 2020. 'The Propaganda Pipeline: The ISIS Fuouaris Upload Network on Facebook'. Institute for Strategic Dialogue. Available at: <https://www .isdglobal.org/wp-content/uploads/2020/07/The-Propaganda-Pipeline -1.pdf> (last accessed 14 June 2022).

Baker-Beall, C., Heath-Kelly C. and Jarvis, L. (eds). 2016. *Counter-radicalisation: Critical Perspectives*. London and New York: Routledge.

BBC. 2018. 'The Rise and Fall of Islamic State's Propaganda Machine'. *BBC News*, 2 February. Available at: <https://www.bbc.com/news/av/world -middle-east-42824374> (last accessed 14 June 2022).

BBC. 2020. 'Islamic State "Beatles" in Court over US Hostages' Deaths'. *BBC News*, 7 October. Available at: <https://www.bbc.com/news/uk-54 449482> (last accessed 14 June 2022).

Bigo, D. and Tsukala, A. (eds). 2008. *Terror, Insecurity and Liberty: Illiberal Practices of Liberal Regimes after 9/11*. London: Routledge.

Bjola, C. and Pamment, J. (eds). 2019. *Countering Online Propaganda and Extremism: The Dark Side of Digital Diplomacy*. London and New York: Routledge.

Bleiker, R. 2014. 'Visual Assemblages: From Causality to Conditions of Possibility'. In Acuto, M. and Curtis, S. (eds). *Reassembling International Theory: Assemblage Thinking and International Relations*, 75–81. London: Palgrave Macmillan UK.

Boyraz, C. 2021. 'Alternative Political Projects of Territoriality and Governance during the Syrian War: The Caliphate vs Democratic Confederalism'. *Geopolitics* 26 (4): 1095–120. Available at: <https://doi.org/10.1080/14650 045.2020.1855580> (last accessed 14 June 2022).

Breidlid, T. 2021. 'Countering or Contributing to Radicalisation and Violent Extremism in Kenya? A Critical Case Study'. *Critical Studies on Terrorism* 14 (2): 225–46. Available at: <https://doi.org/10.1080/17539153.2021.19 02613> (last accessed 14 June 2022).

Bunzel, C. 2015. 'From Paper State to Caliphate: The Ideology of the Islamic State'. Analysis Paper 15. Washington, D.C.: Brookings Center for Middle East Policy.

Byman, D. 2019. *Road Warriors: Foreign Fighters in the Armies of Jihad.* Oxford: Oxford University Press.

Crone, M. 2014. 'Religion and Violence: Governing Muslim Militancy through Aesthetic Assemblages'. *Millennium: Journal of International Studies* 43 (1): 291–307. Available at: <https://doi.org/10.1177/030582981454 1166> (last accessed 14 June 2022).

Dallal, A. S. 2017. *The Political Theology of ISIS: Prophets, Messiahs, and the Extinction of the Grayzone.* Washington, D.C.: Tadween.

Debrix, F. 2016. *Global Powers of Horror: Security, Politics, and the Body in Pieces.* London: Routledge.

de Goede, M. and Simon, S. 2013. 'Governing Future Radicals in Europe'. *Antipode* 45 (2): 315–35. Available at: <https://doi.org/10.1111/j.1467-83 30.2012.01039.x> (last accessed 14 June 2022).

Deleuze, G. and Guattari, F. 1987. *A Thousand Plateaus: Capitalism and Schizophrenia.* Minneapolis: University of Minnesota Press.

Ditrych, O. 2014. *Tracing the Discourses of Terrorism: Identity, Genealogy and State.* Basingstoke and New York: Palgrave Macmillan.

Europol. 2018. 'Islamic State Propaganda Machine Hit by Law Enforcement in Coordinated Takedown Action'. *Europol,* 27 April. Available at: <https:// www.europol.europa.eu/newsroom/news/islamic-state-propaganda-mac hine-hit-law-enforcement-in-coordinated-takedown-action> (last accessed 14 June 2022).

Foucault, M. 1991. ' Governmentality'. In Burchell, G., Gordon, C. and Miller, P. (eds). *The Foucault Effect: Studies in Governmentality,* 84–104. Chicago: University of Chicago Press.

Friis, S. M. 2015. '"Beyond Anything We Have Ever Seen": Beheading Videos and the Visibility of Violence in the War against ISIS'. *International Affairs* 91 (4): 725–46.

Friis, S. M. 2018. '"Behead, Burn, Crucify, Crush": Theorizing the Islamic

State's Public Displays of Violence'. *European Journal of International Relations* 24 (2): 243–67.

Ginsborg, L. 2021. 'Moving toward the Criminalization of "Pre-Crime": The UN Security Council's Recent Legislative Action on Counterterrorism'. In Vedaschi, A. and Scheppele, K. L. (eds). *9/11 and the Rise of Global Anti-Terrorism Law: How the UN Security Council Rules the World*, 133–54. Cambridge: Cambridge University Press.

Halimi, M. B. H., Bin Sudiman, M. S. A. S. and Bin Hassan, A. S. R. 2019. 'Assessment of Islamic State's Ideological Threat'. *Counter Terrorist Trends and Analyses* 11 (1): 86–90.

Hamdan, A. N. 2016. 'Breaker of Barriers? Notes on the Geopolitics of the Islamic State in Iraq and Sham'. *Geopolitics* 21 (3): 605–27. Available at: <https://doi.org/10.1080/14650045.2016.1138940> (last accessed 14 June 2022).

Heck, A. 2017. 'Images, Visions and Narrative Identity Formation of ISIS'. *Global Discourse* 7 (2–3): 244–59. Available at: <https://doi.org/10.1080/23 269995.2017.1342490> (last accessed 14 June 2022).

Hegghammer, T. (ed.). 2017. *Jihadi Culture: The Art and Social Practices of Militant Islamists*. Cambridge: Cambridge University Press.

Jacoby, T. 2021. 'The Islamic "State": Sovereignty, Territoriality and Governance'. *International Politics* Online First. Available at: <https://doi .org/10.1057/s41311-020-00277-x> (last accessed 14 June 2022).

Kadercan, B. 2018. 'What the ISIS Crisis Means for the Future of the Middle East'. In Yeşiltaş, M. and Kardaş, T. (eds). *Non-state Armed Actors in the Middle East*, 237–60. Cham: Palgrave Macmillan.

Kadercan, B. 2019. 'Territorial Logic of the Islamic State: An Interdisciplinary Approach'. *Territory, Politics, Governance* 9 (1): 94–110.

Koerner, B. I. 2016. 'Why ISIS Is Winning the Social Media War – And How to Fight Back'. *Wired*, April. Available at: <https://www.wired.com/20 16/03/isis-winning-social-media-war-heres-beat/> (last accessed 14 June 2022).

Kraidy, M. M. 2017a. 'Revisiting Hypermedia Space in the Era of the Islamic State'. *The Communication Review* 20 (3): 165–71.

Kraidy, M. M. 2017b. 'The Projectilic Image: Islamic State's Digital Visual Warfare and Global Networked Affect'. *Media, Culture & Society* 39 (8): 1194–209.

Kraidy, M. M. 2018a. 'Fun Against Fear in the Caliphate: Islamic State's Spectacle and Counter-spectacle'. *Critical Studies in Media Communication* 35 (1): 40–56.

Kraidy, M. M. 2018b. 'Terror, Territoriality, Temporality: Hypermedia

Events in the Age of Islamic State'. *Television & New Media* 19 (2): 170–6. Available at: <https://doi.org/10.1177/1527476417697197> (last accessed 14 June 2022).

Kundnani, A. and Hayes, B. 2018. *The Globalisation of Countering Violent Extremism Policies: Undermining Human Rights, Instrumentalising Civil Society.* Amsterdam: Transnational Institute.

Lambach, D. 2020. 'The Territorialization of Cyberspace'. *International Studies Review* 22 (3): 482–506. Available at: <https://doi.org/10.1093/isr/vi z022> (last accessed 14 June 2022).

Leander, A. 2017. 'Digital/Commercial (In)Visibility: The Politics of DAESH Recruitment Videos'. *European Journal of Social Theory* 20 (3): 348–72.

Li, D. 2019. *The Universal Enemy: Jihad, Empire, and the Challenge of Solidarity.* Stanford: Stanford University Press.

Mabon, S. and Royle, S. 2017. *The Origins of ISIS: The Collapse of Nations and Revolution in the Middle East.* London and New York: I. B. Tauris.

Martini, A. 2020. 'Legitimising Countering Extremism at an International Level: The Role of the United Nations Security Council'. In Martini, A., Ford, K. and Jackson, R. (eds). *Encountering Extremism: Theoretical Issues and Local Challenges*, 159–79. Manchester: Manchester University Press.

Martini, A. 2021. *The UN and Counter-terrorism: Global Hegemonies, Power and Identities.* Routledge Critical Terrorism Studies. Abingdon and New York: Routledge.

Matin, K. 2018. 'Lineages of the Islamic State: An International Historical Sociology of State (De-)Formation in Iraq'. *Journal of Historical Sociology* 31 (1): 6–24. Available at: <https://doi.org/10.1111/johs.12188> (last accessed 14 June 2022).

Mello, B. 2018. 'The Islamic State: Violence and Ideology in a Post-Colonial Revolutionary Regime'. *International Political Sociology* 12 (2): 139–55.

Mendelsohn, B. 2012. 'God vs. Westphalia: Radical Islamist Movements and the Battle for Organising the World'. *Review of International Studies* 38 (3): 589–613. Available at: <https://doi.org/10.1017/S0260210511000775> (last accessed 14 June 2022).

Milton, D. 2016. *Communication Breakdown: Unraveling the Islamic State's Media Efforts.* New York: Combating Terrorism Center.

Mohamedou, M. O. 2017. *A Theory of ISIS: Political Violence and the Global Order.* London: Pluto Press.

Möllers, N. 2021. 'Making Digital Territory: Cybersecurity, Techno-Nationalism, and the Moral Boundaries of the State'. *Science, Technology, & Human Values* 46 (1): 112–38. Available at: <https://doi.org/10.1177/016 2243920904436> (last accessed 14 June 2022).

Offenhuber, D. 2018. 'Maps of Daesh: The Cartographic Warfare Surrounding Insurgent Statehood'. *GeoHumanities* 4 (1): 196–219.

Ostřanský, B. 2019. *The Jihadist Preachers of the End Times: ISIS Apocalyptic Propaganda*. Edinburgh: Edinburgh University Press.

Pearson, E. 2018. 'Online as the New Frontline: Affect, Gender, and ISIS-Take-Down on Social Media'. *Studies in Conflict & Terrorism* 41 (11): 850–74. Available at: <https://doi.org/10.1080/1057610X.2017.1352280> (last accessed 14 June 2022).

Richards, I. 2020. *Neoliberalism and Neo-jihadism: Propaganda and Finance in Al Qaeda and Islamic State*. Manchester: Manchester University Press.

Romaniuk, P. and Durner, T. 2018. 'The Politics of Preventing Violent Extremism: The Case of Uganda'. *Conflict, Security & Development* 18 (2): 159–79. Available at: <https://doi.org/10.1080/14678802.2018.1447863> (last accessed 14 June 2022).

Roy, O. 2004. *Globalized Islam: The Search for a New Ummah*. New York: Columbia University Press.

Roy, O. 2017. *Jihad and Death: The Global Appeal of Islamic State*. Oxford: Oxford University Press.

Shirk, M. 2019. 'The Universal Eye: Anarchist "Propaganda of the Deed" and Development of the Modern Surveillance State'. *International Studies Quarterly* 63 (2): 334–45. Available at: <https://doi.org/10.1093/isq/sqy062> (last accessed 14 June 2022).

Steinbach, M. 2016. 'ISIL Online: Countering Terrorist Radicalization and Recruitment on the Internet and Social Media'. Federal Bureau of Investigation. 6 July. Available at: <https://www.fbi.gov/news/testimony/isil-online-countering-terrorist-radicalization-and-recruitment-on-the-internet-and-social-media-> (last accessed 14 June 2022).

Sukarieh, M. and Tannock, S. 2018. 'The Global Securitisation of Youth'. *Third World Quarterly* 39 (5): 854–70. Available at: <https://doi.org/10.1080/01436597.2017.1369038> (last accessed 14 June 2022).

Thiessen, C. 2019. 'The Strategic Ambiguity of the United Nations Approach to Preventing Violent Extremism'. *Studies in Conflict & Terrorism* Online First. Available at: <https://doi.org/10.1080/1057610X.2019.1647685> (last accessed 14 June 2022).

Truong, F. 2018. *Radicalized Loyalties: Becoming Muslim in the West*. Translated by Seth Ackerman. Cambridge: Polity.

Ucko, D. H. 2018. 'Preventing Violent Extremism through the United Nations: The Rise and Fall of a Good Idea'. *International Affairs* 94 (2): 251–70. Available at: <https://doi.org/10.1093/ia/iix235> (last accessed 14 June 2022).

UN GA. 2015. 'Plan of Action to Prevent Violent Extremism: Report of the Secretary-General'. United Nations General Assembly. Available at: <https://undocs.org/en/A/70/674> (last accessed 14 June 2022).

UN SC. 2014. 'United Nations Security Council Resolution 2178'. United Nations Security Council. Available at: <https://undocs.org/S/RES/2178 (2014)> (last accessed 14 June 2022).

UN SC. 2015. 'United Nations Security Council Resolution 2249'. United Nations Security Council. Available at: <https://www.securitycouncilre port.org/atf/cf/%7B65BFCF9B-6D27-4E9C-8CD3-CF6E4FF96FF9%7D /s_res_2249.pdf> (last accessed 14 June 2022).

UN SC. 2017. 'United Nations Security Council Resolution 2354'. United Nations Security Council. Available at: <https://undocs.org/en/S/RES /2354(2017)> (last accessed 14 June 2022).

UNDP. 2017a. 'Journey to Extremism in Africa'. United Nations Development Programme. Available at: <https://journey-to-extremism.undp.org/con tent/downloads/UNDP-JourneyToExtremism-report-2017-english.pdf> (last accessed 14 June 2022).

UNDP. 2017b. 'Preventing Violent Extremism through Promoting Inclusive Development, Tolerance and Respect for Diversity'. United Nations Development Programme. Available at: <https://www1.undp.org/content /dam/undp/library/Democratic%20Governance/OGC/UNDP%20OGC _PVE%20report_Final_web.pdf> (last accessed 14 June 2022).

Vu, T. and Van Orden, P. 2020. 'Revolution and World Order: The Case of the Islamic State (ISIS)'. *International Politics* 57 (1): 57–78. Available at: <https://doi.org/10.1057/s41311-019-00176-w> (last accessed 14 June 2022).

Ward, A. 2018. 'ISIS's Social Media Use Still Poses a Threat to Stability in the Middle East and Africa'. RAND Corporation. Available at: <https://www .rand.org/blog/2018/12/isiss-use-of-social-media-still-poses-a-threat-to- stability.html> (last accessed 14 June 2022).

Westall, S. 2014. 'After Iraq Gains, Qaeda Offshoot Claims Islamic "Caliphate"'. *Reuters*, 30 June. Available at: <https://www.reuters.com/article/us-syria- crisis-iraq-idUSKBN0F40SL20140630> (last accessed 14 June 2022).

Whiteside, C. 2016. 'New Masters of Revolutionary Warfare: The Islamic State Movement (2002–2016)'. *Perspectives on Terrorism* 10 (4): 4–18.

Zenn, J. 2019. 'The Islamic State's Provinces on the Peripheries: Juxtaposing the Pledges from Boko Haram in Nigeria and Abu Sayyaf and Maute Group in the Philippines'. *Perspectives on Terrorism* 13 (1): 87–104.

5

On Top of the Revolutionary Game: Uncovering the 'Islamic State's' Revolutionary Message

Miriam M. Müller-Rensch

Revolutionary violence is 'the highest [that is divine] manifestation of unalloyed violence by man'.

Walter Benjamin, *Critique of Violence*, 1921

This uprising to which we invite the umma [global Muslim community] must possess the essential elements of success. There must first occur a revolution at the plane of thought and awareness so that the masses are prepared for the next stage, so that they know why they must revolt, **and when revolt they do, they must know their ultimate destination**.

Hamza bin Ladin
Son of Osama bin Ladin, presenting al-Qaʻida
as the Guardian of the revolution,
7 November 2017

Since its formation, the social movement of Jihadi-Salafism (Bonner, 2006; Cook, 2009; Meijer, 2009) has consistently advocated nothing less than an 'alternative modernity' where a new 'imagined world order' would supplant and finally replace the international system of nation states, the global economic system of capitalism, and the effects of liberal democratic values and lifestyles. This ultimate goal of Jihadi-Salafism has, however, taken a back seat in public perception. The movement's most prominent face of the early 2000s, the al-Qaʻida network, exclusively concentrated its efforts on its 'global jihad' against the 'far enemy' through its clandestine cell activities (Gerges, 2005). But while the al-Qaʻida mother network postponed until very recently the establishment of the 'global Caliphate' to an imagined future (Staffel and Aqan, 2016, p. 15), their regional offshoot, the so-called 'Islamic State' (Daesh or ISIS),[1] not only made this imagined future their priority from the very beginning, but success-fully took the first steps to make it a reality: Even though short-lived, Daesh's governance of social life in Iraqi and Syrian territory between 2013 and 2017 offered a first glimpse of how the global Jihadi-Salafist project might look.

Connecting perspectives that have come to understand Jihadi-Salafism as a social movement (Hegghammer, 2009a; Meijer, 2009; Westphal, 2018), that reject Jihadi-Salafism's singularity in favour of considering it 'part of globalized modernity' (Meijer, 2007, p. 423; Hegghammer, 2009b, p. 245), and that accept the movement's revolutionary character (Atran, 2016; Cockburn, 2015; Fall, 2015; Ingram, 2016; Mello, 2018; Walt, 2015; Whiteside, 2016), this chapter explicitly supports the incentive of this volume to de-exceptionalise Daesh (cf. Ditrych et al., this volume) and aims to uncover Daesh's revolution-ary message as crucial for its ongoing global success.

Building on Ditrych et al.'s framework (Ditrych et al., this volume), which connects revolutionary hybrid subjectivity and Deleuze and Guattari's 'war machine', as well as Richards's theoretical confrontation of IS organisational hybridity with its neoliberal methods of statist governance (Richards, this volume), the argument first retraces the ultimate revolutionary goal of Jihadi-Salafism in the movement's history to connect the dots between the revolution-ary dimensions of Marxism–Leninism, political Islam and Jihadi-Salafism with a specific focus on Daesh's upgraded version of this 'revolutionary' dimension. Then, Rod Aya's processual understanding of the revolutionary (Aya, 2015a) is applied to Daesh's revolutionary hybrid subjectivity. To grapple with Daesh's revolutionary character beyond the structure–agency binary, three dimensions of the revolutionary as a social phenomenon are identified: revolutionary intent, revolutionary situation and revolutionary outcome (Aya, 1979, p. 40). A crit-ical reinterpretation of 'revolutionary situation' as 'opportunity' then sets the stage to reconstruct the genealogy of Daesh's rise as a revolutionary actor that successfully joined independent elements of two different ontological orders: those of 'state' and 'war machine'. By recoding these previously irreconcilable elements, Daesh aimed to create an assemblage in its own logic (Ditrych et al., this volume; on Deleuze and Guattari 1987, p. 43), an alternative modernity as the revolutionary outcome, the group's ultimate revolutionary goal.

Uncovering Connections Between Revolutionary Marxism and the Jihadi-Salafist Project

To grasp Daesh's revolutionary call to action – that is, their revolutionary intent as a belief system's integration of revolutionary message and strategic outlook – the following subsection briefly explores the possible connection between Marxism, Sayyid Qutb's writings as chief ideologue of the Muslim Brotherhood (Al-Ikhwan) and Jihadi-Salafism through some of the 'inelimina-ble' revolutionary core concepts of Marxism–Leninism (Freeden, 1996, p. 62).

While Jihadi-Salafist influencers and ideologues have regularly explicitly rejected Marxism–Leninism as 'Westernised', atheist and thus anti-Muslim, there is no doubt that the majority of them have studied and discussed this body of thought (Orbach, 2012, p. 966), especially as Arab Nationalism, Arab Socialism and political Islam originated from the same intellectual circles in the Levant between the 1920s and 1960s (Choueiri, 2000). With a sideways glance at the impact of Marxist theories on Arab communism, it is likely that Jihadi-Salafist theorists were less invested in the 'intellectual advancement of Marxist and Socialist discourse' (Ismael, 2005, p. 103) and, rather, focused on the writings of classical 'dialectical materialism' (Hansen and Kainz, 2007).

Accordingly, we can identify two 'core elements' concerned with the ontology and agency of Marxist–Leninist ideology, which have been recoded and absorbed by Qutb and his admirers:

1. A deterministic view of history, according to which sociopolitical evo-lution necessarily follows a predetermined pattern of stages, in which the 'state' is merely considered one temporary, though necessary, stage among many (Marx 1973 [1875], p. 25; Lenin, 1917, Ch. 1). This logic of order allows us to conceptualise the Marxist–Leninist-inspired movement in any stage of development from group to statehood and beyond with a hybrid revolutionary subjectivity.
2. The essentialised roles of the 'rank-and-file members of the proletarian working class' and the 'political elite' in this process, which deduce their agency and fundamentally different abilities from the 'revolutionary histor-ical consciousness' of the 'elite' as a leading vanguard which is prescribed *a priori* (Lenin, 1917, Ch. 1; Davidshofer, 2014, p. 17).

The leadership role of the vanguard then connects the logic of order with the logic of agency as the vanguard is defined as both push and pull, as driver and leader, to overcome the current (and rejected) stage of society and realise the utopian society as the ultimate objective of all efforts while relying on the creation of the 'new human' (Segert and Zierke, 1998, pp. 171, 177). It is the vanguard as the inevitable protagonist to realise the revolutionary goal that connects the strategic outlook with the revolutionary message – a message which includes the diagnosis of the current condition as a problem with the revolutionary goal as the ideal situation where this problem has been solved. The vanguard is presented as the only protagonist able to realise this goal –

usually through violence. These three – problem, solution (goal) and call to action (how-to) as the revolutionary message – are 'ineliminable' concepts of any revolutionary belief system (Freeden, 1996).

Where to begin looking for hallmarks of these Marxist-inspired concepts among the vast array of influencers who inspired Jihadi-Salafist ideologies is indeed challenging. The political thinkers Abul Ala Maududi and Sayyid Qutb are regularly referred to when the theoretical groundwork for political Islam is examined, but they have also played a significant role in Jihadi-Salafism (Musallam, 2005).

Maududi and Qutb both wrote their texts in response to colonial rule and their systems of belief were shaped by a strong image of the coloniser as the adversary of Islam. Consequently, their bodies of thought should be read as a reaction to, or colonial 'resentment' at, the combination of their personal experience of oppression and their maltreatment and the general *Zeitgeist* among the occupied populations of colonial societies at the time (Fanon, 2004 [1961], p. 89; also see Mello, 2018, p. 150ff.). Pakistani journalist Maududi translated a thirteenth-century reading of the life of the Prophet Muhammad and his contemporaries for the audience of the modern world (Bowering, 2013, p. 269f.; Cheema, 2013). Also, he rephrased Islam as an all-embracing *Weltanschauung* superior to all other interpretations of this world in its 'epistemological finality' (Safdar, 2013, p. 202). Similarly, his contemporary and Muslim Brotherhood's chief ideologue Qutb successfully merged selected religious doctrines and concepts of Islam and the critique of nineteenth-century Muslim reformers with the logic of political ideologies of the twentieth century (Carré, 1984).

The notions formulated by Maududi and Qutb more than accommodated incentives of political action. However, it was Qutb who explicitly called for violence as the necessary means to realise what he labelled the 'Islamic State' ('*al-daula al-islamīyya*') – an undeniably revolutionary message recoding sovereignty:

> [T]here is no deity except God. [. . .] [The Arabs] [. . .] realized that ascribing sovereignty only to God meant that the authority would be taken away from the priests, the leaders of tribes, the wealthy and the rulers, and would revert to God. [. . .] [And they] knew the real meaning for the message, 'La alah illa Allah' – what its significance was in relation to their traditions, their rule and their power. [T]hey greeted this call – the revolutionary message – with anger. (Qutb, 2015 [1966], p. 16)

Even though Qutb explicitly rejected both communism and nationalism as a source of inspiration or driving force of social change, he still reconsidered and reframed the concepts and logics they provided. In Qutb's *ma'alim fi-l-tariq* – or Milestones, as it is often translated – he defines the revolutionary message, diagnosing a problem and suggesting a solution (goal), including a call to action (how-to) for his version of a 'vanguard' (Qutb, 2015 [1966], pp. 25f., 36). According to Qutb, due to Western colonial rule and the moral decay of Muslim rulers, '*jahiliyya*' had returned, the time of ignorance and darkness, the time before the Prophet Muhammad revealed his message to humankind (problem). For him, it is in the hands of a Muslim vanguard (*taliy'a*) to lead the *umma* out of this dark place of ignorance. '[A]uthority would be taken away' from all blasphemous and established leaders in the current stage of society, not too different from Marx's 'bourgeoisie', to be wielded by God alone as the ultimate sovereign. This revolution would be realised by a vanguard of (pure/pious) Arabs modelled on the *salaf al-saleh*, the 'pious forebears' of Muhammad. To this pious vanguard had been revealed true knowledge, or consciousness to do 'the right deed at the right time' (short: *'amr bil m'aruf*)[2] (call to action) and realise a better world in the guise of an 'Islamic State' (*al-daula al-islamiyya*) (solution). In the sense of Hobsbawm and Ranger's (1983) *Invention of Tradition*, this 'Islamic Body Politic' as a universal system of social and political governance would realise a Medinean utopia modelled on the imagined past of the first Muslim community in Yathrib under Muhammad's leadership, including recoded sovereignty in *hakimiyya*, as an alternative form of governance with Allah as the sovereign, the ultimate law-giver, arbiter and decision-maker.

While the revolutionary dimension of Qutb's thought is regularly a mere undercurrent in the work of later Jihadi-Salafist thinkers, we can find exceptions: Yusuf al-Uyairi, the first leader of al-Qa'eda on the Arabian Peninsula, and Abu Bakr Naji, very likely a pseudonym for one of al-Qa'eda's most active propagandists of the 2000s. The ideas of both authors have the potential to be identified as jigsaw pieces in the 'missing link' between Marxist–Leninist ideology, Qutb's thought, Jihadi-Salafist discourse and finally Daesh's revolutionary ontology:

Al-Uyairi introduces the 'praxis between theory (tanẓir) and implementation (tatbiq)' as a dialectical process (Meijer, 2007, p. 450) in the classical Marxist sense, and thus argues for nothing less than a 'permanent revolution' (Marx and Engels, 1850), an unending process of becoming of state. For him, 'violence remains as [the only] form of resistance' (Meijer, 2007, p. 457), exerted by a vanguard formed by mujāhids deserving 'to be at the forefront of the permanent revolution to change reality in accordance with the will of God' (Meijer, 2007, p. 422). A similar logic can be identified in Hamza bin Ladin's speeches (for example, bin Ladin, 2017).

Naji, on the other hand, even includes extensive direct quotations from Qutb's 'In the Shade of Quran':

> He exposes its **vanguards** to a long trial and delays their victory, decreases their numbers, and makes the people withhold their support for them **until He knows that they have been patient and steadfast and that they are ready and fit because they are the firm base, pure, aware, and trustworthy**. (Naji, 2004, p. 58)

This suggests the author's preference for the revolutionary aspects of Qutb's work, while lending additional credibility to Naji's case for establishing a body politic where he imagines 'God' as the true sovereign and realising a recoded sovereignty of the state in *ḥākimīyya*.

As political ideologies invariably take decades to crystallise, and bearing in mind Qutb's Marxist wording, Al-Uyairi's dialectical conceptualisation of *praxis* and Naji drawing legitimacy from Qutb in the style of Islamic juris-prudence, it is highly likely that Jihadi-Salafism has been influenced by both Marxist and twentieth-century revolutionary theories. Daesh merely had to upgrade the 'revolutionary' dimension of Jihadi-Salafist thought from a theo-retical undercurrent to a driving-force characteristic.

Daesh's Revolutionary Intent and Message

The revolutionary intent of Daesh as part of the Jihadi-Salafist movement can be identified by comparing its representations of what it intends to do (revo-lutionary message) with its actions, or what the group actually does (strategic outlook). Qutb, inspired by the political ideologies of his time, had diagnosed the return of '*jahilīyya*'. To end this unbearable situation, Qutb called for an 'Islamic world revolution' (Qutb, 1979, p. 173), a call which echoes in all official speeches delivered by Daesh's representatives. Daesh's version of the 'Islamic world revolution' is directed at the establishment of a state-like entity beyond the rules of the international system of nation states (Caliphate) and its permanent expansion on a global scale in the sense of 'Empire' by vio-lence or, as Richards puts it, 'a territorialised global sovereignty' (Richards, this volume).

The social and political entity as it had been established by proclamation in 2014 is ruled based on the logic of its very own comprehensive belief system, including the radical change of society. From the group's perspec-tive, the revolutionary situation had to be created and exploited by Daesh as the revolutionary vanguard through violence. This vanguard is constructed as the 'spearhead in this war [. . .] of the people of faith against the people of disbelief' (Al-Baghdadi, 2015), just as Naji's strategy for the establishment of the 'Islamic State' suggests. Naji's ontology follows the deterministic logic of Qutb, but expands its temporal trajectory: In Stage 1 (Vexation and Exhaustion) on the 'Path for Establishing an Islamic State' (Naji, 2004, p. 15), the revolutionary group is advised to seize situations of regime transition or change and escalate them beyond the logic of 'state' to reach a 'state of savagery' by tapping into the arsenal of the 'war machine'. This 'Stage of Savagery' should then be administered by this group (Stage 2 – Administration of Savagery) finally to establish the 'Islamic State' (Stage 3), all three stages being nothing less than different versions of assemblage drawing from 'state' and 'war machine'.

Thus, for Daesh, it was crucial to install the realisation of the 'Caliphate' at the top of its agenda, a clear revolutionary goal which set Daesh apart from other Jihadi-Salafist groups on the one hand and on the other legitimated Daesh's demand for *baī'a*, the vow of allegiance to its Caliph:

> We clarify to the Muslims that with this declaration of khilāfah, it is incumbent upon all Muslims to pledge allegiance to the khalīfah Ibrahim and support him (may Allah preserve him). The legality of all emirates, groups, states, and organizations, becomes null by the expansion of the khilāfah's authority and arrival of its troops to their areas.' (Al-Baghdadi, 2014)

It is hard to argue against a connection with the echo of Qutb's words in mind, when 'the authority would be taken away from the priests, the leaders of tribes, the wealthy and the rulers' (Qutb, 2015 [1966], p. 16) to be bestowed on God only. Also, this quotation highlights the tautological logic of Daesh's system of belief based on Jihadi-Salafist thought: legitimated by what is presented as Allah's will, any 'devout Muslim', as part of the vanguard, is obliged to swear allegiance to the Caliph and his Caliphate and, if physically able, join the small jihad to establish it; otherwise he (or she) does not qualify as a 'devout Muslim'. The binary between 'inside' and 'outside' of this territorial Caliphate, however, defines anything and anyone outside it as a threat, so that jihad has to continue as part of the 'permanent revolution' (Marx and Engels, 1850; Meijer, 2007, p. 422) to keep the Caliphate safe. Consequently, the eternal incentive and necessity to fight for the Caliphate has to result in its permanent expansion, with the globe as its only spatial limit and the apocalypse and final battle before the day of judgement as its only temporal one.

Concluding, we can identify one blatant difference in the revolutionary message of political Islam, Jihadi-Salafism and secularised Marxism–Leninism:

the connection between political ideology and religious doctrine allows Jihadi-Salafist thought to escape and transcend the limitations of this world, so that Daesh's political mission is without spatial and temporal limits, a political agenda based on a transcendent justification and eternal truth. Again, looking into Qutb's 'Milestones' is helpful in recognising the sociopolitical power lying in the merger of religious and ideological references and legitimisation of the doctrinal concepts of a system of belief. Based on *tauḥīd*, the oneness of God that also refers to the ideal of unity of the *umma* and is one of the central dogmas of Muslim belief, *ḥākimīya* is deduced in a coherent and logical manner from a core belief of Islam. Curiously, we can rediscover *ḥākimīya* as a core concept of Daesh's system of belief, regardless of the group's outright hostility towards today's Muslim Brotherhood and that group's traditions.

By merging Qutb's interpretation of Quranic concepts of political rule and their exegesis with the modern idea of the nation state, Daesh has created a chimera that simultaneously opposes and rephrases the concept of the nation state, while recoding sovereignty for its own purposes. This manifests in the group's demand for ultimate authority, as displayed in the quotation above and the exclusive claim for the concept of '*al-daula al-islamīyya*', 'Islamic State', for the Caliphate. The notion is clearly formulated for a modern audience, resonating with people's sociopolitical lifeworld and experiences of today, and thus can be presented as an alternative to and an antithesis of the international community and its nation states. Meanwhile, the term 'Caliphate' bestows meaning upon the modern construct of the 'Islamic State' beyond its current condition, contextualising it in the past and legitimising its future. *Ḥākimīya* then specifies the nature of political and religious rule and authority in this Caliphate without being too definite, so that any Muslim can imagine the Caliphate as his or her ideal political community. This 'imagined community' (Anderson, 1983), based on the 'invention of tradition' (Hobsbawm and Ranger, 1983), is embedded as a core concept in Daesh's system of belief and defines the character and rules of the ideal 'religious' community, and also of the 'political' and the 'social' community, brought together under the roof of an 'Islamic State' with God as its only sovereign claiming ultimate '*ḥākimīya*' (Lohlker, 2009, p. 69). In doing so, Daesh embraces and exceeds the logic of 'state apparatus', as it does not merely include religion as a 'piece in the state apparatus', but uses the power of transcendence 'to elevate this model to the level of the universal or to constitute an absolute Imperium' (Deleuze and Guattari, 1987, p. 383; also see Richards, this volume).

'Social Movements' – the Most Likely Revolutionary Actor

This fundamental change of 'state and class structures', however, demands several preconditions even to begin to unfold first and foremost intent-driven and able revolutionary actors. These are, in numerous cases, the individual or group actor who either has unchallenged access to or wields state power, on the one hand, and their adversary or adversaries who challenge this situation, on the other. To put it more simply, the most relevant actors in revolutionary situations are 'the state' and its representatives and the forces that challenge their position, opposing but also complementing each other, just like Deleuze and Guattari's 'state' and 'war machine'. Consequently, a situation can never become revolutionary without 'state' explicitly being challenged by what 'state' itself labels its (nomadic) adversaries residing in the plane of 'war machine'. However, and as will be discussed further later on, the successful revolutionary hybrid is characterised by its ability to draw from both planes, 'state' and 'war machine'.

Apart from established and organised state-related or non-state actors like political parties or military elites, the most common contenders for political power, and thus the most frequent revolutionary driving forces, are social movements. As 'sustained campaigns of claim making, using repeated performances that advertise that claim, based on organizations, networks, traditions, and solidarities that sustain these activities' (Tilly and Tarrow, 2015, p. 237), social movements differ widely in their operational range and supportive constituency. Despite the initial interdependence with their sociopolitical context of origin, social movements can develop into highly autonomous actors sufficiently independent from this very context and thus even from the context they are operating in – groups emerging as a social condensation of these movements being the final stage of autonomy. Michael Walzer describes social movements that drive a revolutionary situation as 'a concerted effort to change government, regime, society or all three by violence' (Aya, 2015a [2005], p. 90; Walzer, 1998). The moment a revolutionary group emerges not only separate and 'exterior' to the state, but countering 'the state as an apparatus of power distinct from the societies it governs' through violence, not to 'ward off' but to undo the 'very process of state formation', we witness the rebirth of Deleuze's 'war machine' (Reid, 2003, p. 61f.). Thus, and following Walzer, a social movement is defined as 'revolutionary' based not on success or the outcome of its action, but on the intent of the movement's actions and its resort to violence to realise this intent in opposition to the 'state apparatus'.

How Revolutionary Situation Transforms into Revolutionary Opportunity

However, for Aya, revolutionary intent and ability of the actor itself are never sufficient for revolution to unfold. In his ground-breaking article 'Theories of Revolution Reconsidered' (Aya, 1979, p. 40), Aya understands 'revolution' as a 'revolutionary situation' relegating both revolutionary intent and social and institutional outcomes of the revolutionary situation to the back-bench of historical variables. In doing so, he emphasises the genuinely political character of the revolutionary situation as 'an open-ended situation of violent struggle, wherein one set of contenders attempts (successfully or unsuccessfully) to displace another from state power', creating a state of 'dual power' or 'multiple sovereignty' in its wake. Interestingly, this recoding of sovereignty in the revolutionary situation resembles Naji's theorem of transitional stages from 'foreign' Western rule to an 'Islamic State', whereby situations of social change are to be exploited 'by means of groups and separate cells in every region of the Islamic world [. . .] until the anticipated chaos and savagery breaks out [. . .]' (Naji, 2004 p. 17). In conclusion, a revolutionary situation has to present itself to the intent and able revolutionary actor or be provoked by it.

Intent and ability of the revolutionary actor, as well as the revolutionary situation, are mutually dependent. But how do they relate to one another? First, Thucydides points out 'hope of success' as *conditio sine qua non* for any revolutionary movement to emerge (Aya, 2001, p. 145), which presents itself to the intent and able actor in the revolutionary situation. Second, this hope is necessarily preceded by an obvious weakness of the existing government, as Platon argues (Aya 2015a [2005], p. 90). Thus, the emergence of the revolutionary situation is preceded or accompanied by a moment, or rather time span, during which the hope for success coincides with the apparent or actual degeneration of the government's authority on the relevant territory. Tilly and Tarrow label this moment in time and place the 'political opportunity structure': that is, 'features of regimes and institutions [. . .] that facilitate or inhibit a political actor's collective action.' Instabilities or changes in political constellations take centre stage among these features (Tilly and Tarrow, 2015, p. 238).

From Aya's theoretical perspective, however, the dimension of 'time' has to play a more significant role when explaining the emergence of a concrete empirical 'revolutionary situation', as 'timing' and 'time' complement the factors that determine both structure and agency. McAdam, Tarrow and Tilly have defined the relevant time spans for social change as 'episodes of contention [which] typically grow out of and depend on a perception of significant environmental uncertainty on the part of state and non-state elites and challengers alike' (McAdam et al., 2001, p. 97). To be able to improve analysis and thus comprehension of the 'revolutionary situation' for the adversaries, this approach can benefit significantly from the integration of, and thus emphasis on, the dimensions of 'time' and 'opportunity'. As sociopolitical entrepreneurs, revolutionary movements may 'seize the moment' without even a conscious and / or rational decision-making process. At a certain moment in time, they perceive the 'revolutionary situation' as an 'entrepreneurial opportunity' in which the successful creation of a new means–end framework' appears more likely than (ever) before, whereas the insecurities produced by an unknown future increase the incentive for action, even though 'opportunities differ significantly in expected value [and] are not always profitable' (Shane, 2003, p. 19). This moment in time, which is structured by a significant change in the 'political opportunity structure', is what defines a **'window of opportunity'** (Müller, 2018) in the sense of 'revolutionary opportunity'. Finally, when reconsidering empirical findings – that is, the course of historic events related to revolutions – several of these 'windows' may open for the revolutionary actor(s). Not all opportunities will or can be seized due to the lack of awareness and / or ability or when success is perceived as unlikely.

Daesh's Rise in Iraq: Identifying the First 'Window' of 'Revolutionary Opportunity'

There was and still is controversy about the causes of and explanatory factors for Daesh's successful territorial expansion. How to include the relevant structural preconditions in such an analysis without disregarding Daesh's capabilities as a political actor, and thus the group's agency, is the greatest challenge. The following paragraphs will identify Daesh's successfully seized 'window(s)' of 'revolutionary opportunity' which have emerged from a 'revolutionary situation', and thus analytically describe the revolutionary situation and its provisional revolutionary outcome as it unfolded between 2013 and 2017: the violent seizure of state territory by a non-state actor, followed by attempts to control and govern the respective territory in a state-like manner.

Two regional developments, at first glance unrelated, have played a decisive role in the emergence of the revolutionary situation in geographical proximity to the revolutionary actor. Like other militant terrorist groups in the region, Daesh – at the time al-Qa'ida in Mesopotamia – seized the opportunity after Saddam Hussein's downfall in 2003 to expand its territory and constituency in Iraq. However, a combination of counterintelligence strikes and the US-supported 'bottom-up fight' by the Iraqi *Saḥwa* councils (Lister, 2015) deprived the group of a large number of its leading figures, including

Abu Musab Al-Zarqawi, leader of Daesh's forerunner in Iraq, and from about 2006 to 2010 the 'Islamic State of Iraq' struggled to survive. 'It faced a two-pronged battle in Iraq: one against the predominantly Shia government and the Shia population in general; another against fellow Sunnis who opposed its dark vision and takfiri [*sic!*] ideology,' while the group suffered from 'internal dissension and fragmentation' under the weak leadership of Al-Zarqawi's successor, Abu Hamza Al-Muhajir (Gerges, 2016, pp. 98, 102). The fact that the group did survive in the end is regularly blamed on the withdrawal of the US military. But while this, without a doubt, weakened the *Sahwa* councils, the more complex argument recently presented by Whiteside (2015) is much more convincing, as he bestows agency not only on the external force.

Whiteside paints a convincing picture of a highly embedded struggle between the various factions competing for social and territorial control and draws the conclusion that Daesh's survival and ensuing rise hinged on the group's successful application of 'revolutionary warfare' tactics, as defined by Fall: that is, 'guerrilla warfare plus political action', which results in 'the application of guerrilla methods to the furtherance of an ideology or political system' (Fall, 2015, p. 41). So Daesh escalated existing tensions to further sociopolitical instability in the very sense of Naji's 'State of Savagery.'[3] Importantly, the 'stage of savagery' does not equal chaos. Rather, Naji's Stage of Vexation and Exhaustion means producing a state of 'multiple sovereignties' (Aya, 1979, p. 40), which the revolutionary group successfully exploits to recode sovereignty and position itself as the best alternative.

For Daesh's situation in Iraq, this meant that the aim was, firstly, to remove its rivals from their power positions through a dual strategy of coercion (violence and the threat of violence) and attraction (bribery and the promise of improved living conditions), and secondly, to promote security and welfare by (re-)establishing functional institutions in the war-torn communities of Iraq (Astorino-Courtois, 2017; Müller, 2017; Revkin and McCants, 2015). On the local level, Daesh was able to 'regain a base of political support in the Sunni community' (Whiteside, 2015, p. 749) between 2008 and 2013, which also included the temporary suspension of its ideals for the sake of achieving 'long-term' objectives — something that had regularly been done by most radical liberation movements in the period of decolonialisation (Müller, 2015, pp. 110–22). Also, the group not only successfully established the administrative foundations to develop from 'network to organization', but also the preconditions to integrate its ideas of government into the existing administrative structure in Iraq, and later on in Syria, in a very short period of time (Hashim, 2018, p. 158ff.). Daesh did not emerge separate and 'exterior' to the state, but countered 'the state as an apparatus of power distinct from the societies it governs' through violence, not to 'ward off', but to undo the 'very process of state formation' as a rebirth of Deleuze's 'war machine' (Reid, 2003, p. 61f.).

Daesh's Expansion into Syria: Identifying the Second 'Window' of 'Revolutionary Opportunity'

From its localised base in Iraq's north and east, Daesh was able to seize the moment when a second 'window' of 'revolutionary opportunity' opened in geographically close proximity: in the wake of the Arab uprisings, the destabilisation of the Assad regime's state in Syria offered an opportunity to challenge the pre-existing sociopolitical structures fundamentally.

When the spark of revolution swept ferociously over the Arab world, it remained startlingly quiet on the public squares of Damascus and Aleppo – until Syrian President Bashir Al-Assad finally overdid his strategy of Machiavelli's 'force and fraud' (Machiavelli, 2014, p. 71) to quell public resistance. On the grounds that they had painted graffiti on a school wall in the city of Dar'a – 'the people want the fall of the regime' – eighteen teenage boys were detained and tortured (Müller, 2016). When Assad's state police returned thirteen-year-old Hamza Ali Al-Khateb's dead body to his family as a warning, the latter decided to share their grief with the Syrian public. The commemorative march for Hamza was the beginning of countrywide protests in Syria, protests which Assad again aimed to suppress with excessive state violence. The expressions of opposition spread from Dar'a to Ḥama and Daīr Al-Zūr, 'traditional bastions of Sunni piety resentful of the regime', as well as Ḥoms, 'where sectarian conflict added further fuel to the flames' (Hinnebusch, 2012, p. 107). With governmental violence added to the mix, a second 'window' of 'revolutionary opportunity' opened to satisfy Daesh's hunger for territory.

Daring a backward glance at the story that preceded Daesh's expansion into Syria, one aspect of Assad's mismanagement, or even sociopolitical miscalculation (Hinnebusch, 2012; Gerges 2016, pp. 170–80), emerges as the most relevant for the 'rise' of Daesh among the events and many and diverse challenges in Syrian society at the time: the social, political and economic neglect of Ḥassaka, Raqqa and Daīr Al-Zūr resulted in these eastern provinces being the poorest and socially weakest in Syria (Terc, 2014, p. 136; Gerges, 2016, p. 177). This offered Daesh both a convenient gateway into Syria and a vulnerable space in which to establish a first foothold on Syrian soil. And as Adnan Al-Mhamid from the Syrian opposition argued in our interview,[4] it is by no means a coincidence that the cities of Al-Bū Kamāl and Daīr Al-Zūr and their hinterlands have remained Daesh's last stronghold against the so-called

'Global Coalition against Daesh' (*al-taḥālif al-dawlī ḍidd dāʾesh*). Analogous to its strategy in Iraq, from there Daesh followed a remarkably cautious and pragmatic course of action to expand its influence to Syria: 'During this early phase [between May 2011 and mid-2013, Daesh] avoided flooding Syria with Iraqi fighters and relied instead on Syrian Sunni recruits and local and tribal coalitions, together with foreign volunteers and a few skilled and trusted Iraqi lieutenants' (Gerges, 2016, p. 176).

Not least due to Assad's continued refusal to step down, the uprisings turned into a fully-fledged revolution against the regime, a prime example of Goldstone's 'state breakdown' (Goldstone, 1991), and it is highly likely that Assad's amnesty of hundreds of imprisoned Jihadists not only fuelled the escalation of the protests to justify further violent suppression, but also supplied the clandestine Jihadi groups in Syria and the region with new leaders – an overall policy which very likely served Daesh's expansion into Syria well. Following Tilly, the revolutionary situation in Syria facilitated the emergence and perseverance of 'multiple sovereignties' (Tilly, 1978, pp. 189–222), a process of recoding sovereignty which continues until one recoding prevails. With the benefit of hindsight, we can conclude that Daesh, initially aided by its offshoot, the Nusra Front, seized the opportunity to claim its position successfully among these 'multiple sovereignties'. And while the revolutionary situation in Syria was the second 'window' of 'revolutionary opportunity' for Daesh to join the scene as a revolutionary actor and expand into Syrian territory, it was the temporal and spatial overlap of the first and second 'window[s] of opportunity' that was one of the necessary, though not sufficient, preconditions for a successful challenge to the pre-existing structures of government, regime and society in Iraq and Syria from nomadic 'war machine' to 'state' (Deleuze and Guattari, 1987, pp. 357–423).

Claiming Interstitial Space Between 'State' and 'War Machine': Daesh at the Top of the Revolutionary Game

Both 'revolutionary opportunities' in Iraq and in Syria included 'state' being weakened, causing its revolutionary contenders to 'hope' for success. Daesh's unwavering ambition to challenge and replace the dominant neoliberal system of 'state' and beyond with a new 'imagined world order' of a global Caliphate have forced 'state' and its international community to react to the group as a threat to their very existence (Ditrych et al., this volume). Deconstructing this dominant interpretation of the revolutionary by invoking Deleuze and Guattari's understanding of 'war machine' and 'state' as both distinct and complementary is worthwhile, as the process highlights the dire consequences of depicting 'the revolutionaries as radical others' from the plane of 'war machine' and thus ignoring the hybrid subjectivity of revolutionary actors.

Neither the revolutionary movements defying the 'normative core of order' nor the 'war machine' they supposedly represent reside 'outside' and thus beyond the state or its Westphalian order. Hybrid revolutionary subjectivity is any state's past in the process of becoming a state. Also the revolutionaries' strategies associated with the 'war machine' are an integral part of any state's sovereign strategy of power (cf. Foucault, 1977). Considering space, 'state' and 'war machine' produce 'two different types of space at the interstice of which war takes place' (Deleuze and Guattari, 1987; Ditrych et al., this volume). Now, between 'state' and 'war machine', Daesh successfully claimed intersti-tial space, being both and neither in their current time and space, defying their distinctness – an ability which, indeed, is exclusive to the revolutionary hybrid. Daesh's success may be attributed to this subjectivity, being able to tap into the arsenal of both planes, of 'state' and 'war machine'. This combination of strategies has been a recipe for success for the Taliban in Afghanistan and has been mimicked only recently by other Jihadi-Salafist groups like al-Qaʿida on the Arabian Peninsula in Yemen, adding further proof to this claim.

After waging 'total war', Daesh successfully exerted military and social control over a territory and population of internationally significant size from early 2013 to late 2017. Oral reports and official documents about life on Daesh's former territory convincingly confirm that the group had initiated concrete policy measures to realise their 'revolutionary programme' politically and socially. Public education had been replaced by ideological indoctrina-tion that follows religious precepts (Al-Tamimi, 2015, Specimens L and Z; Al-Tamimi 2017, Specimen 39P) and catalogues of socially adequate behav-iour had been distributed, implemented and enforced by religious police and religious courts (Al-Tamimi, 2015, Specimens 8N and P; Al-Tamimi, 2016, 14C). Nonetheless, Daesh's administrative and political efforts had to build on, or even 'exploit', what was there before, and in the end Daesh's performance of power was not that different from the 'elements of the forms of power they first overthrew' (Richards, this volume).

Without a doubt, Daesh's revolution will have long-term effects on, firstly, the communities in Syria and Iraq which had to live through Daesh's 'alter-native mode of governance'; and secondly, the movement of Jihadi-Salafism itself. At least temporarily, Daesh had recoded sovereignty and claimed and exercised the 'monopoly of violence' on its territory, and the effect of this per-formance of 'state' will remain with people and place. With Daesh successfully seizing and exceeding the territory of two 'state' entities, the dominant global system has been compromised and has become negotiable. The interconnectedness of these two effects is what constitutes the revolutionary outcome: Daesh's ambition to realise an 'alternative mode of governance' in their very own Caliphate does not contend itself with the inside / outside limitations of any political, legal, social or ethnic categories and thus borders (Walker, 1993; Ditrych et al., this volume). Their ultimate goal is nothing less than to replace the dominant neoliberal system and international community of states with their new 'imagined world order' of a global Caliphate – Jihadi-Salafism's alternative version of modernity.

Notes

1. In this text, the problematic term 'Islamic State' is used to refer to the Caliphate project but not to the group itself. This is instead referred to by the Arabic acronym 'Daesh', which is based on the previous name for the group: that is, 'Islamic State in Iraq and the Levant' (Arabic *al-daula al-islamīyya fil-'irāq wa al-shām*). Daesh also literally means 'one who crushes something underfoot' or 'destroyer' in Arabic.
2. This refers to a Quranic doctrine prescribing the right/honourable and forbidding the wrong/dishonourable.
3. The primary goals of Stage 1 are '1 – to exhaust the forces of the enemy and the regimes collaborating with them [. . .]; 2 – to attract new youth to the jihadi work [. . .]; 3 – to dislodge the chosen regions [. . .] from the control of the regimes and then working toward the administration of savagery which will transpire in it [. . .] It is the goal we are publicly proclaiming and which we are determined to carry out, not the outbreak of chaos; 4 – [. . .] to advance the groups of vexation through drilling and operational practice so that they will be prepared psychologically and practically for the stage of the management of savagery' (Naji, 2004, pp. 17, 49).
4. Interview with Adnan Al-Mhamid on 17 May 2017 at the University of Victoria, Canada. Al-Mhamid had been active in the Syrian opposition to the Assad family for quite some time and fled from his home town Dar'a through Daesh's territory in the summer of 2014.

References

Al-Baghdadi, A. 2014. 'This is the Promise of Allah'. Al-Hayat Media Center, 28 June. Available at: <https://ia902505.us.archive.org/28/items/poa_259 84/EN.pdf> (last accessed 3 December 2015).

Al-Baghdadi, A. 2015. 'Call to Arms to All Muslims (March Forward Whether Light or Heavy)'. *Memri.org*, 14 May. Available at: <http://www.memri

jttm.org/in-new-audio-speech-islamic-state-isis-leader-al-baghdadi-issues
-call-to-arms-to-all-muslims.html> (last accessed 3 December 2015).

Al-Tamimi, A. 2015–18. Archive of Islamic State Administrative Documents
(all last accessed 5 August 2022):

Specimen L: Shari'a Session for Teachers, Raqqa Province (announcement
for Saturday, 5 Dhu al-Qa'ada 1435 AH), 27 January 2015. Available at:
<http://www.aymennjawad.org/2015/01/archive-of-islamic-state-ad
ministrative-documents>.

Specimen P: Affirmation of Faith, al-Bab, Aleppo Province (May 2014),
27 January 2015. Available at: <http://www.aymennjawad.org/2015/01
/archive-of-islamic-state-administrative-documents>.

Specimen Z: Call for Repentance of Teachers, Ninawa Province
(December 2014), 27 January 2015. Available at: <http://www.ay
mennjawad.org/2015/01/archive-of-islamic-state-administrative-docu
ments>.

Specimen 8N: Notification to Wanted Person from Islamic Police,
Albukamal (no date). 27 January 2015. Available at: <http://www.ay
mennjawad.org/2015/01/archive-of-islamic-state-administrative-docu
ments>.

Specimen 14C: Prisoner Form, Hasakah Province (accusation: wanting
to abandon jihad), 11 January 2016. Available at: <http://www.aymen
njawad.org/2016/01/archive-of-islamic-state-administrative-documents
-1>.

Specimen 39P: Statement on Education, al-Hajr al-Aswad, south
Damascus (late August 2017), 28 August 2017. Available at: <http://
www.aymennjawad.org/2017/08/archive-of-islamic-state-administr
ative-documents-3>.

Anderson, B. 1983. *Imagined Communities*. London and New York: Verso.

Astorino-Courtois, A. 2017. 'SMA Reachback: Meaning of ISIS Defeat &
Shaping Stability'. Policy Brief Summarizing and Interpreting Accessible
Survey Data, March. Available at: <http://nsiteam.com/social/wp-content
/uploads/2017/03/Rounds-1-3-Questions-Summary-Highlights_FINAL
V4.pdf> (accessed 24 April 2017).

Atran, S. 2016. 'Why ISIS Has the Potential to be a World-altering Revolution'.
Aeon. Available at: <https://aeon.co/essays/why-isis-has-the-potential-to
-be-a-world-altering-revolution> (last accessed 10 October 2016).

Aya, R. 1979. 'Theories of Revolution Reconsidered: Contrasting Models of
Collective Violence'. *Theory and Society* 8 (1): 39–99.

Aya, R. 2001. 'The Third Man; or, Agency in History; or, Rationality in
Revolution'. *History and Theory* 40 (4): 143–52.

Aya, R. 2015a (2005). 'Theory of Revolution: From Thucydides to Tilly'. In Kousis, M. and Tilly, C. (eds). *Economic and Political Contention in Comparative Perspective*, 89–98. New York: Routledge.

Aya, R., 2015b. 'Theories of Revolution'. In Wright, J. D. (ed). *International Encyclopedia of the Social and Behavioural Sciences* 20, 627–32. Amsterdam: Elsevier.

Benjamin, W. 1977 (1921). 'Zur Kritik der Gewalt'. In Walter, B. *Gesammelte Schriften II(1)*. Frankfurt am Main: Suhrkamp.

bin Ladin, H. 2017. 'The Fighter Against Invaders and the Inciter of Rebellion Against Tyrants'. In Orton, K. *Hamza bin Ladin Presents Al-Qaeda as the Guardian of Revolution*. Available from: <https://kyleorton.co.uk/2017/11/10/hamza-bin-ladin-presents-al-qaeda-as-the-guardian-of-revolution/> (last accessed 5 September 2020).

Bonner, M. 2006. *Jihad in Islamic History: Doctrines and Practice*. Princeton: Princeton University Press.

Bowering, G. (ed.). 2013. *The Princeton Encyclopaedia of Islamic Political Thought*. Princeton: Princeton University Press.

Carré, O. 1984. *Mystique et politique: Lecture révolutionnaire du Coran par Sayyid Qutb, frère musulman radical*. Paris: Presses de Sciences Po.

Cheema, S. A. 2013. 'Problematizing the Religious Basis of Maududi's Political Theory'. *Studies on Asia* 3 (2): 52–82.

Choueiri, Y. M. 2000. *Arab Nationalism: A History*. Oxford: Blackwell.

Cockburn, P. 2015. *The Rise of Islamic State: ISIS and the New Sunni Revolution*. Verso: London.

Cook, D. 2009. 'Islamism and Jihadism: The Transformation of Classical Notions of Jihad into an Ideology of Terrorism'. *Totalitarian Movements and Political Religions* 10 (2): 177–87.

Davidshofer, W. J. 2014. *Marxism and the Leninist Revolutionary Model*. New York: Palgrave Macmillan.

Deleuze, G. and Guattari, F. 1987. *A Thousand Plateaus: Capitalism and Schizophrenia*. New York: Vintage Books.

Fall, B. 2015. 'The Theory and Practice of Insurgency and Counterinsurgency'. *Naval War College Review* 95 (5): 40–9.

Fanon, F. 2004 (1961). *The Wretched of the Earth*. New York: Grove Press.

Foucualt, M. 1977. *Discpline and Punish: The Birth of the Prison*. New York: Vintage Books.

Freeden, M. 1996. *Ideologies and Political Theory. A Conceptual Approach*. Oxford: Clarendon Press.

Gerges, F. A. 2005. *The Far Enemy: Why Jihad Went Global*. Cambridge: Cambridge University Press.

Gerges, F. A. 2016. *ISIS: A History*. Princeton: Princeton University Press.

Goldstone, J. A. 1991. *Revolution and Rebellion in the Early Modern World*. Berkeley: University of California Press.

Hansen, H. and Kainz, P. 2007. 'Radical Islamism and Totalitarian Ideology: A Comparison of Sayyid Qutb's Islamism with Marxism and National Socialism'. *Totalitarian Movements and Political Religions* 8 (1): 55–76.

Hashim, A. S. 2018. *The Caliphate at War:. The Ideological and Military Innovations of Islamic State*. London: Hurst.

Hegghammer, T. 2009a. 'Jihad, Yes, But not Revolution: Explaining the Extraversion of Islamist Violence in Saudi Arabia'. *British Journal of Middle Eastern Studies* 36 (3): 395–416.

Hegghammer, T. 2009b. 'Jihadi-Salafis or Revolutionaries? On Religion and Politics in the Study of Militant Extremism'. In Meijer, R. (ed.). *Global Salafism: Islam's New Religious Movement*, 244–66. New York: Columbia University Press.

Hinnebusch, R. 2012. 'Syria: From "Authoritarian Upgrading" to Revolution?' *International Affairs* 88 (1): 95–113.

Hobsbawm, E. and Ranger, T. 1983. *The Invention of Tradition*. Cambridge: Cambridge University Press.

Ingram, H. J. 2016. 'An Analysis of Islamic State's Dabiq Magazine'. *Australian Journal of Political Science* 51: 458–77.

Ismael, T. Y. 2005. *The Communist Movement in the Arab World*. New York: Routledge.

Lenin, W. I. 1917. 'The State and Revolution: The Marxist Theory of the State and the Tasks of the Proletariat in the Revolution'. *Collected Works, Vol. 25*, 381–492. Available at: <https://www.marxists.org/ebooks/lenin/state-and-revolution.pdf> (last accessed 12 February 2017).

Lister, C. R. 2015. *The Islamic State*. Washington, D.C.: Brookings Institution.

Lohlker, R. 2009. *Dschihadismus: Materialien*. Stuttgart: UTB.

McAdam, D., Tarrow, S. and Tilly, C. 2001. *Dynamics of Contention*. Cambridge: Cambridge University Press.

Machiavelli, N. 2014. *The Prince*. New York: Open Road Media.

Marx, K. 1973 (1875). 'Critique of the Gotha Programme'. In Marx, K. and Engels, F. *Selected Works, Vol. 3*, 13–30. Moscow: Progress Publishers.

Marx, K. and Engels, F. 1850. 'Address of the Central Committee to the Communist League'. *Marxists.org*. Available at: <https://www.marxists.org/archive/marx/works/1847/communist-league/1850-ad1.htm> (last accessed 3 April 2021).

Meijer, R. 2007. 'Yūsuf al-'Uyairī and the Making of a Revolutionary Salafi Praxis'. *Die Welt des Islams* 47 (3/4): 422–59.

Meijer, R. (ed). 2009. *Global Salafism: Islam's New Religious Movement.* New York: Columbia University Press.

Mello, B. 2018. 'The Islamic State: Violence and Ideology in a Post-colonial Revolutionary Regime'. *International Political Sociology* 12: 139–55.

Müller, M. M. 2015. *A Spectre Is Haunting Arabia: How the Germans Brought Their Communism to Yemen.* Bielefeld: Transcript.

Müller, M. M. 2016. 'Staatlicher Zerfall und Bürgerkrieg in Syrien seit 1990'. In Lemke, B. (ed.). *Wegweiser zur Geschichte Irak und Syrien der Bundeswehr*, 179–88. Paderborn: Schöningh.

Müller, M. M. 2017. 'Terror or Terrorism? The "Islamic State" Between State and Nonstate Violence'. *Digest of Middle East Studies* 26 (2): 442–62.

Müller, M. M. 2018. 'Einfache Antworten in einer Welt der Krisen? Über Erfolg und Grenzen des "Islamischen Staates"'. In Lutz, R. /Staus, A. (eds). *Tanzende Verhältnisse. Zur Soziologie politischer Krisen*, 190–204. Weinheim: Beltz Juventa.

Musallam, A. 2005. *From Secularism to Jihad: Sayyid Qutb and the Foundations of Radical Islamism.* Westport, CT: Praeger.

Naji, A. B. 2004. 'The Management of Savagery: The Most Critical Stage Through Which the Umma Will Pass', translated by William McCants. John M. Olin Institute for Strategic Studies at Harvard University. Available at: <https://azelin.files.wordpress.com/2010/08/abu-bakr-naji-the-manag ement-of-savagery-the-most-critical-stage-through-which-the-umma-will -pass.pdf> (last accessed 7 February 2018).

Orbach, D. 2012. 'Tyrannicide in Radical Islam: The Case of Sayyid Qutb and Abd al-Salam Faraj'. *Middle Eastern Studies* 48 (6): 961–72.

Qutb, S. 1952–66. 'fī ẓilāl al-qur'ān', translated by M. A. Salahi and A. Shamis. Nairobi: Islamic Foundation. Available at: <http://www.kalamullah.com /shade-of-the-quran.html> (last accessed 8 February 2018).

Qutb, S. 1979. *al-salām al-'ālamī wa al-islām.* Cairo: Dar Al-Shurūq.

Qutb, S. 2015 (1966). 'ma'alim fi-l-tarīq'. No place: Holy Books / Islamic Book Service. Available at: <http://holybooks.lichtenbergpress.netdna-cdn .com/wp-content/uploads/Milestones.pdf> (last accessed 7 October 2016).

Reid, J. 2003. 'Deleuze's War Machine: Nomadism Against the State'. *Millennium: Journal of International Studies* 32 (1): 57–85.

Revkin, M. and McCants, W. 2015. 'Experts Weigh In: Is ISIS Good at Governing?' *Markaz*, 20 November. Available at: <https://www.brookings .edu/blog/markaz/2015/11/20/experts-weigh-in-is-isis-good-at-gover ning/> (last accessed 26 May 2017).

Safdar, A. 2013. *Reform and Modernity in Islam: The Philosophical, Cultural and Political Discourses Among Muslim Reformers.* London: I. B. Tauris.

Segert, A. and Zierke, I. 1998. 'Gesellschaft der DDR: Klassen – Schichten – Kollektive'. In: Judt, M. (ed). *DDR-Geschichte in Dokumenten*, 165–81. Bonn: Bundeszentrale für Politische Bildung.

Shane, S. 2003. *A General Theory of Entrepreneurship: The Individual-Opportunity Nexus*. Cheltenham: Edward Elgar.

Staffel, S. and Aqan, A. N. 2016. 'Introduction'. In Staffel, S. and Aqan, A. N. (eds). *Jihadism Transformed: Al-Qaeda and Islamic State's Battle of Ideas*, 21–34. London: Hurst.

Terc, M. 2014. '"To Promote Volunteerism among School Children" Volunteer Campaigns and Social Stratification in Contemporary Syria'. In Hinnebusch, R. and Zintl, T. (eds). *Syria from Reform to Revolt: Political Economy and International Relations*, Vol. 1, 95–113. Syracuse, NY: Syracuse University Press.

Tilly, C. 1978. *From Mobilization to Revolution*. New York: McGraw Hill.

Tilly, C. and Tarrow, S. 2015. *Contentious Politics*. Oxford: Oxford University Press.

Walker, R. B. J. 1993. *Inside/Outside*. Cambridge Studies in International Relations (No. 24). Cambridge: Cambridge University Press.

Walt, S. 2015. 'ISIS as Revolutionary State'. *Foreign Affairs*, 21 October. Available at: <https://www.foreignaffairs.com/articles/middle-east/isis-revolutionary-state> (last accessed 12 September 2017).

Walzer, M. 1998. 'Intellectuals, Social Classes, and Revolutions'. In Skocpol, T. (ed). *Democracy, Revolution, and History*. Ithaca, NY: Cornell University Press.

Westphal, J., 2018. 'Violence in the Name of God? A Framing Processes Approach to the Islamic State in Iraq and Syria'. *Social Movement Studies* 17 (1): 19–34.

Whiteside, C. 2016. 'The Islamic State and the Return to Revolutionary Warfare'. *Small Wars & Insurgencies* 27 (5): 743–76.

6

'Islamic State' and the Neoliberal War Machine: Power, Resistance and Revolution

Imogen Richards

> War clearly follows the same movement as capitalism: In the same way as the proportion of constant capital keeps growing, war becomes increasingly a 'war of matériel' in which the human being no longer even represents a variable capital of subjection, but is instead a pure element of machinic enslavement.
>
> Deleuze and Guattari, *A Thousand Plateaus*, pp. 514–15

Introduction

Deleuze and Guattari's 'war machine' has been a useful framework through which to conceptualise the relational and processual arrangements of state-like apparatuses such as Islamic State (IS), including in their hybridised dimensions. As Ditrych et al. note (in this volume), the hybrid nomadic and state-like characteristics of IS can be said to characterise Deleuze and Guattari's (1980) theory of state capture and opposition regarding (sometimes non-violent) 'war machine' apparatus. Where the war machine exists exterior to state but remains vulnerable to state co-optation, its non-disciplinary nomadic elements include 'warriors', 'herders', and groups of people who otherwise exist in fleeting organisational hierarchies, as 'rhizomatic' assemblages. As elements of a *war-like* war machine, IS actors within and outside the Middle East can similarly be said to operate on transnational scales that are dynamic and deterritorialising, though at the same time reconstitutive of the broader, state-based, strategic–military game they operate within (Richards, 2020).

This chapter's analysis of IS's neoliberal methods of statist governance in its financial practices and propaganda extends Ditrych et al.'s discussion in this volume of the international, 'revolutionary' aspects of IS, whose transformative potential is likewise mediated by inflammatory counter-IS influences. Also from this volume, it reflects on Müller-Rensch's interrogation of the Marxist–Leninist ideological aspects of IS's spatial and temporal (anti-)neoliberal positioning. These analyses might be situated historically among scholarship after the al-Qaʿida attacks in New York and Washington on 11 September 2001 (9/11) that incorporated philosophical frames to interpret al-Qaʿida's, and then IS's, dialectical relationships with cultural and economic globalisation. In one such example, Boggs and Pollard drew on Baudrillard's notions of hyperreality to highlight a circular causality between 'jihadist' terrorism and globalised modernity, while Giroux (2012) elsewhere incorporated Massumi's (1993) 'mainstream workstations of fear' to examine how the 'visual theatre' of this form of terrorism 'mimics the politics of the 'official' war on terrorism'. In reflecting on 'jihadist' forms of organisational governance and management of finance, Reid (2004), and Barkawi and Laffey (2006) respectively considered how, after the bombings of 11 September 2001, al-Qaʿida became inextricable from the open borders and transnational flows of finance and communications that underwrite the neoliberal international economy. Drawing on Bourdieusian and neo-Marxist ideas, in 2020, I similarly explored how al-Qaʿida and then IS sought to raise and exploit social, symbolic and cultural forms of capital through their propaganda in ways that dialectically responded to US neoliberals and counterterrorists, and that were also, in this respect, correlative with their methods of economic capital distribution (Richards, 2020). Adding to this research, this chapter considers select components of Deleuze and Guattari's (1972, 1980) 'war machine' theory to analyse IS, focusing on its outline of contemporary subjection, conceptualisation of the state form and casting of the war machine as revolutionary.

The discussion in this chapter explores IS as a hybrid actor that exploits but also seeks to overturn a dominant sociopolitical order. In its display of revolutionary and counterrevolutionary tendencies, it considers how IS can be seen to follow a developmental trajectory reminiscent of other hybridised actors in modern history. In some ways recalling post-1917 Bolshevik and 1950s Maoist state-building projects, for example, IS propaganda and violence were predicated on resistance to capitalist systems, despite the organisation's leverage of those systems to attain access to power and government. IS's administration of the Caliphate was also recognised as corrupt and exploitative, in some ways recalling corruption that followed US-backed insurgencies in the European 'Colour Revolutions' in the 2000s (DeFronzo, 2018), albeit in IS's case in a much more brutal fashion. As this chapter shows, IS's statecraft and international activity reinforce the very forms of neoliberal power the organisation sought to oppose, 'neoliberalism' in this instance referring to:

A theory of political economic practices that proposes that human well-being can best be advanced by liberating individual entrepreneurial freedoms and skills within an institutional framework characterized by strong private property rights, free markets, and free trade. The role of the state is to create and preserve an institutional framework appropriate to such practices. (Harvey, 2005, p. 2)

Reflecting on Deleuze and Guattari's extension of Foucaultian tropes on neoliberal ideation, the neoliberal paradigm is in this chapter also taken to represent an 'extension of economic analysis to domains previously considered to be non-economic' (Foucault, 2008 [1978–9], pp. 145, 215). The discussion commences from the position that, rather than resisting state-based sovereignty, as Ditrych et al. observe in this volume, IS seeks to recode state-based rationalities of sovereignty, capitalism and territoriality, often along neoliberal lines. This occurred from IS's founding in 2013, with more than thirty media departments distributing propaganda in more than a dozen languages at its height in 2015 (Zelin, 2015), and through its establishment and governance of a 680 km Syrian and Iraqi quasi-nation state of the 'Caliphate' from June 2014 (Lister, 2014).[1] In these expeditions, IS sought to reinscribe a particular kind of sovereign condition contingent upon its exploitation of existing sociopolitical circumstances both regionally and on an international scale.

This chapter regards the practical circumstance of IS specifically since 2014, investigating how the organisation rhetorically resisted the neocolonial and neoliberal dimensions of US foreign and economic policy, and 'the West' broadly, which are portrayed in European and English-language IS propaganda as homogenous neoliberal capitalist societies. With reference to cases of IS governance and finance, it examines how, in its state- and institution-building, the organisation materially exercises forms of neoliberal power and authoritarian governmentality. These aspects of IS are critically outlined for the purpose of shedding light on some applications and limitations of Deleuze and Guattari's (1972, 1980) 'war machine' theory for hybrid revolutionary actors, in its approach to diverse political movements, the role of religion, and the potential collapse of important class distinctions for understanding these phenomena.

Subjectivation and Machinic Enslavement

To the extent of its primarily capitalist expressions, the war machine is comprised of two components of contemporary subjection; subjectivation, or social subjection, combined with machinic enslavement (Lazzarato, 2006). These attributes of Deleuze and Guattari's (1980) theory can illuminate the explicitly neoliberal ideational dimensions of IS's political–economic behaviours. Subjectivation constitutes identity formation within an individual subject, and the relegation of individual autonomy in the ideological service of some higher power. This process occurs primarily where subjectivity is negotiated in relation to some external referent – interpolated or 'folded' in to give subjective status meaning – such as an ideology or ethic of anti-capitalist resistance as in the 1968 cultural revolutions, or in codes of morality prescribed by Abrahamic religions. The process of 'machinic enslavement', on the other hand, comprises individual subjects acting as part of a machinic assemblage, also extending to the desubjectivisation of individuals when they are incorporated as part of a 'machine' on supra- or sub-individual levels. This loss of individualised subject status occurs where individuals become constituted by their involvement in financial and media institutions or through the collective institutions of the state. The process of enslavement can also extend in the political realm, in concert with individuals' subjectivation, to a form of state capture. Where capitalism exists in its entirety, therefore, neither as an isolated system nor 'mode of production', then the individual subject becomes enslaved to the material and ideological 'machine', to which they are also fundamental (see Lazzarato, 2006).

IS's efforts at international governance and domestic state-building might be interpreted in line with those system-focused aspects of Deleuze and Guattari's capitalist war machine. For example, while, following Foucault, revolutionary thought in Deleuze and Guattari's theory – as 'noology' – itself constitutes a form of war machine, the authors diverge from Foucault in that the violent articulation of 'war' is not understood as fundamental to state power (Deleuze and Guattari, 1980). Rather, it is either a function of states or an expression of the war machine by nomadic forces, though always understood as 'absolute' rather than 'limited' (Deleuze and Guattari, 1980, p. 420). War in the absolute, ideational sense, deriving from Clausewitz (1982), consists of excesses and surpluses constitutive of Deleuze and Guattari's creative dynamics, always exterior to the state and invulnerable to its regulations. In the *war-like* 'war machine', thus:

> There is enslavement when human beings themselves are constituent pieces of a machine that they compose among themselves and with other things (animal, tools), under the control and direction of a higher unity. But there is subjection when the higher unity constitutes the human being as a subject linked to a new exterior object, which can be an animal, a tool, or even a machine. (Deleuze and Guattari, 1980, p. 504)

In applying this theory, one could argue that the war machine of IS functions to regularise both individuals in its former territory and those subject to its wider governance practices, as subjectivised within the state, and products of the wider IS capitalist network's machinic enslavement, through their constitution as human capital (see Deleuze and Guattari, 1980, p. 515; Walshe, this volume). This could be seen as apparent in the wages that IS fighters were paid in 2014 – individually between US$400 and US$1,200, and US$25 for each child, and US$50 for each wife (Al-Tamimi, 2016), which in turn encouraged the growing of large families within the Caliphate, while financial rewards reflect the measure of constitutional value individuals were deemed to provide for the 'assemblage' of IS's state-capitalist apparatus.

This tendency of machinic enslavement combining with entrepreneurial subjects was also recognisable in the measures IS took to encourage competitive marketisation in IS territory. As revealed in one of the organisation's early propaganda magazines, *Islamic State Report*, a Consumer Protection Authority operated within IS territory in Raqqa, Syria, and was described as 'an office that's concerned with protecting shoppers by inspecting the goods being sold in shops, markets, shopping centers, and wholesale outlets, discovering goods that are spoiled or not suitable for sale and taking those responsible for account' (Alexander and Alexander, 2015, p. 112; Al Hayat, 2015c, p. 5). During the persistence of its so-called Caliphate, IS was furthermore recognised as taxing those in its territory as part of a 'protection racket'; after its movement into Syria in 2015, IS used the Popular Credit Bank to facilitate tax administration (Bindner and Poirot, 2016), and US$360 million of IS's annual wealth that year allegedly derived from taxes and extortion imposed on residents in its territories and on those passing through (Swanson, 2015). Demonstrating IS operatives' utility as workers and commitment to external machines of influence, its revenue from oil brought about massive financial windfalls; as much as US$730–1,460 million in 2014 (Brisard and Martinez, 2014, p. 7), US$435–550 million in 2015, and US$200–250 million in 2016 (Heißner et al., 2017).

Although 'machinic enslavement' and 'subjectivation' might therefore characterise aspects of IS's financial and territorial governance, and in particular the reinforcement of a 'regional capitalist coherence' (Jessop, 2006) in relation to its formerly held territory, the Nietzschean understanding of 'enslavement' informing Deleuze and Guattari's theory, on the other hand, limits its characterisation of power differentials extant within IS's organisational hierarchy. IS implemented a broader machinic capitalist apparatus via its adoption of a decentralised, two-tiered system of governance (from 2014 to at least 2017) that RAND Corporation researchers likened to a 'multidivisional-hierarchy form' (or 'M-form') of management, first popularised in the 1920s by Alfred Sloan's

General Motors (Bahney et al., 2010; Simpson, 2014). In this capitalistic two-tiered management system, featured discretely in both Syria and Iraq, there sat the leader Abu Bakr al-Baghdadi and a Cabinet, including a Shura Council and Executive Branch, below which was a Deputy of Iraq and a Deputy of Syria. There were then twelve 'governors' administering Financial, Military, Leadership, Legal, Fighters, Security, Intelligence and Media branches of IS.

Contrary to Deleuze and Guattari's anti-hierarchical aspirations for the war machine, as Sharpe (2021) highlighted with reference to Deleuze's historical work, and Patton (2000, p. 105) observed of Deleuze and Guattari, the actually existing separation between the 'capitalists' and the 'proletarians', and the 'governors' and the 'governed' in the subjects under examination is in some ways obscured by war machine theory. This tendency within Deleuze and Guattari's usage of Nietzsche has also been interpreted to imply rhetorical justification for the protection of the 'strong' against the 'weak', and the moral–political promotion of state capture through portraying as inevitable its coding of sovereignty:

> The extent to which the Nietzschean notion of the slave does not necessarily stand for someone dominated, by fate or social condition, but also characterises the dominators as much as the dominated once the regime of domination comes under the sway of forces which are reactive and not active. Totalitarian regimes are in this sense regimes of slaves, not merely because of the people that they subjugate, but above all because of the type of 'masters' they set up. (Deleuze, 1962, p. xvi cited in Sharpe, 2021, p. 76)

Lazzarato (2006) also highlighted how, for Deleuze and Guattari, capital is 'a process of subjectivation that constitutes all human beings as subjects; but some, the "capitalists", are subjects of enunciation . . . while others, the "proletarians", are subjects of the statement, subjected to the technical machines'. The transformation of the subject into an entrepreneur of herself or himself in Deleuze and Guattari's theory (as with Foucault's *homo economicus*), however, was also recognised in Lazzarato's reading to render them vulnerable to 'identification, subjectivation and exploitation, given that s/he is both her/his own master and slave, a capitalist and proletarian, the subject of enunciation and the subject of the statement' (Lazzarato, 2006). Bringing this into stark relief in IS's case, entrepreneurial measures exemplifying its institutional promotion of literal financial and physical enslavement through state-based social relations include its manipulation of water and wheat resources both as a weapon of war (including manipulating the movement of people as human shields), and through creating scarcity to drive prices of agricultural goods higher (Fick,

2014). Indicating the scale of IS's exploitative agricultural activity, the total value of its wheat production in Syria and Iraq in 2015 almost equalled that of its oil production revenues in late 2014 and early 2015, with a net yield of 2.45 million tonnes (Jaafar and Woertz, 2016).

In concert with the restrictive, conservative codes for subjectivation that IS also made available within the former Caliphate – as in the manner of 'anti-production' (Deleuze and Guattari, 1972) – such examples of the organisation colonising life for war and capitalist ends importantly highlight the realities of the master–slave dialectic for IS. They also illustrate counterrevolutionary tendencies employed but often under-recognised in Deleuze and Guattari's theory. Since its 1972 publication, *Anti-Oedipus* has often been read as fundamentally revolutionary in nature, while for Deleuze historically, following Foucault (2004 [1976]), the concept of *war* itself – and the war machine by extension – was, in many ways, analogous to revolutionary thought. The war machine, in theory at least, outlined an epistemic place for nomadic, often transient and autonomous social movements to resist in thought and deed the oppressive powers of the systems of state and capital (see, for example, Purcell, 2013). Structurally and materially, however, as cases of revolutionary movements in history had been subject to powerful capitalist and state entities' codification, repurposing and co-optation (Bloom, 2016), IS's statecraft transformed its nomadic, resistance ethic into one of domination, while *war* moreover remained its primary means of organisational identification.

Misdirection and the 'catachrestic' use of political terms in Deleuze and Guattari's differential reinterpretation of Nietzsche on war might, then, be viewed as erasing knowledge of the ontological separation between master and slave (Sharpe, 2021), and in particular respect of IS's case, its political–economic derivations. Despite the fact that residents in the Caliphate participated in commercial industry, from localised goods and services, featuring a taxation system, and labour leveraged to benefit IS's extractive management of natural resources, many of those who participated in these programmes did so under extreme duress, and many were subject to literal sexual and physical enslavement. This comprises an important dimension of IS's neoliberal recoding of state-based sovereignty, and again highlights concern with Deleuze and Guattari's inflection of *homo economicus* as articulated in Foucault; in conditions of neoliberal capitalism, the terrorist subject (or those in IS territory) becomes a 'partner of exchange' through their subjectivation and machinic enslavement, though not necessarily an 'entrepreneur of himself' (Foucault, 2008 [1978–9], p. 226).

The negotiations IS strikes between its nomadic war machine aspects and its sedentary, territorial incentives could thus be said to constitute the organisation as fundamentally hybrid, though in ways incorporating both revolutionary and *counter*revolutionary tendencies – which, in turn, paradoxically serve to destabilise the very nature of IS's hybrid form. These tendencies, expressed primarily by means of violent conflict, are hierarchically driven, and for the most part absent Deleuze and Guattari's ideal of the war machine's emancipatory intention. As the discussion below further illustrates, this also occurs through the dominant coding standards IS enforces via media and financial apparatuses that are in some ways rhizomatically distributed, but ultimately also yield vertically integrated production lines.

(De)territorialising in State and Subject

The neoliberal expressions of IS's sovereign economic activity in a theoretical application of the war machine imply that Deleuze and Guattari's conceptualisation of the corresponding state form is fundamental. For the purpose of the analytical comparison, it is also useful that in *A Thousand Plateaus*, the state (as a modern ideal type) is defined as an isomorph, but also a heterogeneous assemblage depending on the expression of state-like qualities in abstract settings. Westphalian states supposedly negotiate this balance by adding and subtracting axioms for the institutional and societal management of social difference, while, according to Deleuze and Guattari's theory (1980), despite the economy's extension beyond the state, the forces of neoliberal and broader forms of capitalism also perform this coding function. The state's drive to repress difference, however, leads to an apparently inevitable situation wherein smooth war machines, exemplified for Deleuze and Guattari by autonomous or nomadic social movements, despite their often erstwhile non-violent political positioning, can variously find themselves in conflict with the striated state. Their goal (or desire) is primarily to deterritorialise sovereign (in international relations theory, government, geographically controlled) boundaries internally and symbolically, but often also through the reclamation of exterior territories to state-based systems. To the extent to which they are not absorbed or eroded by the state form, by attempting to recode or cancel the so-called striated space of states, these movements variously, dialectically, support the legitimacy of the state, and they exist in tension with it.

In properly accounting for IS power differentials and its broader geopolitical aims, a discussion of the organisation's hybrid form must, then, necessarily direct attention toward how its coding devices work to recast IS and its associated networks as both oppositional to the (Westphalian) state form, and reconstitutive of an exteriorising unbounded territory, combined, though, with expressions of a deterritorialised global sovereignty. While these networks for IS in 2014 extended to Boko Haram in Nigeria, Ansar al-Khilafah in the Philippines, East Indonesia Mujahidin in East Timor and Ansar al-Sharia in Yemen, among others (Zahid, 2014), IS also claimed formalised and less for-malised rights to ideational 'sovereign' governance through political violence internationally, and state formation in the Caliphate. To understand its hybrid revolutionary aspect in this frame, wherein forms of state-centric resistance can end up resembling the forms of oppressive, literal sovereign power they try to overthrow, it is necessary to reflect further on ontological dissimilarities between the sovereign state and the nomadic assemblages of the war machine as they are accounted for in Deleuze and Guattari's theory, and its related capacity to explain such hybrid (anti-)state movements.

For Deleuze and Guattari (1980, p. 351), the 'principle elements' of a state apparatus are two heads of a stratum defining political sovereignty, through the 'bond' and the 'pact'. Respectively, they refer to those forces in the state that bind and control, and others that regularise relationships of a more holistic domination, through legislation, administration and organisation. Forces for state violence include the apparatus of law enforcement and judiciary in place of the military, wherein 'war' itself, including in military action, is external to the state, though militaries can be used to serve statist agendas of limited domestic and international conflict. Outside those structures of the state exists the war machine, comprised of non-disciplinary nomadic elements featuring 'warriors' and 'herders', while the groups of people participatory in the war machine are variously described as 'multiplicities', 'packs' or 'bands', and often have horizontal, rhizomatic forms of organisation or fleeting, often localised, organisational hierarchies (Deleuze and Guattari, 1980).

To the degree that the state entity hostile to the war machine is striated, bound or fixed, the impermanence and counterterritorial tendencies of IS might appear at first to preclude it from exhibiting 'state-like' characteristics. As the former discussion of some of IS's governance practices outlined, how-ever, its efforts at legitimacy-building within the Caliphate resemble Deleuze's 'state' in its implementation of rules, restrictions and territorially defined legis-lation, while its performance of statehood accords with Deleuze and Guattari's description of this as processual (1972, 1980). The capitalistic dimensions of IS governance are, on the other hand, readily apparent, as are the neoliberal capitalist aspects of its 'rhizomatic' network. These too might be understood to reflect a 'war machine' aspect of IS's hybrid characteristics. Neoliberalism, like the binding and fixing 'state', here exists in these conditions as a *process* rather than as a *thing*, generating a monetising dynamic that is rhizomatic in its transience, with contingencies, but that can also become arboreal once the processes of striation eliminate rival countertendencies.

IS followed its predecessor and ongoing competitor, al-Qaʻida, by exhibiting rhizomatic tendencies, in terms of both its networks of propaganda distribution and its relatively autonomous modes of decision-making for geographically disparate cells. al-Qaʻida had adopted privatised, outsourced and networked modes of governance, reminiscent of a 'venture capitalist' organisation after the post-2001 US assassination of its leaders (Charette, 2007). IS then, in even more adept fashion, ran more than thirty media departments at its height (Zelin, 2015), and between 2013 and 2019 followers of IS's transnational network, or adherents to its 'brand name', perpetrated more than 143 attacks in 29 countries across four continents (Lister et al., 2018), and according to IS spokespersons, 3,670 attacks in 2018 alone (al-Lami, 2019). Demonstrating IS's networked organisational resilience, in 2019, despite its loss of territory, IS central was estimated to hold between US$50 and US$300 million in financial assets (UNSCR, 2019). As with al-Qaʻida, however, ideological tension existed between the messages of anti-capitalist – anti-imperial and anti-colonial – resistance distributed via IS's rhizomatic networks and propaganda systems, given the late capitalist media apparatus by which they were constituted (Awan, 2014). In distinction from al-Qaʻida, moreover, IS's arboreal, *striating* efforts at state-building characteristics also contrasted with its erstwhile, global, centrifugal or *nomadic* ambitions.

The online, rhizomatic distribution of IS propaganda, produced in a paradoxically hierarchical fashion by formalised media 'departments', and with centralised campaign mediation and content, then, appears to resist US and European, Westphalian conceptions of sovereignty. At the same time, further to its literal state-building, IS seeks through its propaganda to recode the sovereign superiority of the (domestic and eventually international) Caliphate, reinscribing, in doing so, the sovereign and neoliberal forms of violence and domination that first subjugated its target audience. This is demonstrated by audiovisual media oriented toward European and English-speaking audiences, which access ideological tropes of anti-US capitalism resonant within these contexts (Richards, 2020), and is possibly replicated across the organisation's much wider corpus of media that unfortunately cannot be examined here. IS's European-language media, at least, foreground neoliberal dimensions of the international financial system, often in combination with extensive comparative references to sovereignty, land and territoriality.

One IS video comparison of territorial and economic governance between the organisation and the United States was *The Rise of the Khilafah: Return of the Gold Dinar* (Al Hayat, 2015a), a documentary-style production that advocates replacing the US fractional-reserve banking system with a form of economic Sharia predicated on a new form of currency, the 'Islamic dinar'. Throughout a resistance narrative characteristically interspersed with footage of raids, bombings and executions, a North American narrator condemns the US-led international financial system, dialectically incorporating a textual snapshot of US libertarian politician Ron Paul's judgement that a 10 per cent devaluation of the US dollar 'robs' the domestic US population of '10 percent of its accumulated wealth' (Al Hayat, 2015a). Excerpting footage from the US Hollywood production, *Kingdom of Heaven* (2005), the narrator discusses Western imperial and neocolonial forces' historical subjugation of Muslim people, overlaid with footage of armed conflict featuring chariots, cannons and bows, signifying the eleventh-century Christian Crusades. Underlining further what might be understood to represent a capitalistic machinic enslavement for the global *umma* (spuriously casting Muslim people as IS subjects), but also referring to figurative enslavement for people generally living in the United States, he then describes 'the dark rise of bank notes, born out of the Satanic conception of banks, which mutated to a fraudulent and riba-based [usury] financial system of enslavement, orchestrated by the Federal Reserve in America' that would 'deprive the people of their due' (Al Hayat, 2015a).

The notion of a varied international population subjugated by capitalism's destructive forces is in some ways coherent within Deleuze and Guattari's frame of machinic enslavement, particularly resonating with descriptions of the machine as a form of capitalism itself, including: 'whose organization exceeds the State apparatus and passes into energy, military–industrial, and multinational complexes' (Deleuze and Guattari, 1980, p. 387). The military–industrial war machine, perhaps also comparable to a regime of 'primitive' capital accumulation (Boal et al., 2005), was explicitly foregrounded in extensive IS propaganda, including videos and articles featuring a UK journalist held captive by IS, John Cantlie. Cantlie was compelled to produce propaganda that foregrounded US-led 'petrodollar warfare' and its military industries. In the sixth issue of a glossy IS magazine, *Dabiq*, for instance, he wrote:

> In return for using dollars only as the trade currency for oil and investing billions in US bonds, America would provide [Saudi Arabia] military support and protect their oil fields. At Saudi's bidding, the other OPEC countries fell into line, and the petrodollar was born. The dollar had been pinned to gold, now it was pinned to oil. (Al Hayat, 2014b, p. 59)

In their emphasis on geopolitical tensions, other examples from IS media might also be said to evoke the war machine practice to 'make the outside a territory in space; consolidate that territory by the construction of a second, adjacent territory; deterritorialize the enemy by shattering his territory from within; deterritorialize oneself by renouncing, by going elsewhere' (Deleuze and Guattari, 1980, p. 353). Noteworthy cases include in particular statements by the now-deceased former IS leader, Caliph or 'emir' Abu Bakr al-Baghdadi, and his deputy, Abu Muhammad al-Adnani, which tended to situate their conflict with forces opposing IS spatially as a battle between *Dar al-Harb* (the Abode of War) and *Dar al-Islam* (the Abode of Peace) (McCants, 2015). The quasi-state of IS in such statements, and across such videos as *The End of Sykes-Picot* (Al-Hayat, 2014a), can be said to 'code and decode space' through territorialising and deterritorialising methods, ultimately serving to define, though, the capitalist-sovereign limits of IS's 'counter-US' political resistance.

Recoding traits are also apparent by virtue of the geopolitical references replete across IS media, which associate US political–economic incentives for military–counterterrorist action with the country's multilateral alliances, transnational commercial partnerships, and the way US political–economic hegemony and an international neoliberal capitalist order are reinforced through the 'bond' and 'pact' of states. The video *No Respite* (Al-Hayat, 2015b), for example, elaborates an account of US-directed military activity in the Middle East against IS and its strategic fallout, extending to the trillion-dollar war expense of the United States, suicides of US soldiers, and diplomatic loss of face following America's unsuccessful and brutal military campaigns. The video dialogue opens with a declaration that the Caliphate was built on 'the prophetic methodology . . . not a secular state built on man-made laws'. Here, the laws that define capitalist (and stated 'Western') conceptions of nationhood are rejected, while IS's very selective interpolation of religion into its mode of government is promoted, reinscribing a form of state-based sovereignty, and reflecting Deleuze and Guattari's additional statement that 'religion' can act as 'a piece in the state apparatus (in both of its forms, the "bond" and the "pact or alliance", even if it has within itself the power to elevate this model to the level of the universal or to constitute an absolute *Imperium*' (1980, p. 383).

It is important to note that IS's exploitation of religious tropes and terms is almost consistent with the statement above, despite IS being an organisation that should not be considered a 'religious' movement as such. Its militant quasi-Islamism, as the non-religious politicisation of Islam, was questionably interpolated to establish authority and institutional legitimation serving the organisation's distinctly late modern capitalist governance apparatus and its territorial ambition. As Gunning and Jackson (2011) have observed, those movements that cite the broad religion of Islam as justification for violence often do so in conflictual ways, while the 'war on terror' resembled the rationale of asymmetric conflict more than it did 'cosmic war'. In this chapter's reading,

IS's application of so-called 'Sharia law' in reality derived inspiration from corporations and nation states, and it was pursued according to the dominant coding standards of Deleuze and Guattari's modern state. Further problematising the applicability of Deleuze and Guattari's theory in this regard is their citation of *Imperium*, possibly representing Francis Parker Yockey's 1948 fascist opus; again, either way, demonstrating rhetorical but potentially meaningful elision of the actual–material manner in which classist differentiation plays into the formation of myriad violent politics.

Here, it is worth reflecting again on Sharpe's (2021) note about Deleuze's historical obscuration of class-based oppressions instantiated in the machineries of institutional capitalism, by casting each of those implicated in master–slave dialectics as *mutually* (if not equally) enslaved or subjugated by the machinic apparatus of which they are constitutively a part. Within the Caliphate, drivers for violent conflict are mediated materially by IS's quest for a restrictive monopoly over social relations, and its enactment of enslavement and subjugation, hierarchised according to the state form. Escaping activist definitions of the war machine as a 'metamorphosis-machine', or 'difference engine' (Robinson, 2010), the organisation epitomises striated capitalism by reinforcing dominant coding standards along vertically integrated production lines. A critical reading of the war machine applied to IS must, then, take account of distributed power if it is to avoid inadvertently supporting the imperial sign regime associated with the state apparatus in Deleuze and Guattari's theory. As the final comment below illustrates, this must also entail accounting for practical as well as associational, ideational connections between IS and its state-based opposition, literally represented by their shared wartime apparatus of military–industrial assemblages (see also Richards, 2020).

IS at the Margins

IS's engagement with its US, neoliberal and military opposition has been characterised by reflexivity on its part, sustained by dialectical and ideational engagements, as well as organisational mirroring. In the context of Deleuze and Guattari's theory, this helps to explain how IS might be described as a hybrid revolutionary actor, negotiating a relationship of 'complementarity' between the state and war machine 'that further plays out in representations of clashes between celerity and gravity, obscurity and clarity, violent and calm, the fearsome and the regulated, bond and pact' (Ditrych et al., in this volume). In their revolutionary dimensions, the state-forming practices of IS are often those that erode its (declared) emancipatory potential. The negotiations IS strikes between its 'nomadic' war machine aspects and its 'sedentary', territorial incentives are conducted in symbolic ways by the spectre of the 'state form', related to its quest for a hierarchical monopoly over social relations. Unlike some progressivist forms of anti-state resistance, IS reinforces dominant coding standards through the forms of 'despotic signification' (Deuchars, 2011) it imposes, through rhizomatic but centrally coordinated propaganda networks, and formalised methods of governance employed as 'state' laws and regulations in IS-held territory.

IS's dialectical engagements with US military and counterterrorism, though, escape even those hybridities set out in Deleuze and Guattari's theory. Considered in terms of Deleuze and Guattari's extension of Clausewitz's (1982) 'absolute war', wherein the 'war on terror' can be said to operate in Deleuzian terms well beyond the sovereign interests of America (Fischer, 2011), neoliberal capitalism cannot be understood as an essentialist exigency of nomadism rather than as fundamental to modern militaristic statism. The political–economic activity underwriting contemporary forms of militarism related to the role of the economy in (anti-)state conflict destabilise the historical comparison set out here. It is not through IS's participation in the 'war on terror' that it diverges from a recoding of neoliberal statehood, as against the state apparatus – as described in Deleuze and Guattari's theory – but rather through the neoliberal expressions of its organisational management in the context of the war that IS resists nomadism, adhering, in fact, in both practical and ideational terms, to a post-Westphalian state-based order. Although IS might have been understood in more binary terms through a Deleuzian frame as 'irreducible to sovereignty and prior to its law' (Reid, 2003, p. 65), IS's enactment of *actual* war, despite its somewhat paradoxical ideations, leveraged existing geo- and sociopolitical conditions both in the Middle East and internationally to stake its legitimacy and capacity for sovereign status. This example not only problematises Deleuze and Guattari's claim that sedentarisation provides stoppage which settles the nomads; it also, conversely, puts paid to the limits of possibility for state-based hybridisation – where war machines as 'revolutionary' cannot be sustained beyond the processes of striation.

Building on other contributions to this volume, this chapter showed how war machine theory can usefully elaborate some aspects of IS's organisational hybridity and its dialectical pro- and counterrevolutionary tendencies. Limitations of the theory were argued to risk elision between what can be interpreted as class-based power differentials underwriting heterogeneous forms of political violence. To the extent of its possible Nietzschean amoral programme, such theory, applied to existing movements, could be read to obscure fundamental difference, despite Deleuze and Guattari's countervening political incentives, and in so doing contribute to such perspectivist sociopolitical conditions as justify the installation of, for example, 'imperium'. As the discussion showed, a critical application of war machine theory requires attention to extant power differentials supporting IS's imperialist tendencies, taking into account their contribution to the unsettled and destabilising nature of the organisation's hybridity. Insofar as Deleuze and Guattari's theory can describe the processual and relational character of each of their respective (for example, state, war machine, capitalism) categories, its instrumental application can demonstrate from a process-philosophical perspective how the apparatus of power and resistance is, as in history, mutually constitutive and always contingent, where the relative negotiations of statehood and capital underwrite this principle.

Note

1. IS lost territory against US coalition airstrikes and Kurdish forces in the Middle East from 2016 and 2017, finally losing the last of its Syrian territory in 2019.

References

Al Hayat. 2014a. *The End of Sykes–Picot*, 29 June. Available at: <http:// jihad ology.net/2014/06/29/al-%E1%B8%A5ayat-media-center-presents-a-new -video-message-from-the-islamic-state-of-iraq-and-al-sham-the-end-of-sykes-picot/> (last accessed 10 May 2017).

Al Hayat. 2014b. *Al-Qa'idah of Waziristan: A Testimony from Within. Dabiq* 6. Available at: <https://clarionproject.org/docs/ISIS-isil-islamic-state-magaz ine-issue-6-al-qaeda-of-waziristan.pdf> (last accessed 10 May 2017).

Al Hayat. 2015a. *The Rise of the Khilafah: Return of the Gold Dinar*, 29 August. Available at: <https://archive.org/details/TheRiseOfTheKhilafah AndTheReturnOfTheGoldDinar> (last accessed 10 February 2016).

Al Hayat. 2015b. *No Respite*, 24 November. Available at: <http://heavy .com/news/2015/11/new-ISIS-islamic-state-news-pictures-videos-no-res pite-englishlanguage-propaganda-full-uncensored-youtube-daesh/> (last accessed 10 May 2016).

Al Hayat. 2015c. 'Islamic State Report: An Insight into the Islamic State: Issue 1'. *Al Hayat*. Available at: <https://azelin.files.wordpress.com/ 2014/06/ islamic-state-of-iraq-and-al-shc481m-22islamic-state-report-122.pdf> (last accessed 10 February 2017).

Al-Lami, M. 2019. 'Where Is the Islamic State Group Still Active Around the World?' *BBC News*, 27 March. Available at: <www.bbc.com/news/world-middle-east-47691006> (last accessed 29 December 2019).

Al-Tamimi, A. 2016. 'Archive of Islamic State Administrative Documents (cont.)', 11 January. Available at: <www.aymennjawad.org/2016/01/arc hive-of-islamic-state-administrative-documents-1> (last accessed 10 May 2017).

Alexander, Y. and Alexander, D. 2015. *The Islamic State: Combating the Caliphate Without Borders*. Lanham: Lexington Books.

Awan, A. 2014. 'Terrorism Craves an Audience and We Are Playing into Islamic State's Hands by Watching'. *New Internationalist*. Available at: <http://works.bepress.com/akil_awan/15> (last accessed 10 May 2017).

Bahney, B., Shatz, H., Ganier, C., McPherson, R. and Sude, B. 2010. *An Economic Analysis of the Financial Records of Al-Qaida in Iraq*. Rand Corporation. Available at: <www.rand.org/content/dam/rand/pubs/mo nographs/ 2010/RAND_MG1026.pdf> (last accessed 10 May 2017).

Barkawi, T. and Laffey, M. 2006. 'The Postcolonial Moment in Security Studies'. *Review of International Studies* 32 (2): 329–52.

Bindner, L. and Poirot, G. 2016. *ISIS Financing: 2015*, ed. J.-C. Brisard and D. Martinez. Center for the Analysis of Terrorism. Available at: <www.cat -int.org/wp-content/uploads/2016/06/ISIS-Financing-2015-Report.pdf> (last accessed 10 May 2017).

Bloom, P. 2016. *Beyond Power and Resistance: Politics at the Radical Limits*. London: Rowman and Littlefield.

Boal, I., Clark, T., Matthews, J. and Watts, M. 2005. *Afflicted Powers: Capital and Spectacle in a New Age of War*. London and New York: Verso.

Boggs, C., and Pollard, T. 2006. 'Hollywood and the Spectacle of Terrorism'. *New Political Science* 28 (3): 335–51.

Brisard, J.-C. and Martinez, D. 2014. *Islamic State: The Economy-based Terrorist Funding*. Reuters, Center for the Analysis of Terrorism, October. Available at: <http://cat-int.org/wp-content/uploads/2016/06/White-Paper-IS -Funding_Final.pdf> (last accessed 10 May 2017).

Charette, R. 2007. 'Al-Qaeda: Venture Capitalists of Terror: A Q&A with Lawrence Husick on How Insurgents Spread Their Message via the Web'. *Spectrum*, 1 November. Available at: <http://spectrum.ieee.org/telecom/ security/alqaeda-venture-capitalists-of-terror> (last accessed 10 May 2017).

Clausewitz, C. 1982. *On War*. New York: Penguin.

DeFronzo, J. 2018. *Revolutions and Revolutionary Movements*. London: Routledge.

Deleuze, G. 1962. *Nietzsche and Philosophy*. New York: Columbia University Press.

Deleuze, G. and Guattari, F. 1972. *Anti-Oedipus: Capitalism and Schizophrenia*. New York: Viking Press.

Deleuze, G. and Guattari, F. 1980. *A Thousand Plateaus: Capitalism and Schizophrenia*. London: Bloomsbury.

Deleuze, G. and Guattari, F. 1986. *Nomadology: The War Machine*. Boston: MIT Press.

Deuchars, R. 2011. 'Creating Lines of Flight and Activating Resistance: Deleuze and Guattari's War Machine'. *AntePodium* 1–28.

Fick, M. 2014. *Special Report: Islamic State Uses Grain to Tighten Grip in Iraq*. Reuters, 30 September. Available at: <www.reuters.com/article/us-mide ast-crisis-wheat/special-report-islamic-state-uses-grain-to-tighten-grip-in -iraq-idUSKCN0HP12J20140930> (last accessed 10 May 2017).

Fischer, R. 2011. 'Response to Robert Deuchars: The War Machine, Power and Humans as Social Animals', in Deuchars, R. 'Creating Lines of Flight and Activating Resistance'. *AntePodium* 35–8.

Foucault, M. 2004. *'Society Must Be Defended': Lectures at the Collège de France, 1975–1976*. New York: Penguin Books.

Foucault, M. 2008. [1978–9], *The Birth of Biopolitics: Lectures at the Collège de France, 1978–1979*. London: Palgrave Macmillan.

Giroux, H. 2012. 'Disturbing Pleasures: Murderous Images and the Aesthetics of Depravity'. *Third Text* 26 (3): 259–73.

Gunning, J. and Jackson, R. 2011. 'What's So "Religious" About "Religious Terrorism"?' *Critical Studies on Terrorism* 4 (3): 369–88.

Harvey, D. 2005. *A Brief History of Neoliberalism*. Oxford: Oxford University Press.

Heißner, S., Neumann P., Holland-McCown, J. and Basra, R. 2017. *Caliphate in Decline: An Estimate of Islamic State's Financial Fortunes*. International Centre for the Study of Radicalisation and Political Violence, King's College, London. Available at: <http://icsr.info/wp-content/uploads/20 17/02/ICSR-Report-Caliphate-in-Decline-An-Estimate-of-Islamic-States -Financial-Fortunes.pdf> (last accessed 10 December 2017).

Jaafar, H. and Woertz, E. 2016. 'Agriculture as a Funding Source of ISIS: A GIS and Remote Sensing Analysis'. *Food Policy* 64: 14–25.

Jessop, B. 2006. 'Spatial Fixes, Temporal Fixes and Spatio-temporal Fixes'. In Castree, N. and Gregory, D. (eds). *David Harvey: A Critical Reader*, 142–66. Oxford: Blackwell.

Kingdom of Heaven. 2005, motion picture, Scott Free Productions. Distributed by 20th Century Fox.

Lazzarato, M. 2006. *The Machine*. European Institute for Progressive Cultural Politics, October. Available at: <http://asounder.org/resources/lazzarato _themachine.pdf> (last accessed 1 October 2020).

Lister, C. 2014. *Profiling the Islamic State*. Doha: Brookings Doha Center.

Lister, T., Sanches, R., Bixler, M., O'Key, S., Hogenmiller, M. and Tawfeeq, M. 2018. 'ISIS Goes Global: 143 Attacks in 29 countries Have Killed 2,043'. *CNN*, 12 February. Available at: <https://edition.cnn.com/2015/12/17/world/mapping-isis-attacks-around-the-world/index.html> (last accessed 29 December 2019).

McCants, W. 2015. *The ISIS Apocalypse: The History, Strategy, and Doomsday Vision of the Islamic State*. London: Macmillan.

Massumi, B. 1993. *The Politics of Everyday Fear*. Minneapolis: University of Minnesota Press.

Patton, P. 2000. *Deleuze and the Political*. London: Psychology Press.

Purcell, M. 2013. 'A New Land: Deleuze and Guattari and Planning'. *Planning Theory and Practice* 14 (1): 20–38.

Reid, J. 2003. 'Deleuze's War Machine: Nomadism Against the State'. *Millennium: Journal of International Studies* 32 (1): 57–85.

Reid, J. 2004. 'Architecture, Al-Qaeda, and the World Trade Center: Rethinking Relations Between War, Modernity, and City Spaces after 9/11'. *Space and Culture* 7 (4): 396–408.

Richards, I. 2020. *Neoliberalism and Neo-jihadism: Propaganda and Finance in Al Qaeda and Islamic State*. Manchester: Manchester University Press.

Robinson, A. 2010. 'In Theory: Why Deleuze (Still) Matters: States, War-machines and Radical Transformation'. *Ceasefire*, 10 September. Available at: <https://ceasefiremagazine.co.uk/in-theory-deleuze-war-machine/> (last accessed 1 October 2020).

Sharpe, M. 2021. 'Golden Calf: Deleuze's Nietzsche in the Time of Trump'. *Thesis Eleven*, 163 (1): 71–88.

Simpson, C. 2014. 'The Banality of Islamic State'. *Bloomberg Business*, 20 November. Available at: <www.bloomberg.com/graphics/2014-the-business-of-ISIS-spreadsheets-annual-reports-and-terror/#/> (last accessed 10 May 2017).

Swanson, A. 2015. 'How the Islamic State Makes Its Money'. *Washington Post*, 18 November. Available at: <www.washingtonpost.com/news/wonk/wp/2015/11/18/how-ISIS-makes-its-money/?utm_term=.f184decbadff> (last accessed 10 May 2017).

UNSCR. 2019. *Letter Dated 15 July 2019 from the Chair of the Security Council Committee Pursuant to Resolutions 1267 (1999), 1989 (2011) and 2243 (2015) Concerning Islamic State in Iraq and the Levant (Da'esh), Al-Qaida and Associated Individuals, Groups, Undertakings and Entities Addressed to the President of the Security Council*, 15 July. Available at: <https:// undocs.org/S/2019/570> (last accessed 29 December 2019).

Yockey, F. P. 1948. *Imperium: The Philosophy of History and Politics*. Abergele: The Palingenesis Project / Wermod and Wermod.

Zahid, F. 2014. *The Expanding World of ISIS: Affiliates and Associates*. Islamabad: Center for Research and Security Studies.

Zelin, A. 2015. 'Picture or It Didn't Happen: A Snapshot of the Islamic State's Official Media Output'. *Perspectives on Terrorism* 9 (4): 85–97.

Part III

. . . And Not That Exceptional?

7

The Typical Troublemakers: Bolsheviks as Hybrid Revolutionaries

Ondrej Ditrych, Miroslava Kul'ková and Alexander Ščerbak

When alternatives to the system of domination are created, they always occur during singular moments. The revolutions were singular moments that lasted days, weeks, months or years. This amounts to saying that the normal order of things was interrupted, that, at certain times, the normal rules disappear, that time is suspended and at the same time accelerates because the movements generate high speeds,

Rancière noted recently (Gavroche, 2018). The Bolshevik Revolution represents a paradigmatic case of an attempted upheaval of a sociopolitical order. It was driven by a political utopia based on a radically different notion of collective emancipation when compared to Wilson's liberal internationalism or exclusionary nationalism, which it competed with after World War I. It promised a millennium that would be a negation of the mundane time of catastrophes. Where the liberal utopia was provided as a regulative for mundane history, the communist utopia radicalised it, directing (linear) time toward the actualisation of the realm of freedom and equality, later simulating its actual presence. Yet, conventional geopolitical thought and strategies constituted elements of Bolshevik international practice along non-linear instruments of expansion, mobilising transnational class solidarity in the labour movement (which was divided among the Bolshevik Revolution's support). Moreover, the restoration of centralised territorial governance domestically – including at the expense of ideological collectives represented by local councils (*soviets*) – also signalled that territory was never waived as a political technology (Elden, 2013).

This chapter seeks to make Bolshevik revolutionary practice intelligible by deploying the book's conceptual toolbox. It points to the coalescence of a space of spaces and spaces of flows (Ruggie, 1993) in Bolshevik practice, or of the Bolshevik war machine that contested the Westphalian order's dominant spatiality and temporality, relating to the outside milieu without horizon while also re-enacting territorialised and despotic state elements, even prior to the 'sedentarisation' in the form of the USSR. It attends to key futures in the constitution of the Bolshevik subject, whose genesis it traces to the decades prior to the Red October (1917). It interrogates the Bolsheviks' hybrid practice following the revolution, its international 'subject effects', and similarly a hybrid counterrevolutionary action from a limited armed intervention and occupation combined with support to an array of local actors in the erstwhile Tzardom. By means of these investigations, the chapter seeks to contribute to a more nuanced, theoretically anchored history of (counter)revolutionary action and challenge: among other things, ISIS's exceptionalism in showing similarities in the recurrence of a revolutionary practice that is historically contingent yet also deeply embedded in the *longue durée* sociopolitical structures of the Westphalian social time.

And So It Becomes

First, how can the constitution of the Bolshevik subject – whose genesis may be traced back to around the Brussels and London summit (1902) in which key discursive rules and practices were established, and whose important milestone was the Prague conference (1912) in which the major transformation of a 'party of the new type' took place – be read using this volume's toolbox? In what follows, we focus on specific points and discursive practices at the time of this emergence, not venturing into a total history of the party as a vanguard of the proletariat, the workers who have no country (cf. McAdams, 2017, p. 3) and following its development into a global institution with a multiplicity of forms. Rather, the emphasis is placed on situating the narrative of the proletarian(s), corresponding to basic discourses and rhetorical devices through which the strategic vision of the party was conveyed in this early period.

The vehicle for establishing radical alterity in the constitution of the Bolshevik subject, as a means to convey the political utopia of an order different from the *status quo*, was the idea of *class* as establishing primary relations of association and dissociation. The concept of class in the Bolshevik understanding is fundamentally relational – it is defined by common interests linked to a certain relation to the means of production and opposed to the other social groups with different economic interests linked to their own relations.[1] As Giddens notes, it is also basically dichotomous along the lines of haves / have nots – 'All class societies are built around a primary line of division between two antagonistic classes, one dominant and the other subordinate' (Giddens, 1973, p. 35). The mobilising potential of this division is clearly echoed by Stalin in this respect: 'Bourgeoisie, our irreconcilable enemy, their riches based on our poverty and their happiness on our grief. It is obvious that their existing representatives will be our sworn enemies who will try to consciously destroy us' (Stalin, 1954b [1905]). The relationship is one of absolute enmity, even though the figure of the *proletarian* is purely ideological – it does not have specific qualities related to race, politics, language or nationality. It is a pure identity standing opposed to the *capitalist* and the *bourgeois*, a negative definition and an unsaturated function. The proletarian does not know what he *is*; he knows only what *he is not*. As Deleuze and Guattari suggest in *A Thousand Plateaus* (1987), one can understand class theory only through the prism of nomadic science. A proletarian must accept a vision of the world that is embedded in the general knowledge accepted and promoted by the state but at the same time as something that needs to be abolished and destroyed. It is necessary to verify the proletarian's position on the grid of the social field but also as something that is in a state of (suspended) elimination since, with the success of the revolution, this and other relational positions are to be negated – it is both the inner and the outer surface of the matter: a Möbius strip of a kind.

In this positioning, and in the whole ideological concept of the proletarians and their world, the key role is played by the party. The party is the heart of the political, ideological and strategical body of the proletarian. It is the mechanism that unites proletarians and, as the *vanguard* of the proletariat, provides a sense of strategic, depersonalised orientation to class struggle. The party is a body – poetically, as for Mayakovsky, identical with Lenin's – yet one without organs, as a war machine is expected to be, and the proletarian is its stretched hand, a fist of justice that delivers the strike. The party cannot exist without the proletarian – it needs the oppressed class and the relationship between them to create a symbiotic double bind that forms, and at the same time verifies, its war machine function. Both are nomadic in the sense of their radical opposition to the state apparatus and sovereign power as such, which oppresses the proletarian class in both material and ideological ways. The proletarian becomes akin to the nomadic warrior, challenging private property as the foundation stone of existing social relations and political order(s), with even sovereignty, as the basic ordering norm of the international order, traced back to it (Ruggie, 1993; Onuf, 1998; for discussion see Holland, 2010). From this position, the proletarian engages in political violence out of necessity – unlike, for example, the *bandit*, whose violence is embedded in the existing paradigm and serves only to satisfy his or her own needs – and to further the class struggle. He is a *go* piece on a *chessboard* – its specific value cannot be manifested on the chessboard unless a new rule set is established – and this is the exact force that brings the war machine vehicle into momentum; it makes it emerge. The party's appeal is that of the vanguard, a progressive movement which advances a cause superior to all individual members, allowing them to participate in a drama of grand historical proportions (McAdams, 2017, p. 5). It is the community of those who have the *virtue* to transcend their individual needs and desires, and the *sight* to see the inevitable course of history.

Their assumed gift of (fore)sight notwithstanding, the party discourse featured some notable controversies. A key one centred on the position toward the rival revolutionary idea of an alternative political order based on the principle of *national*, rather than class, emancipation. Confronting this alternative shaped both the process of Bolshevik becoming and the hybrid nature of their rule following the revolution (see below). In the early years, Bolshevik elites, including Lenin, Stalin and Rosa Luxemburg, were sceptical of strong nationalist inclinations in the revolutionary movement – stirred by Polish, Georgian, Ukrainian or Armenian national aspirations, the attraction of Austromarxism, and the high degree of centralisation by the imperial government (Zajaczkowski, 2009) in the empire. It was decisively established at the Second Congress (1903) that workers' parties would not be established on a national basis. Yet, Lenin or Stalin also understood nationalism as a progressive event and believed that the colonial struggle for national determination could be tactically exploited for the sake of world revolution (cf. Lenin, 1916) – even if the nation was to be dialectically overcome in the end. Bourgeois nationalism and proletarian internationalism were opposed to one another as two irreconcilably hostile worldviews. Nonetheless, (non-exclusive) national emancipation and the principle of the equality of all nations were to be appropriated, in a distinctly hybrid form, as part of the generalised struggle for human emancipation – universally applicable because of the proletarian's pure identity – and an element in the Bolsheviks' distinct vision of a global, revolutionary, democratising movement. The denial of separation is part and parcel of bourgeois oppression: '[I]n a capitalist state, the denial of freedom of self-determination, that is, secession of nations, means only the protection of the privileges of the ruling nation and police methods of government' (Lenin, 1972 [1914], p. 396).[2] However, if the demand for national, democratic emancipation were to be *particular* – 'a particle [that] contradicts the whole' (Stalin, 1954a [1913]) – it would need to be rejected.

Formally, the party as a war machine betrays distinct rhizomatic structural features. It is dispersed in separate cells which were not specialised but mimicked each other, emitting the same activity and sharing the same strategic narrative, notwithstanding particular conditions related to the specific location, country or political system in which they were operating – it was an ideological, deterritorialised form. Interestingly, money flows to the central committee of the Russian Social Democratic Labour Party (of which the Bolsheviks were a part) were made subject to oversight by the recognised personalities of German Social Democracy (Kautsky, Zetkin, Mehring), invited to play the role of controllers. This occurred, even though Lenin did not appreciate the initiative to establish these foreigners in such positions. At the same time, while even its organisational form serves as a marker of radical opposition to the organisational form it sought to break ('disorganise'),[3] it was also distinguished by a closed structure with strict discipline and a clear strategic orientation toward the use of radical revolutionary methods. Like modern militaries (cf. DeLanda, 1991) – the war machines appropriated by the states – the party imposes limits on its dispersal, limiting its reliance on local, tactical initiatives.

As noted above, the proletarian's pure identity is conditioned on a complex interrelationship between the dominant and alternative knowledge of the world. Like other revolutionaries, the Bolsheviks, moreover, appropriated and operationalised knowledge of modern revolution, a distinct *tradition* developed since the Great French Revolution (1789), relying on and relating to, for instance, the experience of Jacobin radicals. Theirs was also, in Lenin's words (Engels et al., 2017), 'applied' Marxism as knowledge formation that was radical yet clearly entangled with the Western *epistémé*, which the Bolsheviks were to adapt to the conditions of their time and space. Born from the tradition of European Social Democracy, Bolshevik discourse centred around concepts of social justice and democracy, relating Bolshevik practice to both the premodern and the modern democratic tradition. The Bolsheviks, however, radicalised related discourses to differentiate themselves clearly from other elements of the broader revolutionary fields, both in Russia and internationally – for instance, by articulating the 'dictatorship of the proletariat' as an objective and deploying a variety of symbolic repertoires to establish a radical difference between, on one hand, *bourgeois, philistines, priests, oprichniks* and the *rotten throne of the Romanovs* and, on the other hand, the *liberation movement* that remembered its *fallen*, stood for *light* and even represented Russians as *godly people* (Bunin and Marullo, 1998) in direct relation to Russia's spiritual and moral exceptionalism, even later supporting the export of the revolution (see below). The Bolsheviks took pains, however, to accommodate their radicalism with a simulation of authentic proletarian democracy and formulating mythological narratives of power related to it – Lenin is one of the people but also has remarkable powers, for example, to create peace with a single signature, something bourgeois statesmen can never hope to achieve, and this commands obedience.

This radical positioning and use of familiar, yet repacked and repurposed, repertoires facilitated communication with the masses, who were yet to recognise themselves as part of the proletariat. Familiar, mobilising rhetorical devices such as repetition, exaggeration and shock strategy were part and parcel of Bolshevik speech that, when directed to these masses, accentuated the association of words and deeds and the practical application of revolutionary knowledge. Meanwhile, Bolsheviks could similarly adopt traditional juridical registers when speaking to an educated public, for instance, when reproducing the democratic myth:

> Being a good ruler means to know how to rule. In order to control the fates of such a colossal republic, even a union of republics, we need extremely acute, extremely diverse knowledge . . . for every citizen, in our true democracy, must be a participant in the government of the country. (Lunacharsky, 1919)

Visual rhetoric was conceived as a particularly important means of communication with the 'savage' masses in Russia – 'a wild country in which the masses were robbed of education, light and knowledge' (Lenin, 1977 [1913]) – by the Bolsheviks. It was via visual propaganda that the image of the Bolsheviks as the vanguard of the proletarian that a new, modern person in the world was to be established, and the call to action to the masses to partake in the making of the brave new world was issued and serially reproduced. In doing so, bricolages were made comprising heterogeneous codes and hybridisations of elements in the cognitive field through which the radical novelty was to be made intelligible – premised on the triadic relation to the sign always involving the interpreting agency too (see Švantner, this volume) – by means of familiar scripts.

Bolshevik visual practices follow the principle of binary opposition discussed in relation to speech above. They also embody many of the features noted regarding the constitution of the Bolshevik subject and that of the proletarian. The latter carry no specific signs (gender, age, clothing), representing their essential function (see above), which can be filled by anyone and everyone. An exception is that they carry tools or weapons, representing them as people of action. The field of vision comprises the individual but also a mass – the party – in which individual proletarians unite and the symbiotic double binds between them. Both the individual and the mass are in movement, emitting activity and making decisions – contrasting with the figure of the enemy, the bourgeois, whose attributes, like fatness or stillness, represent both the exploitive nature of his character but also the contrast with the Bolshevik war machine's dynamic becoming.

Red is the colour of revolution and it dominates Bolshevik visual imagery. It is in constant contrast with other colours in the image, asserting dominance and capturing the attention. The figure representation is often large, even gargantuan – representing how a mass of people can be enrolled for the grand revolutionary project, changing the entire world while becoming one universal body. Leaders – the particular bodies – are visible and recognisable (with a special status awarded to Lenin's body in relation to the body of the party, as noted above). Yet, as in textual codes constitutive of the Bolshevik mythology of power, they are represented as regular party members working toward achieving a common revolutionary goal.

In the World of States

The hybrid constitution of the Bolsheviks was inscribed in their practice immediately following their seizure of power in Russia in the Red Revolution (1917). Even before Bolshevism was domesticated as 'socialism in one country' in the 1920s, this practice featured some rather conventional, and distinctly *territorialising*, (geo)political and diplomatic strategies. Bolsheviks sought, ultimately successfully, to collect most pieces of the Tzarist empire together in the civil war. Instead of forming it into a smooth space without enclosures, they subjected it to a rather conventional, centralised and *imperial* sovereign rule, erasing local soviets' autonomy as heterogenous spaces for authentic, non-alienated human existence. The Soviet state was, ultimately, organised as an abstract space in which rational economic calculation and the exercise of power at a distance was possible, as was mass mobilisation, state intervention, social engineering and biopolitical population surveillance – a continuation, rather than a rupture, in the project of modern statehood (Holquist, 2002, Neumann and Willimott, 2018; cf. Viola, 2002).

Bolshevik Rule: A Hybrid Political Order

The Bolsheviks never waived territory as a political technology (Elden, 2013). They had enacted a transnational space of flows through which the intersubjective political utopia of a global, classless society was to come to be. The Cominform was founded (1919) to this end, as a deterritorialised empire of sorts – as Lenin put it, 'the founding of an international soviet republic is on the way' (cited in McAdams, 2017, p. 102). This was not to be, not only because of local counterrevolution (brutally enacted, for example, by the Freikorps in Germany) but also because of failed strategies – including favouring mass mobilisation over the vanguard in Germany, and the bizarre, incompetent and

fleeting rule of terror under Bela Kun's Republic of Councils in Hungary[4] –
or internal divisions. This aside, the geopolitical anchor of the state and the
conventional sovereignty of the state over territory (and the mutual relationship between the two) were manifest in the practices of consolidation during
the civil war, and linear territorial expansion both to protect and to push forward the revolution's reach by means of dominion over a spatial extension.
Following a (partial) internal consolidation, this ambition guided the Polish
campaign, followed by a retrenchment that eventually resulted in diplomatic
agreements on the borders with Persia, Turkey, Poland, the United Kingdom
and Germany, intended to give the Bolsheviks time to breathe while they
consolidated their hold over the former empire.

     Therefore, in parallel to the radical reinterpretation of the sovereignty norm
and collective emancipation that competed with the period of nationalism and
liberal internationalism, the Bolsheviks also enacted a distinct space of spaces.
Moreover, notwithstanding their clear assimilative posture toward otherness,
the Bolshevik leadership constantly showed a readiness to coexist with the
capitalist world and engage in diplomacy as a practice of mediating estrangement with capitalist powers – whose embassies remained in Russia after the
revolution, but for a time communicated with the Bolsheviks by means of
informal agents (Engelstein, 2017, p. 383). Before the Brest-Litovsk separate
peace agreement with Germany in March 1918, recognising that the revolution could not be defended internationally, the Bolsheviks seriously con-
templated receiving aid from Western capitalist powers.[5] Even after this, the
Murmansk soviet sanctioned the landing of British marines, and later French
and American troops, to defend a strategic railway against nearby Germans
and Finns. Since the Germans disrespected the conditions of the Brest-Litovsk
agreement in spring 1918, the possibility of receiving support from Western
capitalist powers – which remained keen on reopening the eastern front –
continued to be considered by the Bolsheviks, while the British cabinet played
with the idea of renewing a formal alliance with Russia (Engelstein, 2017,
p. 387). Lenin's position that the peace with Germany was paramount ultimately prevailed, however, and further Western support was rejected, even
though the Bolsheviks were divided on the matter. Lenin then unsuccessfully attempted to enlist German business interests to check German military
engagement in Eastern Europe while seeking economic assistance from the
German state – his strategy now premised on the expectation of a socialist
revolution in Germany.

     To ensure their political survival, the Bolsheviks thus entertained not just
one but *several* diverse strategies of engagement with Western powers during
this period, reaching out to both the Entente powers and Germany – the

German state capitalism model, Lenin believed, should be appropriated and transposed to the political conditions now established in Russia to remake the country as a modern industrial society. Even after the civil war, the importance of external recognition was embedded in the Westphalian grid of intelligibility rather than in some radically different ordering of international politics. This was manifested, for example, in Lenin's claim (1921) that the Bolsheviks had now 'won the fight for an independent existence' and established a 'basis in the international sense' (quoted in Jacobson, 1994, p. 14); or the assertions by Chicherin, the first people's foreign commissioner, that great powers do not need recognition but declare their own existence – and history would force the imperialists to recognise the Bolshevik government.

Could this be merely a tactical, temporarily bounded stage in the time flow of inevitable historical progress toward a world free of politics and time – the proper nomad's world? Was Bolshevik diplomacy only a clever dissimulation intended to trick their capitalist enemies, a rational strategy intended to reduce or defer the costs of the revolution? Indeed, it was justified as such. Lenin argued, among other things, that since the world revolution had not materialised, 'a highly protracted situation' came to be, which necessitated establishing a (temporary) equilibrium. Examining the practice of Bolshevik rule, however, also points to something else: the inability to escape the confines of the Westphalian *epistémé*, of the territorial concept of authority, as well as representations and operationalisations of political authority, and of the common sense and routines of mediation of estrangement that *reified*, rather than erased, the boundaries between human associations.

The becoming of Bolshevik hybrid rule was not the result of some master plan but rather of contingency, pragmatism and the need to resolve immediate controversies – to manage tensions between Grand Russia conceptions alive in the party and the expectations of allies from other nationalities in the civil war, or to ensure stability even after the war was over in the 1920s since the control of some territories (such as Siberia) remained only nominal for the new state and resistance persevered (Zajaczkowski, 2009). As noted above, national liberation was integrated into the Bolshevik vision of a global revolution, even as this was a pragmatic move and nation as a form of bounded human collectivity was to be dialectically overcome, eventually. Immediately after the revolution, this pragmatism was manifested in the *Declaration of the Rights of the Peoples of Russia* – and during the war in promises made to nationalist movements within the former empire. (In marked contrast, the conservative Whites showed a manifest lack of practical understanding for these aspirations and, as a result, confronted not just Bolsheviks but national forces during the civil war, particularly in Russia's South.)

Bolsheviks thus demonstrated a tactical ability to enrol moderate nationalist forces – and drive a wedge between them and the more radical nationalists – even though nationalism posed one of the alternative political utopias for the organisation of political life both in the former Tzardom and internationally – in which the *people* emanated from the nation, whose historicity they recognised rather than class. In Russia, this utopia was ultimately unsuccessful, just like the conservative utopia of the restitution of the *ancien* empire. Yet, both served as sources of elements repacked and repurposed as the Bolsheviks devised a political design for their rule that combined new imperialism with the application of the nationalist grid in the USSR's federal model.

The federal model featured (multilevel) national autonomy in which nationality was the basic organisational principle of government. Indeed, real political autonomy was illusory, yet the governing machine was productive in terms of nationalities, operating by means of schools, newspapers, street signs, administrative censuses or the scholarly design of literary languages. (The productive nature of this governing machine can be illustrated in Soviet Central Asia, where there had never previously been a state that would emerge from linking an ethnic group and a territory. Traditional forms, however, were not erased but rather hybridised. Kishlak, a traditional form of rural settlement linked to the governing of irrigation channels in valleys, was thus duly transformed into *kolkhoz*, but neither its economic nor its political function was substantially changed (Roy, 2000, p. 2; Olcott, 1994; Bacon, 1966)). This enterprise was further governed by the expediency of communicating the Bolshevik doctrine to the peoples of the erstwhile empire. The degree of centralisation increased over time while the diversity of recognised nationalities with a political status was reduced. Nonetheless, the nation as political technology was never erased from the Bolshevik mode of government, manifested in the federal design's durability and living through materialities like the *nacionalnost* rubric in personal documents – as Zajaczkowski (2009) notes, this was more important from a security perspective than even class – deportations based on a national key to 'clean' the frontiers (a practice inherited from imperial times), or ethnic purges during the Great Terror.

Counterrevolution Limited

At first, the dominant problematisation of the Red October events was related to the impact of the revolution on the fates of the allies as World War I remained all but decided on the Western front.[6] It was only later that securitisation practices were refocused on the substance of the revolution as a threat to the global normative order and the possible export of revolutionary activity under the conditions of political, economic and social turmoil after World War I – not even a year had passed since *Aurora*'s shots were fired before the *New York Times* (21 Sept. 2018) warned that the Bolsheviks engaged in 'mass terrorism' and general activity that 'civilisation' could only look at with 'aversion'. The corresponding discourse of danger and exclusion could draw on familiar patterns of association and dissociation in the discourse of civilisation and barbarism (Salter, 2002), but also particular repertoires of establishing Russia's inferiority in cultural terms – as one of Europe's many Easts (Wolffe, 1994). The 'Motionless Mongol', as Marx had called it, refused to be tamed, however – and the export of the Bolshevik revolution was further justified on cultural grounds in a discourse that rendered Russia and its spiritual (that is, *religious*) 'idea' – an established repertoire also featuring apocalyptic messianism that Bolsheviks recoded and repurposed – superior to decadent capitalist civilisation (Tsygankov, 2008). More intriguing still, this spiritual core of the Bolshevik political utopia, and the moral superiority claimed over generations by *homo sovieticus*, can be traced not only to local religious ideas but also to German idealist philosophy (Chamberlain, 2017). Meanwhile, the tension between a permanent revolution and socialism in one country mirrors the dilemma found in Russia's exceptionalism (even at present, cf. Rojek, 2015; Nowak, 2010) between isolationism – that is, the idea of Russia as an island, articulated by Zamyatin or Cimbursky – and the expansionism advocated by Kurbsky or, more recently, Dugin.

This gradual and variable problematisation of the revolution abroad – due to other (post-)World War I concerns but also a limited situational awareness – combined with the pursuit of parochial national political and economic interests in the erstwhile Tzarist empire and elsewhere in Eastern Europe shaped the scope and intensity of counterrevolutionary intervention. It explains why it ultimately ended in abject failure, despite an ambitious attempt at joint command operations among a number of nations and, importantly, at a great distance (Moffat, 2015). It also suggests how the very parochialism generated by dominant ordering practices in the Westphalian epochal time frame curbed the response against the threat Bolsheviks posed to the hegemonic order.

The intervention, initially to keep Russia in the war against Germany, then intended to convince Bolsheviks to reopen the Eastern front and only later – mainly after the Compiègne armistice but even before with the British landing in Archangelsk in August 1918 – to prevent the consolidation of Bolshevik rule, followed a distinctly *geopolitical* script, including in terms of carving out pieces of the former empire's territories, as illustrated by the declaration of the Japanese protectorate in Vladivostok or Turkish advances in Kars, Ardahan and Batumi. It was also a fragmented, heterogeneous enterprise featuring numerous actors adopting different and incoherent responses when confronting local realities, internal controversies and disputes while also featuring distinct elements of asymmetric warfare. The latter combined limited armed intervention and occupation in parts of northern Russia, Ukraine (Odessa), Siberia and the Caucasus with support given to an array of local actors seeking to perform rule over territory. These actors varied from diverse White armies to separatist groups – proxies supported by various outside powers that were often found to be in opposition or direct confrontation, which promoted further rivalry among these powers and distracted them from the strategic objective of defeating the Bolshevik Revolution. A curious hybrid actor in this theatre was the Czechoslovak Legion, created shortly before the Bolshevik Revolution under the authority of the Czechoslovak National Council – not a formal government of a state that did not yet exist.[7] Not keen at first to engage the Bolsheviks – it was meant to reach the battlefield in France by Vladivostok and Panama – the legionnaires were drawn into the unrolling conflict as the Germans advanced. Eventually, their progress along the Trans-Siberian Railway transformed – following a chain of events after the Chelyabinsk incident – into their control of the line in a rather *rhizomatic* form.[8]

Controversies and divergences in strategy abounded among the allies – the only reluctantly intervening United States (cf. Miller Unterberger, 1987), the Japanese (supporting rebels in Siberia fighting Kolchak's government, which was hostile to the Bolsheviks and lending only limited support to the Czechoslovak Legion), the British and the French (for a comprehensive overview of these controversies, see Thompson, 1967). The French presented several plans at the Paris Peace Conference for major armed intervention in Russia with Poland or Romania as launching bases – and, by extension, to ensure French hegemony over Eastern Europe. However, the Americans were more inclined toward diplomacy: to wit, the Prinkipo conference proposal to bring together the warring factions in Russia, which failed due to French resistance, and Bullit's mission in March 1919 to broker an agreement to end the civil war and withdraw the allied troops from Russia. It was ironic that the resistance to a more substantial intervention by Wilson – a proponent of the liberal internationalist ordering alternative – and his wariness about forcing regime change in Russia were probably the decisive causes of the international counterrevolution's failure to defeat the Bolsheviks; in the end, after the outside powers withdrew, it resulted in containment of the revolution to the territory reclaimed by the Bolsheviks in the civil war and the defeat of revolutions elsewhere by either social democrat or conservative reactionary forces. For a time, relief (humanitarian assistance) was identified as a means to contain the spread of the Bolshevik revolution, 'of bringing about normal conditions of life which will enable the people to choose a representative government', in the words of a US official (quoted in Barry, 1998, p. 5). As such, it prefigured both the Marshall Plan and contemporary deradicalisation programmes, but it ultimately collided with the rationale of the penal peace imposed on losing parties – not least to satisfy US creditors.[9]

Even this limited intervention produced real political effects inside Russia. It internally reinforced the Bolsheviks by lending credibility to their analysis of international relations in which the revolution in Russia – on to which various political objectives were projected from a plethora of sides before the regime's authoritarian consolidation – was threatened by Western imperialism. As a result, some previously antagonistic political forces would join the Bolsheviks, particularly after the Brest-Litovsk peace was rendered moot, or would withdraw from actively contesting them.

Conversely, while a 'protracted situation' followed Red October rather than a global proletarian revolution, some distinct subject effects of revolutionary events can be traced to outside Russia too. Even the limited securitisation narratives at the Peace Conference concerning the risks of Bolshevik penetration of Central Europe played a part in supporting the idea of a *cordon sanitaire* of newly independent states that would serve both to isolate against the red danger and to prevent German advances to the east (cf. Gerwarth and Horne, 2012, p. 43). Later, the threat representation of the Bolshevik war machine informed (geo)political responses to interwar continental dynamics, producing a more favourable reception of a consolidated Germany – as a barrier against the Bolshevik menace – in Britain, or of Franco's party in the Spanish Civil War (1936–9). It also had disciplining effects for the domestic political orders of the capitalist powers as societies were to be protected against the 'nihilist forces of disorder' threatened by the Bolsheviks (Moffat, 2015; cf. also Little, 1988) – to the point that 'Bolshevism' became an overarching ideograph for any radical threat to the *status quo* political order (Gerwarth and Horne, 2012, p. 44) that not only served to suppress dissent but also provided legitimacy to nationalist authoritarian regimes on the continent. Even in liberal countries such as the United States, new security legislation was passed, such as the Espionage Act (1917) and Sedition Act (1918), previewing the Patriot Act following 9/11, labour strikes were framed as 'terrorism' (Ditrych, 2014), and anxiety and xenophobia drove the government security practice of countering violent radicals but also political *status quo* dissenters (Cole, 2020) by means, for example, of targeting immigrants as a population – deploying at large a guilt by association and acting to purify the political community of corrosive ideas.

Conclusion

The Bolsheviks were the first modern revolutionary actor with a truly transnational subjectivity and a global reach, one for whom violence played a crucial role in the enactment of their political utopia. At the centenary of the Bolshevik Revolution in Russia, it remains a piece of living history that continues to inform political narratives of the present. This chapter does not aspire to supply a new and comprehensive narrative of the revolution (see Wade, 2017; for earlier accounts Carr, 1979; Pipes, 1996; or Read, 2002). It instead proposes a particular reading of the Bolsheviks as hybrid revolutionaries, pointing out the becoming of their (despotic) war machine, intended to 'kill the dream', to borrow from Czech poet Jiří Wolker, of a socialist utopia so as to make it true in a timeless, apolitical state of the 'government of things'. This reading underscores the multiplicity in the processes of its constitution, repacking and repurposing the repertoires of the normative order Bolsheviks aimed to overturn, and later also the alloyed practice of consolidation of the revolutionary government that operated with the repacked and repurposed concept of sovereignty entailing spatial totality (constitution of an ample interior space to be filled with power) and temporal adjustment (attunement to a common historical time). The Bolsheviks thus appropriated and recoded existing patterns of governance in a specific continuation of modern statehood projects while engaging in both linear and non-linear practices of expanding the revolution abroad by means of an unbundled network of emergent local communities as diverse as the Hungarian Republic of Councils or the Limerick Soviet ('Sóibhéid Luimnigh').

This reading is intended as an intervention in the dominant representation of the Bolshevik Revolution as a radical break with the past, with the global reach of its political utopia and inspiration of translocal revolutionary practice (Daly and Trofimov, 2017; Ulam, 1998; Carr, 1979, Halliday, 1999 Lawson, 2015, McAdams, 2017). It also shows that conventional geopolitical rationalities combined with hybrid warfare modalities in *counterrevolutionary* action and the subject effects of the Bolshevik Revolution as a historical event, even in absence of its universalisation. Resisting facile analogies and the concept of history as playing according to a universal tune, the Bolshevik war machine and that of ISIS show not only how, in the modern epochal time frame, hybrid revolutionaries occupying distinct spacetimes may exhibit similar tensions in their hybrid constitution between radical political utopia and nomadic war machine features, but also how various entanglements emerged within the order they sought to revolutionise. In both cases, the failure to realise this political utopia notwithstanding, the emergence of these hybrid revolutionar-

ies shaped the international order in lasting ways, even if not in the ways they
have foreseen or desired.

Notes

1. The class can be *working* and *exploited*, and connote *proletarians, capitalists, kulaks, bourgeoisie* or *exploiters* (cf. Preobrazhensky, 1958).
2. Lenin here employs the metaphor of marriage – in the bourgeois version, based on privilege and corruption – and divorce.
3. 'If societies, classes, groups collide destructively, disorganizing each other, it is precisely because each such a collective strives to organize the world and humanity for itself, in its own way,' as Bogdanov (1996) paraphrased Lenin.
4. Born out of misery after the war and incompetent liberal leadership, while this second soviet state overtly embraced the idea of world revolution, it pursued – incompetently – a nationalist revisionist agenda, first by invading newly founded Czechoslovakia and setting up an emphemeral soviet republic there (1919) before being forced to retreat; it then made the fatal decision to launch a war on Romania, inviting the latter's intervention.
5. Lenin insisted that Trotsky be authorised to 'accept the assistance of the brigands of French imperialism against the German brigands' (Engelstein, 2017, p. 384).
6. In February 2018 – that is, shortly before the Brest-Litovsk separate peace agreement – Wilson rejected the idea of a regime change in Russia and in a message to Bolsheviks supported Russia's 'complete sovereignty and independence in her own affairs' (Engelstein, 2017, p. 386).
7. The declaration of independence of Czechoslovakia was made only in October 1918.
8. It only added to the messy picture because the Red Army conscripts they faced were often prisoners of war from Germany and Austria.
9. Some proposals for moderate peace, such as Lloyd George's in his Fontainebleau Memorandum, were, moreover, founded on securitisation from the geopolitical perspective of the prospective alliance of an alienated Germany with the Bolsheviks.

References

Bacon, E. E. 1966. *Central Asians Under Russian Rule: A Study in Culture Change*. Ithaca, NY: Cornell University Press.

Barry, J. 1998. 'Deja Vu in 1946: Reinterpreting the Origins of Containment'.

Honors Theses 252. Available at: <https://digitalcommons.colby.edu/honor stheses/252> (last accessed 14 June 2022).

Bogdanov, A. A. 1996. *Tektologia: Universal Organizational Science*. Hull: Centre for Systems Studies Press.

Bunin, I. and Marullo, T. 1998. *Cursed Days*. Lanham, MD: Ivan R. Dee.

Carr, E. H. 1979. *The Russian Revolution from Lenin to Stalin 1917–1929*. London: Macmillan.

Chamberlain, L. 2017. *Arc of Utopia: The Beautiful Story of the Russian Revolution*. London: Reaktion.

Cole, D. D. 2020. 'Reflections on Immigration One Hundred Years After the Red Scare'. *NYLS Law Review* 65 (2): 171–94.

Daly, J. and Trofimov, L. 2017. *The Russian Revolution and Its Global Impact: A Short History with Documents*. Indianapolis: Hackett.

DeLanda, M. 1991. *War in the Age of Intelligent Machines*. New York: Swerve.

Deleuze, G. and Guattari, F. 1987. *A Thousand Plateaus: Capitalism and Schizophrenia*. London: Continuum.

Ditrych, O. 2014. *Tracing the Discourses of Terrorism: Genealogy, Identity and State*. London: Palgrave Macmillan.

Elden, S. 2013. *The Birth of Territory*. Chicago: University of Chicago Press.

Engels, F., Lenin, V. I. and Marx, K. 2017. *The Communist Manifesto / The April Theses*. London: Verso.

Engelstein, L. 2017. *Russia in Flames: War, Revolution, Civil War, 1914–1921*. Oxford: Oxford University Press.

Gavroche, J. 2019. 'Interview with Jacques Rancière'. *Autonomies*. Available at: <http://autonomies.org/2019/08/jacques-ranciere-the-singularity-of -rebellion-and-autonomy/> (last accessed 14 June 2022).

Gerwarth, R. and Horne, J. (eds). 2012. *War in Peace: Paramilitary Violence in Europe After the Great War*. Oxford: Oxford University Press.

Giddens, A. 1973. *Capitalism and Modern Social Theory*. Cambridge: Cambridge University Press.

Halliday, F. 1999. *Revolution and World Politics: The Rise and Fall of the Sixth Great Power*. Durham, NC: Duke University Press.

Holland, B. 2010. 'Sovereignty as Dominium? Reconstructing the Constructivist Roman Law Thesis'. *International Studies Quarterly* 54 (2): 449–80.

Holquist, P. 2002. *Making War, Forging Revolution: Russia's Continuum of Crisis, 1914–1921*. Cambridge, MA: Harvard University Press.

Jacobson, J. 1994. *When the Soviet Union Entered World Politics*. Berkeley: University of California Press.

Lawson, G. 2015. 'Revolutions and the International'. *Theory and Society* 44 (4): 299–319.

Lenin, V. I. 1963 [1916]. 'Imperialism, the Highest Stage of Capitalism'. In *Selected Works* 1: 667–766.

Lenin, V. I. 1972 [1914]. 'The Right of Nations to Self-Determination'. *Collected Works* 20: 393–454.

Lenin, V. I. 1977 [1913]. 'The Question of Ministry of Education Policy'. *Collected Works* 19: 137–46.

Little, D. 1988. 'Red Scare, 1936: Anti-Bolshevism and the Origins of British Non-intervention in the Spanish Civil War'. *Journal of Contemporary History* 23 (2): 291–314.

Lunacharsky A. V. 1919. Radio record transcription.

McAdams, J. A. 2017. *Vanguard of the Revolution: The Global Idea of the Communist Party*. Princeton: Princeton University Press.

Mayakovsky, V. 1973. 'Vladimir Ilyich Lenin'. *The Works of Vladimir Mayakovsky*. Moscow: Pravda, 1973.

Miller Unterberger, B. 1987. 'Woodrow Wilson and the Bolsheviks: The "Acid Test" of Soviet-American Relations'. *Diplomatic History* 11 (2): 71–90.

Moffat, I. C. D. 2015. *The Allied Intervention in Russia, 1918–1920: The Diplomacy of Chaos*. Basingstoke: Palgrave Macmillan.

Neumann, M. and Willimott, A. 2008. *Rethinking the Russian Revolution as Historical Divide*. Abingdon: Routledge.

Nowak, A. 2010. *Impérium a ti druzí*. Brno: Centrum pro studium demokracie a kultury.

Olcott, M. B. 1994. 'Ceremony and Substance: The Illusion of Unity in Central Asia'. In Mandelbaum, M. (ed.). *Central Asia and the World*. New York: Council on Foreign Relations.

Onuf, N. 1998. *The Republican Legacy in International Thought*. Cambridge: Cambridge University Press.

Pipes, R. 1996. *A Concise History of the Russian Revolution*. New York: Vintage Books.

Preobrazhensky, A. G. (ed). 1958. *Etymological Dictionary of the Russian Language*. Moscow: Publishing House of Foreign and National Dictionaries.

Read, C. 2002. *From Tsar to Soviets: The Russian People and Their Revolution, 1917–21*. London: UCL Press.

Rojek, P. 2015. *Prokletí Impéria*. Brno: Centrum pro studium demokracie a kultury.

Roy, O. 2000. *The New Central Asia: The Creation of Nations*. London: I. B. Tauris.

Ruggie, J. 1993. 'Territoriality and Beyond: Problematizing Modernity in International Relations'. *International Organisation* 47 (1): 139–74.

Salter, M. B. 2002. *Barbarians and Civilisation in International Relations*. London: Pluto Press.

Stalin, I. V. 1954a [1913]. *Marxism and the National Question*. Moscow: Foreign Languages Publishing House.

Stalin, I. V. 1954b [1905]. 'The Bourgeoisie is Laying a Trap'. *Works 1*. Moscow: Foreign Languages Publishing House.

Thompson, J. M. 1967. *Russia, Bolshevism, and the Versailles Peace*. Princeton: Princeton University Press.

Tsygankov, A. P. 2008. 'Self and Other in International Relations Theory: Learning from Russian Civilizational Debates'. *International Studies Review* 10 (4): 762–75.

Ulam, A. B. 1998. *The Bolsheviks: The Intellectual and Political History of the Triumph of Communism in Russia*. Cambridge, MA: Harvard University Press.

Viola, L. (ed). 2002. *Contending with Stalinism: Soviet Power and Popular Resistance in the 1930s*. Ithaca, NY: Cornell University Press.

Wade, R. A. 2017. *The Russian Revolution, 1917*. Cambridge: Cambridge University Press.

Wolffe, L. 1994. *Inventing Eastern Europe*. Stanford: Stanford University Press.

Zajaczkowski, W. 2009. *Rosja i Narody: Ósmy Kontyntent*. Warsaw: Wydawnictwo MG.

8

First 'International Terrorists' or Local Non-recognised Government? Palestinians and Hybrid Sovereignty

Jakub Záhora

Introduction

This chapter makes the case for conceptualising the Palestinian national movement through the prism of hybrid sovereignty. Building on works that have
shown that the ideal of sovereignty as full control over territory and wielding
legitimate violence does not do justice to the multiplicity of observed structures and practices of governance, power and authority, I argue that revisiting episodes within the Palestinian national movement in the 1960s and the
1970s can demonstrate how seemingly disparate actions converge to give rise
to sovereign claims. The point of departure of the present analysis is the fragmentation of the movement in the 1960s and the 1970s along various lines
– ideological, geographical, strategic and tactical, among others. While some
scholars and commentators have characterised this as hindering Palestinian
political goals (for example, Krause, 2017; Pearlman, 2012; Hilal, 2018), in
this chapter I provide a different perspective on the practices that different
Palestinian factions adopted during this period. Using a Deleuzian conceptual framework, I argue that the diffraction of the Palestinian groups' political
activities should be read within a unitary frame of hybrid sovereignty: that is,
one in which claims to represent a body politic-in-the-making are expressed
through spatially dispersed practices.

The decades following Nakba witnessed a gradual fragmentation of the
Palestinian national movement as various groups adopted highly divergent
political outlooks (from pan-Arabism to communism to Palestine-centred
nationalism) and approaches to accomplishing their goals. It is not possible to
do justice to the complexity of this history here, though others have eloquently
done so (Y. Sayigh, 2004; R. Sayigh, 2007; Kimmerling and Migdal, 2009;

Ghanem, 2013). What is important for the present discussion is that many commentators argue that this fragmentation was highly detrimental for the Palestinian national goals because it prevented different factions from working together towards their common aims. For example, Krause (2017) proposes that the Palestinian movement became efficient only when it was unified under the coherent leadership of Fatah during the 1980s, which enabled it to achieve the formal recognition of its aspirations by Israel. The Oslo accords of the mid-1990s then represented the first opportunity for the Palestinians to exercise self-autonomy (in the Gaza Strip and parts of the West Bank), with the vision of becoming an independent sovereign state. However, there is an increasing recognition that the accords in their specific articulations only provided a fig leaf for the continuation of Israeli dominance and outsourcing of its responsibilities to the newly established Palestinian Authority (Gordon, 2002; Tartir, 2017), and as such the Palestinian national demands could not possibly have been achieved within this framework.

By contrast, inspired by the present volume's departure from the traditional framing of political subjectivity and its refusal of clear-cut categories, in this chapter I provide an alternative reading of Palestinian politics in the 1960s and 1970s by conceiving the different strands of Palestinian political agency within a unitary frame of hybrid sovereignty. I argue that adopting this analytical perspective sensitises us to the various ways in which Palestinian groups were effectively exercising sovereignty before Oslo – although in forms unrecognisable to the global community. Specifically, I focus on two aspects of the Palestinian historical experience during the 1960s and the 1970s: the spectacular acts of violence (which became known as terrorism in the West) conducted by Palestinian groups, and Palestinian self-governance in the refugee camps, especially those in Lebanon, where, at least for a time, the Palestinians exercised the greatest autonomy. Juxtaposing these two examples highlights how Palestinians engaged in a plethora of practices that are usually associated with states. These actions defied not only statist but also national boundaries: they created proto-state structures and apparatuses within the territory of an internationally recognised state, and they conducted transnational operations. This chapter pushes the debates on hybrid sovereignty by showing not only that sovereign practices can be decoupled from a (recognised) state apparatus but that, in line with the Deleuzian framework, they may be dispersed across various sites and manifest themselves in different intensities.

In the following, I first briefly recount developments after the 1948 War / Nakba and the fragmentation of the Palestinian national movement. The next two sections discuss, respectively, the violent transnational practices conducted by the Palestinian groups in the 1960s and the 1970s and Palestinian self-governance in refugee camps in Lebanon during the same period. The Conclusion jumps temporally to argue that the Oslo accords with Israel marked the taming of the Palestinian revolutionary project of hybrid sovereignty.

The Palestinian National Movement(s) and Hybrid Sovereignty

Following the events of the Nakba that marked the establishment of the State of Israel and precipitated a wave of Palestinian refugees, the national aspirations of the Palestinians were shattered. During the 1950s, various groups in neighbouring Arab countries sought to form a movement which would be able to reclaim historical Palestine, but their efforts were largely hampered by respective host states' governments (Kimmerling and Migdal, 2009, pp. 214–39). It was Fatah, established in 1959 by a group of young revolutionaries, that gradually became the major Palestinian actor and effectively took control over the Palestine Liberation Organisation (PLO) (see, for example, Baumgarten, 2005, pp. 31–7). Following the 1967 War and Israeli occupation of the West Bank and Gaza, Palestinian *fedayeen* were forced to retreat to neighbouring Egypt and Jordan, with the latter becoming the centre of Fatah's militant operations.

Many authors argue that the turning point for the Palestinian movement was the so-called 'battle of Karameh' in 1968, during which Palestinian militia in Jordan clashed with Israeli forces conducting a punitive strike against the Palestinian *fedayeen* who had been attacking Israeli targets in the West Bank. Although the Palestinian casualties were much higher than the Israeli ones, the Fatah-led militia managed to prevent the Israel Defense Forces (IDF) from capturing the town of Karameh, where its local headquarters were located. After the disaster of the 1967 War, the images of retreating Israeli forces captured the attention of the Arab public and catapulted the Palestinian group into the regional limelight. The resulting political capital bestowed upon Fatah and its militias allowed them both to recruit new members and to reduce their dependency on the hosting governments (Y. Sayigh, 2004, pp. 174–9).

These emancipation efforts and the project of Palestinian state sovereignty found their most urgent expression during what became known as Black September. The growing aspirations of the Fatah leadership, coupled with and enhanced by the demographic composition of the Jordanian population (most of which is of Palestinian origin), led to increasing tensions between the Palestinian political leaders and the Hashemite rulers of the Jordanian kingdom. The state aspirations of the PLO and the survival instinct of the Jordanian Hashemite regime came to a head in the autumn of 1970. The immediate trigger for hostilities was the hijacking of three planes by the Popular Front for the Liberation of Palestine (PFLP), which they landed on Jordanian soil at Dawson

Field, near Zarqa. Enraged by such a blatant breach of Jordanian sovereignty and the international dimension of the incident, King Hussein ordered the Jordanian army to subdue the Palestinian armed groups. Over the subsequent months, in what effectively escalated into a civil war and involved a Syrian intervention, the Hashemite regime and its armed forces managed violently to dismantle the *fedayeen*'s infrastructure (albeit with a diplomatic hiatus induced by pressure from other Arab states). The conflict ended in July 1971 with the Palestinian surrender and the expulsion of their leaders to Lebanon (Nevo, 2008).

According to some accounts, the events of Black September and the ousting of the Fatah leadership marked yet another failure to establish national Palestinian sovereignty over a defined territory. But while it is true that the Palestinian leadership did not manage to secure the normative status of state actor, too much emphasis on this failure conceals the already ongoing practices which effectively manifested sovereign power in the terms evoked by Robert Warrior while discussing the sovereignty of indigenous populations under postcolonial conditions: 'a process of asserting the power we possess as communities and individuals to make decisions that affect our lives' (cited in Cattelino, 2008, p. 129).

In the popular imagination, as well as mainstream scholarship, sovereignty is still very much associated with the state as the main actor in international politics (cf. Aalberts, 2016; Bartelson, 2014). However, more nuanced accounts highlight the historical contingency of this understanding, along with the diverse set of practices which contribute to establishing an actor as *a* (rather than *the*) sovereign. In their ethnographically informed take on sovereignty, Hansen and Stepputat rightly criticise the usual understanding of 'sovereignty as a formal, de jure property whose efficacy to a large extent is derived from being externally recognized by other states as both sovereign and legitimate' (Hansen and Stepputat, 2005, p. 2). In a similar vein, the politics typically practised by indigenous peoples demonstrate that the dominant understandings of sovereignty do not capture the full spectrum of political realities that characterise contestations of self-rule in contexts of ongoing political disenfranchisement and dispossession of minorities. Despite this more nuanced approach, Hansen and Stepputat still define sovereignty as 'the ability and the will to employ overwhelming violence and to decide on life and death' (Hansen and Stepputat, 2005, p. 1), which is accepted as legitimate in the given social and political milieu, even if enacted by non-state actors. While I agree that the use of violence is an inherent and highly salient component of sovereign power, I argue that the latter cannot be reduced to the former because sovereignty stands for 'shared assertions, everyday processes, intellectual projects, and lived experiences of political distinctiveness' (Cattelino, 2008, p. 129).

My proposal that the Palestinian national movement should be understood in terms of hybrid sovereignty builds on works which have argued that the dominant notion of sovereignty in mainstream scholarship, as well as in dominant Western policy-making circles and forums, does not capture political realities across much of the world (Tholens, 2017; Bacik, 2008; Fregonese, 2012) and, moreover, that 'any binary opposition between state and nonstate, legitimate and irregular violence' limits our understanding of sovereignty (Ramadan and Fregonese, 2017, p. 952). Thinking in terms of hybridity shows that the ideal of unitary sovereign power is at odds with the conditions in 'which state and non-state actors interact in ways that defy conventional expectations based on the sovereign nation-state' (Tholens, 2017, p. 867).

While I take inspiration from this literature on the hybridity of sovereignty, I seek to nuance the concept further by treating sovereignty as spatially dispersed and manifesting in often disjointed practices. Here, I take inspiration from the Deleuzian conceptual apparatus and propose that sovereignty can be profitably conceived of as an assemblage, a nomadic mode of political existence. Utilising this perspective helps us to grasp how diverse actors, including non-state ones, constitute sovereignty through a range of activities. I propose that the nomadic framework enables us to comprehend the dispersed nature of projects of sovereignty better across spatial, modal and organisational divisions. In short, while scholarship on hybrid sovereignty has highlighted the multiplicity of overlapping sovereign claims and the resulting 'cross-contamination of different state and non-state actors, to the point that the state and the non-state become difficult to distinguish', which leads to 'new entities [being] produced' (Fregonese, 2012, p. 658), mobilising a Deleuzian conceptual toolbox (Deleuze and Guattari, 1987) enables us to conceive of sovereignty as a series of diverse practices and aspirations, exercised by different groups, which nonetheless constitute a coherent political project.

I seek to reconceptualise hybrid sovereigns as situated between the war machine and a state form. In their work, Deleuze and Guattari distinguish these two modes in order to arrive at a classification of different constellations and arrangements between forms of power and the social. For Deleuze and Guattari (1987), the state is 'an apparatus of power distinct from the societies it governs and with the means for its own preservation and conservation' (Reid, 2003, pp. 62–3), a striated structure which strives for 'strategization of thought, movement and disposition' (Reid, 2003, p. 63). As such, their notion of the state goes beyond the set of institutions and entities usually understood as a 'state' and denotes a much more general system of power which desires to tame social and political movements and turn them into rigid institutions. While war is usually seen as an expression of state power, Deleuze and Guattari (Deleuze and Guattari, 1987) draw on historical and anthropological research to argue that the war machine was a mode of existence employed by nomadic societies to defy the imposition of control by state apparatuses. As summarised earlier in this volume, the war machine is thus a set of dispositions and ideas which seek to 'resist, over the course of history, appropriation by the state'.

As this volume's theoretical summary notes, hybrid revolutionaries generally seek to recode the norms of sovereignty rather than reject it outright. They seek to enact elements of state sovereignty, thus drawing on the repertoires of the current order, but refuse to replicate some of its founding principles. In the case of the Palestinian national movement and the various actors who compose it, the vision of state sovereignty is on the political horizon while the means they employ fall outside the state mode of power. To put this slightly differently, hybrid sovereigns combine elements of both state and war machine modes of social and political organisation. While 'the sovereign power of the state is ultimately based on forming some kind of relation to the war machine' (Reid, 2003, p. 64), the case of the Palestinian national movement shows how hybrid sovereigns alter the very relationship between state and war machine modes of social and political organisation. I further emphasise the multifaceted nature of sovereignty, which is composed not only of performative acts of violence but also of mundane activities of organising the polity's everyday life. In 'traditional' understandings of sovereignty these features are connected through the governing (state) apparatus, but as I show below, hybrid sovereigns – situated between the war machine and the state forms – can enact these practices in a diffracted and dispersed manner.

To illuminate these processes further, and building on the Deleuzian proposition that the war machine is an assemblage, an emergent constellation of heterogenous elements (for a more thorough introduction, see DeLanda, 2016), I conceive of hybrid sovereigns in general, and the Palestinian national movement in particular, in these terms. While thinking with assemblages 'offers an approach that is capable of accommodating the various hybrids of material, biological, social and technological components that populate our world' (Acuto and Curtis, 2014, p. 2), in this chapter I do not focus on the involvement of non-human actants. Rather, I seek to discern how various elements, components and relationships come together to form novel articulations of sovereign projects which depart from the classical understanding of this political form. The assemblage perspective helps capture the dynamics in which various practices constituting sovereign claims 'behave according to a central logic that structures the movement of parts' (Bleiker, 2015, p. 882), even if they are spatially disjointed and have different political effects. In other words, what stems from an understanding of sovereignty in terms of assemblages is that this framework allows for capturing dispersed actions within one field of vision (cf. DeLanda, 2016). It further enables us to discern how these actions relate to other political projects, including ones that seek to disrupt the international system of hierarchies and norms, such as the Third World liberation movement.

In sum, I argue that the various political actions and practices of diverse Palestinian factions in the 1960s and the 1970s, although fragmented spatially, tactically and strategically, combined to form a project of hybrid sovereignty, a project that sought to reclaim the political subjectivity of the Palestinian people as a subject capable of shaping its political fate. To highlight the hybrid nature of this project, I focus on two registers: violent manifestations of sovereign aspirations and everyday governance in refugee camps.

Transnational Violence and Transnational Solidarity

While today Palestinian militant action is associated with rock-throwing youngsters wearing *keffiyeh*, suicide attackers or short-ranged rocket attacks, in the late 1960s and the 1970s the Palestinian movement was largely identified in the popular consciousness with what became known as international terrorism. Faced with the reality of Israeli military superiority that rendered Fatah's guerrilla incursions into historic Palestine largely ineffectual (Byman, 2011, p. 40), more fringe Palestinian groups like the PFLP resorted to other, international, forms of political violence which defied neat categorisations.

In July 1968, members of the PFLP seized control of a passenger jet belonging to El Al, the Israeli national carrier, on its way from London to Tel Aviv. This incident marked the beginning of a decade of plane hijackings conducted by various Palestinian groups, among them the Dawson Field hijackings that triggered the events of Black September. In total, various Palestinian groups hijacked sixteen planes between 1968 and 1976 (Byman, 2011, p. 40) in operations which left a deep impression on global audiences. Even more infamously, some Palestinian groups and their allies resorted to direct attacks against Israeli and other civilian targets. In May 1972, members of the Japanese Red Army recruited by a Palestinian faction opened fire at Lod airport in Israel, killing twenty-six people and injuring some eighty more. A few months later, the Black September group conducted an operation with global repercussions: the kidnapping of Israeli athletes during the Olympic Games in Munich that ended with the massacre of eleven hostages.

Byman argues that it was these actions, rather than *fedayeen* cross-border operations, which 'would transfix the world and shape attitudes toward the Israeli–Arab dispute' (Byman, 2011, p. 40). Accordingly, the Palestinian actions are said to constitute the first instances of an international terrorism (Hoffman, 2006, p. 63). Not only did these practices ignore national boundaries, but they also tied into transnational solidarities, as I will discuss below. According to Chamberlin, 'The hijacking signaled a new direction in the armed struggle, with alarming implications for an increasingly interconnected international system. By attacking civil aviation, Third World liberation fighters had transferred their guerrilla war "from the forests to the skies"' (Chamberlin, 2012, p. 72). Others have argued that attacking 'soft' targets was the only option available for Palestinian groups faced with the overwhelming conventional power of the Israeli security apparatus and its Western sponsors (Byman, 2011, pp. 29–57), and as such the only possible retaliation against the colonising forces (Y. Sayigh, 2004). But these actions also tell us something about the Palestinian political project and its sovereign aspirations.

As noted above, sovereignty should not be reduced to the exercise of violence. Nevertheless, this aspect is still most salient in public understandings of state governance. For this reason, violent and visible actions like hijackings, kidnappings and executions were very effective in establishing the agency of the Palestinians despite their condition of statelessness. Although fleeting and highly localised, these moments of violence not only reversed the positions of dominated and dominating, but they further manifested the Palestinian capacity for translating their sovereign aspirations into specific actions. Palestine – as a political project of reclaiming control over the national fate – was actualised through these practices. This even goes for plane hijackings, which were relatively non-violent (especially compared to the 1972 Munich massacre and Lod shooting), as they demonstrated that even in the absence of the state, the Palestinians were capable of imposing their political programme in the form of visible actions.

While this argument risks rendering literally any exercise of violence as a manifestation of sovereign power, the prism of hybridity helps show how Palestinian actions in the 1960s and the 1970s undermine the notion that 'the legitimate use of violence by a state apparatus' is the common marker of sovereignty. While sovereignty goes beyond physical force, it is established 'through the exercise of violence over bodies and populations' (Hansen and Stepputat, 2005, p. 2) by various actors. Far from being acts of 'senseless violence', the Palestinian hijackings and attacks were performative acts that sought to demonstrate the capacity to project violence, an attribute of a sovereign actor, even if these acts were not (yet) linked to particular territory and to particular populations. Put differently, the Palestinian armed groups did not claim sovereign control over bodies on which the (semi-)sovereign violence was imposed. Rather, these violent actions were aimed at manifesting the capacity to project violence associated with sovereign aspirations *per se* at dispersed sites.

Crucially, the Palestinian actions were embedded in a much wider context. Although these operations were part of the Palestinian national struggle, they were, at the same time, closely linked within the international political and sociotechnical orders. These features thus highlight the hybridity at the core of the Palestinian political project in the 1960s when they found themselves situated in transnational processes which transgressed the project of reclaiming the historical homeland, while the latter still oriented these practices. As such, the case of the Palestinian political efforts in the 1960s and the 1970s is illustrative of the tensions between the war machine and state forms.

Specifically, the spectacular plane hijackings tapped into the novel means of airborne transport, which at the time symbolised global interconnectedness (Adey, 2004, p. 1368). Similarly, Munich and Lod received wide resonance thanks to modern technologies and the possibilities afforded by the nascent globalisation, as embodied by the still-famous images of the Palestinian attackers on the hotel balcony, images that were consumed by global audiences in real time (Galily et al., 2015). Furthermore, by exploiting these new transport infrastructures, the 'PFLP moved its regional struggle into the international sphere not just in the ideological dimension [. . .] but in a physical sense' too (Chamberlin, 2012, p. 72). The Palestinian groups thus tapped into the emerging infrastructural and technological webs of a nascent globalisation, as 'Palestinian gunmen began to move across a terrain that was inherently transnational [as] civil aviation existed quite literally in the space between nations' (Chamberlin, 2012, p. 72). In a manner bearing echoes of how ISIS would rely on modern means of communication in spite of its proclaimed rejections of the current order, the Palestinian groups used international means and channels to propagate their claims for sovereignty conceived in highly territorialised form. As such, the Palestinian quest for self-determination cannot be divorced from the means which enabled it to be translated into political practice.

The hybrid nature of the Palestinian political project was further underscored by the fact that the Palestinian armed groups became part of an international movement challenging the existing global order – namely, the anti-colonial movement (see, for example, Chamberlin, 2011). So while the factions' acts were a part of the territorial project of establishing a national state, their attacks ignore state boundaries, and they were also embedded within global Third World anti-colonialism efforts: according to the PFLP's worldview, the Israeli state not only was an agent of national dispossession but was also at 'a centre of imperialist and world capitalist interests' (Y. Sayigh, 2004, 214). This was then translated into close cooperation between the Palestinian groups and other elements discontented with the global order, as testified to by the Lyd attack conducted by a Japanese group, or the PFLP demand for the release of members of the German Red Army Faction after the former's operatives hijacked the Lufthansa flight in October 1977 (Hughes, 2015, pp. 460–2). This again illustrates their defiance of the (international) state form and highlights the inherently hybrid constitution of the Palestinian claims to sovereignty. Because 'the Palestinian armed struggle [was located] within the broad complex of liberationist forces scattered throughout the international system of the Cold War world' (Chamberlin, 2012, p. 3), it clearly exceeded the project of (re)constructing the national homeland.

It is this coming together – indeed, assemblage – of novel technologies, exploitation of the smooth space of air travel, and efforts to establish a coherent national body politic that highlight the inherent tensions in construing hybrid sovereignty. The Palestinians – and the larger movement they were a part of – rejected the global order of the day, an order that placed them at the bottom of its hierarchy. However, they sought to reverse this order by exploiting the mechanisms that upheld it. Likewise, Palestinian political ambitions were directed towards establishing a certain state form – a national state with its inherent sedentarisation – through practices which were deeply antithetical to this form. The war machine materialised in defiance of the very sovereign norms it ultimately sought to achieve. It is here that the hybrid nature of the Palestinian sovereign project becomes clear, a notion which becomes even more pronounced when these actions are juxtaposed with the much more mundane practices of governance that were happening at the same time.

Local Governance and Local Sovereignty

While the PFLP and other Palestinian factions were engaged in transnational practices that defied the global order, the PLO, increasingly under the control of Fatah, engaged in vastly different activities in the refugee camps in Lebanon. Since the late 1960s and well into the 1970s, the organisation and its officials performed a myriad of functions which effectively established sovereign claims: in Lebanon, the Palestinian actors sought to cultivate 'latent' sovereignty (cf. Feldman, 2008) by shaping both the everyday contours and ideological underpinnings of the body politic.

The groundwork for these practices was laid down in the Cairo Agreement of 1969, signed between PLO chairman Yasser Arafat and Lebanese army chief official Emile Bustani, which acknowledged the presence and activities of the

Palestinian groups operating in Lebanon. As a result, the PLO, and to a lesser extent other Palestinian factions, were effectively given free rein to manage the everyday governance of the refugee camps. This ranged from providing internal security and resolving disputes to building infrastructure and providing services such as schooling. With 'a budget bigger than that of many small sovereign states' (Khalidi, 1985, p. 59), the PLO could indeed significantly shape the everyday lives of the camps' inhabitants. For example, by the late 1970s the Palestinian Red Crescent, largely financed by the PLO, 'operated no less than 10 hospitals and 30 clinics in the Lebanese camps, 2 physiotherapy centers, a residential rehabilitation center, an orthopedic workshop, a nursing school, and multiple pharmacies', while non-Fatah-affiliated groups ran almost fifty more clinics (Brynen, 1990, p. 140).

The Palestinians' state-like practices were further consolidated during the civil war that began in 1975, as Lebanese state institutions essentially withdrew and were replaced by localised and communitarian projects. As a result, rubbish collection, schooling, health care provision and road paving became situated within the matrix of overlapping sovereignty claims, wherein Lebanese state sovereignty was enacted by a number of actors (Ramadan and Fregonese, 2017; Fregonese, 2012). Nonetheless, my focus here is not on the hybrid conditions of sovereignty that these overlapping claims engendered but rather on how these practices effectively established a notion of Palestinian self-governance, something that was at the heart of Palestinian aspirations.

Inherent in the national project is control over political matters, even those pertaining to mundane aspects of social life. While, as discussed above, sovereignty is often associated with exercise of violence and visible acts which demonstrate the power of the state apparatus, as noted by Cattelino, 'overly juridical and unitary understanding of sovereignty blinds us to the lived experiences and multiplicities of sovereignty' (Cattelino, 2008, p. 129). While she makes these remarks with regard to American indigenous politics, they are apt for coming to terms with the Palestinian state-like practices in the Lebanese camps as well: even Hansen and Stepputat, who emphasise the role of violence in constructing sovereignty, argue that this mode of power 'should be studied as practices dispersed throughout, and across, societies' (Hansen and Stepputat, 2005, p. 3) rather than *a priori* located in state structures. By providing basic services to its inhabitants, the Palestinian protagonists effectively established a particular form of sovereignty under the conditions available to them.

Importantly for the discussion of sovereignty, these self-governing practices were still linked to nationalistic symbols and imaginaries. Yearning for the land of Palestine, the core of national identity (Khalidi, 1998), was materialised in the camps through numerous maps of historical Palestine, Palestinian flags, and the keys to homes lost in the Nakba of 1948. Further practices, such as naming camp neighbourhoods after lost pre-1948 communities in Palestine, served to actualise national longing in the here and now (Ramadan, 2009; Khalili, 2007). Everyday practices also possessed a highly affective dimension, as Rosemary Sayigh illustrates in her account of the atmosphere in a Palestinian camp in the early 1970s:

> The first moment I got down from the car I saw the Palestinian flag instead of the Lebanese flag, and a group of Palestinians in *fedayeen* clothes instead of the Lebanese police. As I moved through the camp I saw the happiness on people's faces, and in the schools there wasn't the frustration of before. [. . .] Before, there had been a political and ideological siege around us, but now the camp radio played revolutionary songs and speeches. In the homes, mothers spoke clearly with their children about Palestine – before this was only done in a whisper. (R. Sayigh, 2007, p. 174)

Pertinently, the nationalistic sentiments materialised in the camps were further amplified by armed struggle, although in a different manner from the political violence discussed in the previous section. While hijackings, kidnappings and shootings served to manifest political agency and the ability to exercise regulative violence, cross-border operations and armed resistance against the Israeli state cemented the notion of national cohesion, thus contributing to the formation of the (sovereign) body politic. The battle of Karameh and other actions and events in which the *fedayeen* challenged the military superiority of the Israeli state led to 'a renewed sense of pride and autonomy, helping to rekindle a Palestinian national consciousness, battered in the decades since the Arab Revolt' (Kimmerling and Migdal, 2009, p. 257). The mundane matters of governing everyday life thus fused with the efforts to reclaim the national homeland (Peteet, 2005), in the process showing how the project of sovereignty is composed – or assembled – through a myriad of practices that defy neat categorisation.

Arguably, these practices gradually grew in a way which made the PLO recognisable as a *de facto* state actor. Whereas the Palestinian factions oriented towards social and / or political liberation still maintained a discourse of resistance, during the first half of the 1970s the PLO was increasingly manifesting 'statist ambition' (Y. Sayigh, 2004, p. 202) and in many regards became 'state-within-a-state in Lebanon' (Kimmerling and Migdal 2009, 263). As Khalili notes, 'The extent of the shift was such that by the end of the 1970s, the PLO headquarters in West Beirut was labelled "the Fakihani Republic" after the neighbourhood which hosted the buildings and offices of the PLO' (Khalili,

2007, p. 48). Nonetheless, even under these conditions the PLO did not fully adhere to the state form. Even as it established offices and introduced public services in a manner mimicking the state apparatus, it remained distinct from the archetypal state in that it lacked a clearly demarcated territory over which it exerted full control. Again, the revolutionaries find themselves at the interstice between war machine and state, between the nomadic and the sedentary.

Conclusion: Hybridity, Sovereignty, Normalisation

More than two decades after the plane hijackings and the height of activities in the Palestinian camps in Lebanon, the Oslo accords between the PLO as the representative of the Palestinian people and Israel were signed. At the time they were heralded as the culmination of the Palestinian national struggle and were supposed to lead to the establishment of the Palestinian state. However, it gradually became obvious that the promise of sovereignty was illusory. On the contrary, the Oslo process marked the taming of the Palestinian national movement and its incorporation into the dominant framework of international politics, though without the capacities of the (idealised) sovereign state.

This chapter has sought to reframe and complicate the narrative of the Palestinian quest for sovereignty by utilising a Deleuzian perspective. Adopting this conceptual apparatus, I have argued, helps to capture the various practices that come together to form sovereign projects beyond the conventional state forms. By juxtaposing spectacular and often violent actions on the one hand, and the mundane organising of the everyday on the other, I have showed that even actions dispersed globally can combine to constitute sovereignty – in terms of both performative violence and demonstrating the capacity to decide on the polity's futures. It is this assemblage of hybrid sovereignties which enables a better understanding of how various practices coalesce.

Nonetheless, the case of the Palestinian national movement demonstrates that adopting a Deleuzian perspective also provides a political lesson concerning the risks of sedentarisation. Not only is it obvious that the Oslo accords did not lead to the successful attainment of Palestinian sovereign ambitions; they also led to the Palestinian Authority gradually turning into a bureaucratised, repressive apparatus that has little in common with the liberatory ambitions of its antecedents (Tartir, 2017; Gordon, 2002). It is no coincidence that there are now calls to abolish the Palestinian Authority and again empower the PLO as the representative of the Palestinian people. As such, the trajectories of the Palestinian national movement show that statist aspirations can backfire; revolutionaries should be always careful what they wish for.

References

Aalberts, T. 2016. 'Sovereignty'. In Berenskoetter, F. (ed). *Concepts in World Politics*, 183–99. Los Angeles: Sage.

Acuto, M. and Curtis, S. 2014. 'Assemblage Thinking and International Relations'. In Acuto, M. and Curtis, S. (eds). *Reassembling International Theory: Assemblage Thinking and International Relations*, 1–15. London: Palgrave Macmillan.

Adey, P. 2004. 'Surveillance at the Airport: Surveilling Mobility / Mobilising Surveillance'. *Environment and Planning A* 36 (8): 1365–80.

Bacik, G. 2008. *Hybrid Sovereignty in the Arab Middle East: The Cases of Kuwait, Jordan, and Iraq*. New York: Palgrave Macmillan.

Bartelson, J. 2014. *Sovereignty as Symbolic Form*. London and New York: Routledge.

Baumgarten, H. 2005. 'The Three Faces / Phases of Palestinian Nationalism, 1948–2005'. *Journal of Palestine Studies* 34 (4): 25–48.

Bleiker, R. 2015. 'Pluralist Methods for Visual Global Politics'. *Millennium: Journal of International Studies* 43 (3): 872–90. Available at: <https://doi.org/10.1177/0305829815583084> (last accessed 14 June 2022).

Brynen, R. 1990. *Sanctuary and Survival: The PLO In Lebanon*. Boulder, CO, and San Francisco: Westview Press.

Byman, D. 2011. *A High Price: The Triumphs and Failures of Israeli Counterterrorism*. Oxford: Oxford University Press.

Cattelino, J. 2008. *High Stakes: Florida Seminole Gaming and Sovereignty*. Durham, NC: Duke University Press.

Chamberlin, P. 2011. 'The Struggle Against Oppression Everywhere: The Global Politics of Palestinian Liberation'. *Middle Eastern Studies* 47 (1): 25–41.

Chamberlin, P. 2012. *The Global Offensive: The United States, the Palestine Liberation Organization, and the Making of the Post-Cold War Order*. Oxford: Oxford University Press.

DeLanda, M. 2016. *Assemblage Theory*. Edinburgh: Edinburgh University Press.

Deleuze, G. and Guattari, F. 1987. *A Thousand Plateaus: Capitalism and Schizophrenia*. London: Continuum.

Feldman, I. 2008. 'Waiting for Palestine: Refracted Citizenship and Latent Sovereignty in Gaza'. *Citizenship Studies* 12 (5): 447–63. Available at: <https://doi.org/10.1080/13621020802337816> (last accessed 14 June 2022).

Fregonese, S. 2012. 'Beyond the "Weak State": Hybrid Sovereignties in Beirut'. *Environment and Planning D: Society and Space* 30 (4): 655–74.

Galily, Y., Yarchi, M. and Tamir, I. 2015. 'From Munich to Boston, and from Theater to Social Media: The Evolutionary Landscape of World Sporting Terror'. *Studies in Conflict & Terrorism* 38 (12): 998–1007. Available at: <https://doi.org/10.1080/1057610X.2015.1076640> (last accessed 14 June 2022).

Ghanem, A. 2013. 'Palestinian Nationalism: An Overview'. *Israel Studies* 18 (2): 11–29. Available at: <https://doi.org/10.2979/israelstudies.18.2.11> (last accessed 14 June 2022).

Gordon, N. 2002. 'Outsourcing Violations: The Israeli Case'. *Journal of Human Rights* 1 (3): 321–37.

Hansen, T. B. and Stepputat, F. (eds). 2005. *Sovereign Bodies: Citizens, Migrants, and States in the Postcolonial World*. Princeton: Princeton University Press.

Hilal, J. 2018. 'The Fragmentation of the Palestinian Political Field: Sources and Ramifications'. *Contemporary Arab Affairs* 11 (1–2): 189–216.

Hoffman, B. 2006. *Inside Terrorism*. New York: Columbia University Press.

Hughes, G. 2015. 'International Terrorism'. In Law, R. D. (ed.). *The Routledge History of Terrorism*, 456–69. Abingdon and New York: Routledge.

Khalidi, R. 1985. *Under Siege: PLO Decisionmaking During the 1982 War*. New York: Columbia University Press.

Khalidi, R. 1998. *Palestinian Identity: The Construction of Modern National Consciousness*. New York: Columbia University Press.

Khalili, L. 2007. *Heroes and Martyrs of Palestine: The Politics of National Commemoration*. Cambridge: Cambridge University Press.

Kimmerling, B. and Migdal, J. 2009. *The Palestinian People: A History*. Cambridge, MA: Harvard University Press.

Krause, P. 2017. *Rebel Power: Why National Movements Compete, Fight, and Win*. Ithaca, NY: Cornell University Press.

Nevo, J. 2008. 'September 1970 in Jordan: A Civil War?' *Civil Wars* 10 (3): 217–30. Available at: <https://doi.org/10.1080/13698240802168056> (last accessed 14 June 2022).

Pearlman, W. 2012. 'The Palestinian National Movement'. In Shlaim, A. and Louis, W. M. (eds). *The 1967 Arab-Israeli War: Origins and Consequences*, 126–48. Cambridge: Cambridge University Press. Available at: <https://doi.org/10.1017/CBO9780511751431.007> (last accessed 14 June 2022).

Peteet, J. 2005. *Landscape of Hope and Despair: Palestinian Refugee Camps*. Philadelphia: University of Pennsylvania Press.

Ramadan, A. 2009. 'A Refugee Landscape: Writing Palestinian Nationalisms in Lebanon'. *ACME: An International Journal for Critical Geographies* 8 (1): 69–99.

Ramadan, A. and Fregonese, S. 2017. 'Hybrid Sovereignty and the State of

Exception in the Palestinian Refugee Camps in Lebanon'. *Annals of the American Association of Geographers* 107 (4): 949–63.

Reid, J. 2003. 'Deleuze's War Machine: Nomadism Against the State'. *Millennium: Journal of International Studies* 32 (1): 57–85. Available at: <https://doi.org/10.1177/03058298030320010301> (last accessed 14 June 2022).

Sayigh, R. 2007. *The Palestinians: From Peasants to Revolutionaries*. 2nd edn. London: Zed Books.

Sayigh, Y. 2004. *Armed Struggle and the Search for State: The Palestinian National Movement, 1949–1993*. Oxford: Oxford University Press.

Tartir, A. 2017. 'The Palestinian Authority Security Forces: Whose Security?' Al-Shabaka. Available at: <https://al-shabaka.org/briefs/palestinian-autho rity-security-forces-whose-security/> (last accessed 14 June 2022).

Tholens, S. 2017. 'Border Management in an Era of "Statebuilding Lite": Security Assistance and Lebanon's Hybrid Sovereignty'. *International Affairs* 93 (4): 865–82.

9

The Khomeinists: Between Sedentarisation and Perpetual Revolution

Jakub Koláček

The Iranian Revolution of 1979 often stands out – perhaps along with the French and Bolshevik Revolutions – as a paramount example of a fully-fledged revolutionary event in world history, due to both the extent of the mass mobilisation involved and the velocity and gravity of the change it spurred. It precipitated the fall of the Pahlavi monarchy, under which the often secularist and Western-educated elite attempted to steer Iran on to the path of modernisation and nation state-building for more than half a century, shaking off the country's past weaknesses vis-à-vis colonising powers and winning it an equal standing on the regional and world stage. It replaced these attempts with a system which drew on an ostentatiously different imagery of legitimisation and reasoning, at the centre of which was the idea of an eternal and just order prescribed to his believers by God himself.

Gaining power in 1979, the revolutionaries attempted to restructure the Iranian state along this new path by means of the institution of the 'theocratic' Islamic Republic, which – with minor adjustments – has existed for more than forty years now. Nevertheless, the revolution not only brought about an internal change for Iran; its repercussions were also broader on a regional and, indeed, international scale.

Some of these might been expected, as with the exchange of the ruling regime, a shift in the foreign policy of the whole state naturally occurred as well. Still other changes, however, were altogether unexpected. Already during the first year after the demise of the Pahlavi monarchy, the new ruling establishment began to engage in policies which can, by all means, be considered radical. Beginning with the takeover of the US embassy in Tehran in November 1979 and the detainment of US diplomats, these policies, over the following ten years, included: the direct support of a number of armed groups operating in the territories of Middle Eastern states and often engaging in violent armed struggle against the local governments; a costly and bloody protraction of the war with neighbouring Iraq; an appeal to execute a British novelist and citizen residing in London; and an almost continuous flow of threats and recriminations directed towards near or more distant foreign countries. Through these deeds and still other endeavours, the Iranian Revolution trespassed on the narrow confines of one state and changed the geopolitical landscape of the Middle East, in some cases setting the stage for long-term conflicts which continue to this day.

The tendency to transcend local context and affect the broader international or even global political environment is, as has been demonstrated elsewhere (see 'War Machines' in this volume), rather typical of major revolutionary events. Yet what was the mechanism behind this 'spillover' in the Iranian case? The answer also depends, at least partially, on the conceptual means of theorisation applied to it. The conventional view typically relies on established categories of political science, most importantly *the state* as a definite entity possessing its interior and exterior as different theatres of political action. A revolution is viewed primarily and overwhelmingly as an intra-state affair which only indirectly affects its 'exterior': namely, by means of the foreign policy-making of the revolutionary state with an altered ideological orientation. Nevertheless, as is pointed out several times in this volume, neither the category of the state nor the division between 'interior' and 'exterior' can be taken as epistemologically neutral and for granted, as they are themselves a point of contestation and conflict in international politics – the contestation in which the phenomenon of revolutionary agency plays a central role.

In what follows, I will argue against the prevailing perspective which locks the Iranian Revolution into the state and explains its ramifications primarily with reference to the state, if only to render it subsequently a delinquent one (see Combes, this volume). This is because the state was contested in this particular case as well. The contestation of the state and related structures, however, did not occur naturally or spontaneously. It was connected to the agency of mainly one actor. This actor was the Islamic movement led by Ruhollah Khomeini, which eventually acquired hegemony over the revolutionary uprising and shaped its course and outcome to a great degree.

Throughout this chapter, I will focus on the *Khomeinists* as a central agent of revolutionary change in Iran and trace their evolution from the pre-revolutionary period up to the 1980s, when they became a principal actor in Middle Eastern politics through the successful seizure of state power in Iran. As will be argued, the Khomeinists emerged as an actor radically opposed to the established structures of the state and the international order, yet were later forced to compromise their commitments during the revolution and its aftermath. The bulk of the chapter will focus on the dilemmas faced by the Khomeinists as a revolutionary actor operating in Iran and elsewhere, and the way in which they resolved these dilemmas through strategic choices.

Drawing on that, it will be argued that the Khomeinists, as a principal actor of the Iranian Revolution, did not substantially differ from other *hybrid revolutionary actors* examined in this volume (see 'War Machines'). While they became 'sedentarised' in their own state of the Islamic Republic, they also struggled to perpetuate the revolution at home and abroad, combining seemingly incongruent, yet in fact complementary, repertoires of action. In what follows, I will attempt to illustrate how this peculiar form of agency shaped post-revolutionary Iran as well as broader Middle Eastern politics, which up to this day bear the tangible stamp of Khomeinist revolutionary action.

The Khomeinists and Their Project

In this study, I use the term 'Khomeinism', proposed by Ervand Abrahamian (1993) to refer to the phenomena I intend to describe and analyse. The author himself uses this term mainly to characterise 'Khomeini, his ideas and his movement' in terms of more general phenomena of populism (Abrahamian, 1993, pp. 2, 13–38). While such usage is not objectionable *per se*, my focus will be different. In what follows, I will use a more concrete form of the term, the 'Khomeinists', to refer to an actor and movement tied together by a distinct political subjectivity and exerting political agency in various spatial domains over a prolonged period of time. The term thus points to the distinctiveness of the Khomeinists as a historically individuated actor and a 'social assemblage' distinct from other assemblages (DeLanda, 2016, pp. 13–14). Among these, there are two which are particularly important as Khomeinism emerged within their immediate context. The first is transnational Islamic political activism (representing a more 'rhizomatic' and deterritorialised phenomenon) and the second is the bounded entity of the Iranian territorial nation state (representing more of a stratum; DeLanda, 2016, pp. 18–19; Deleuze and Guattari, 1987).

The origins of Khomeinism date back to the political activism of Ruhollah Khomeini, which he initiated in the early 1960s. Khomeini protested against the modernisation reforms of Reza Shah Pahlavi and foreign interference in the country. His protests at the time, however, had little immediate impact and resulted in his exile. It was only with the advent of the revolutionary uprising in 1978 that things changed and the elderly *āyatollāh*, posing as a representative of the traditional Iranian Shi'i clergy, emerged as the charismatic leader of the revolution, after which he effectively replaced the Shah as head of the Iranian state. As already mentioned, he subsequently used this position to transform the state, ostensibly according to the tenets of the indigenous Shi'i religio-political doctrine.

This all serves as the basis for perceiving the Khomeinists and Khomeinism as largely an Iranian phenomenon – a domestic political movement which grew out of local clericalism and, after a period of marginality, eventually utilised the momentum of broader social discontent to impose its own rule. Such a view is, after all, widely represented in Iranian historiography (see, for example, the influential account of Dabashi, 1993).

There are, however, certain grounds upon which this can be disputed or at least viewed as incomplete. Perhaps the most important of these is the overall and apparent orientation of the whole movement towards issues which transcended the immediate Iranian context. These are represented, as will be further discussed, in Khomeini's pre-revolutionary discourse, his religious doctrine (which, in its radicalism and novelty, in fact largely diverted from what was hitherto considered Shi'a 'tradition'; see Arjomand, 1988, pp. 177–82; Sabet, 2013, pp. 69–75) and, perhaps most significantly, the nature of the movement's post-revolutionary policies directed abroad, in which the Khomeinists engaged almost immediately after seizing power, often to the detriment of a narrowly defined national interest (cf. Hunter, 2010, pp. 27–8).

To comprehend these traits, it is necessary to see Khomeinism in its second important context, and that is the transnational phenomenon of 'Islamism': engagement in the name and for the sake of Islam, mostly in confrontation with the secularising and colonising forces of the West, proliferating across the Muslim world from the end of the nineteenth century onwards (see Enayat, 2001). In fact, Khomeini, together with others like Sayyid Qutb in Egypt (who operated on the distinct Sunni side of the doctrinal spectrum, yet whose thinking was also known and resonated in Iran; see Arjomand, 1988, p. 97; Ghamari-Tabrizi, 2008, pp. 28–35), pushed this activism towards new expressions and became one of the principal instigators (cf. Roy, 1994, pp. 35–47; Azani, 2011, pp. 36–41) of its ascent to the role of a major cultural and political force in the Middle East and beyond from the 1970s / 1980s onwards – which was greatly accelerated by the Iranian Revolution itself (Sidahmed and Ehteshami, 2018, pp. 7–8).

Khomeini first fully expressed his novel ideas in his 1970 seminal treatise, *Islamic Government*, which introduced two concomitant doctrinal tenets. The first one comprised embracing a revolutionary strategy for the Islamic political movement while the second focused on raising the demand for a distinctively Islamic form of government (governed according to Khomeini's theory of *vilāyat-i faqīh*) which would be established by this strategy (Khomeini, 1981; cf.

Sabet, 2013). Both of these tenets equipped the Khomeinist movement with a relatively definite agenda, which was partly realised in the post-revolutionary period. What is often missed, however, is that Khomeini, as an integral part of this project, conceived it as a programme for the entire Muslim community and made this meaning congruent with a number of distinct motives which appeared – and kept resurfacing later – in his discourse: the invocation of a strong animus against the West and 'imperialism' (Khomeini, 1981, pp. 27–39), the accentuation of the politically universalist meaning of *umma* (Khomeini, 1981, pp. 48–9), and also, for example, the assertion of the possibility of an armed jihad against the 'idolatrous' (*ṭāghūt*) regimes all over the Muslim world (Khomeini, 1981, pp. 48, 108, 114–15). Overall, these motives underwent a further evolution in line with various expressions of radical Islamism towards the end of the twentieth century.

As will be further argued, this aspect of the Khomeinist doctrine must not be seen as merely accidental, as it constituted the very basis of the political subjectivity of the nascent movement. From the beginning, this was grounded not only in the utopian–revolutionary appeal for substantive political and social change (reforming society into a virtuous and prosperous form under just Islamic rule), but also in the sense of (at least within Islam) universal significance and validity of its aims. As it was this universalism which played a crucial role in the *differentiation* of the movement as a political actor from others, it could not be easily revoked.

Nevertheless, while Khomeini stated before the revolution that it is the 'duty' of Muslims to overthrow the 'criminal regimes' in 'every one of the Muslim countries' in order to 'assure unity of the Islamic umma' (Khomeini, 1981, pp. 48–9), the post-revolutionary Khomeinist regime, despite its adventurism, largely remained locked within the boundaries of Khomeini's native Iran – renowned more as an experiment of the 'Islamism in one country' scenario (cf. Esposito and Voll, 1996, p. 52; Osman, 2016, pp. 173–95) rather than a paragon of jihadi internationalism (though the issue is arguably more complex). In the rest of this chapter, I will attempt to conceptualise this development in terms of the *hybridisation* of Khomeinist political subjectivity ensuing from the movement's participation in the real political process which confronted it with significant obstacles for the realisation of its vision.

The Dilemma of the State

The Iranian Revolution of 1978/9 played a crucial and indispensable role in the Khomeinist ascent to power and their capacity to exert political agency on the level of state politics and beyond. In the 1970s, the movement consisted of only a relatively small number of Khomeini's devotees, who shared with him his fate of being a political outsider and possessing only limited influence in society (cf. Arjomand, 1988, pp. 94–9). Khomeini and his aides could not possibly have planned for the course of the revolution and its aftermath. Their participation in it thus occurred as a series of decisions taken vis-à-vis the rapidly changing conditions. This naturally affected the subjectivity of the movement, which began to be defined by these decisions, especially when principal matters were at stake.

This process had already started during the phase of mobilisation of the revolution. Then, it became primarily influenced by the fact that the Khomeinists did not stand alone in facing the Shah and his formidable security apparatus. The success of the uprising was contingent on the existence of a broad revolutionary coalition (an assemblage of parties, movements, communities, unions, individuals and objects) with which they effectively merged during the critical period between the autumn of 1978 and spring 1979. Over this period, Khomeini apparently suppressed his radical political postures in favour of a more 'spiritual' facet of his personal identity, which resonated with the revolutionary fervour and enabled him to pose as a consensual and, indeed, charismatic leader (see Arjomand, 1988, pp. 100–1; here, the origins of the Khomeinist populist mobilisation must also be seen; see Panah, 2007, pp. 42–3; Abrahamian, 1993, pp. 2–3). This was, however, a rather temporary compromise, which ended as soon as the common enemy dissipated and the 'moderate Islamic', leftist and other factions began to stand in the way of Khomeini's schemes.

A far more consequential series of compromises appeared on a different level and can be most generally conceptualised as the *transition of the Khomeinists from a non-state to a stately existence*. As has been expounded, the Khomeinist pre-revolutionary ideology and identity were based on universalist claims and had explicitly pan-Islamic connotations. As such, it clearly implied antagonism to the modern nation state.[1] Arguably, the most remarkable outcome of the revolution led by Khomeini was that it had virtually decomposed the pre-revolutionary Pahlavi state. The winter months of 1978/9 saw an almost complete deterritorialisation of state institutions.[2] In one of the most fateful and impactful decisions, Khomeini opted for the reterritorialisation of the state. His appointment of Mehdi Bazargan's provisional government on 5 February secured the continuity of the state bureaucracy, and over the following months, a constitutive process was initiated to adopt a new legal framework for the political system in the country. The Khomeinists eventually utilised this process to assert their control over the state (see Randjbar-Daemi, 2013).

In doing so, the Khomeinists cast their lot with the Iranian territorial nation state and laid the groundwork for what is usually seen as the pragmatic character of their politics (Ghamari-Tabrizi, 2008, p. 41; Abrahamian, 1993, pp. 13–17).

This, however, does not mean that the Khomeinist pre-revolutionary subjectivity ceased to exist. The political vision around which the whole movement coalesced implied commitments. These consisted especially in delivering the promised change, as well as in fighting and resisting the political structures against which this whole political project was set and which it rendered corrupt and illegitimate; it was not a mere change in the administration of the country. Moreover, this change was promoted as acquiring a universal importance. If the Khomeinists had just assumed the role of a new 'regime' in Iran, their subjectivity would have been mostly negated.

In this situation, the Khomeinist agency took a couple of distinct forms. On the one hand, in a rather typical way, it resulted in an attempt to transform the Iranian nation state in line with revolutionary aspirations. This tenet was overtly expressed in the 1979 Constitution, which defined the new-born Islamic Republic as an *iswa* ('paragon') Islamic state and society (see 'The Form of Governance in Islam'). Practically, it included the adoption of a specific constitutional system mirroring in part the *vilāyat-i faqīh* doctrine, the attempt to 'Islamise' the legal system, and various other adjustments in the realms of cultural and educational policies and the state's identity and symbolism. This practice, however, seems to have been the least effective, as the institutional structures of the state and the necessities of its administration often prevailed over the 'Islamic' principles (see, for example, Arjomand, 1988, pp. 173–4, 177–88; Ghamari-Tabrizi, 2008). As will be further clarified, the Khomeinist appropriation of the state also became a principal factor in the movement's 'sedentarisation' (in a way, its 'capture' by the state; cf. Deleuze and Guattari, 1987), as it naturally created new commitments which were directly opposed to the perpetuation of the revolution beyond the national territory.

Nevertheless, the Khomeinists simultaneously attempted to tame this effect, at least partially. Despite the fact that, perhaps as early as at the end of 1979, they held decisive control over the state and its institutions, the Khomeinists showed a reluctance simply to merge with the state organisationally, and instead retained a partially (if rather formally) *extrinsic* relation to it. Instead of creating a strictly centralised and formalised party-state structure, they established a number of parallel institutions (see Boroujerdi and Rahimkhani, 2018, pp. 34–6) which overlapped in function with the 'national' bureaucracy inherited from the Pahlavi regime (controlled by the presidency) and put it more directly under the authority of the 'theocratic' branch of the government (thus mirroring the duality incorporated into the constitutional system itself).

While these 'Khomeinist' institutions covered a wide-ranging agenda (not least redistributing social goods as one of the important promises of the revolution and providing upward social mobility for the cadres; see Harris,

2017, pp. 101–15), the Islamic Revolutionary Guard Corps (IRGC) must be regarded as their most important constituent. Established as early as February 1979 (see Ostovar, 2016, pp. 41–54), the IRGC became the main aegis of the Khomeinist rule and enabled the movement to avoid relying on the army (*artesh*), a 'national institution *par excellence*' (Arendt, 1973, p. 259).[3] Yet most importantly, what the Khomeinists procured in the IRGC was their own *war machine*, which was subsequently deployed to implement their revolutionary agency beyond the Iranian national boundaries. This can be seen as the third and final strategy to preserve the Khomeinists' universalist subjectivity in defiance of the 'apparatuses of capture'.

Khomeinist Foreign Policy

Events from the beginning of 1979 created the impression that the revolutionary upheaval in Iran would eventually result in only an intra-state change. Khomeini's acquiescence to the preservation of the essential continuity of governmental institutions also ensured the continuity of the foreign relations of the Iranian state, which – despite some shifts (such as Iran's withdrawal from the CENTO pact on 11 March and a wave of nationalisation of foreign assets) – initially remained more or less intact (see Murray, 2010, pp. 25–9; Gillespie, 1990, pp. 18–20; cf. Rubinstein, 1981, pp. 599–600).[4] This had one significant long-term effect: even after the Khomeinist takeover, the new regime did not have to appeal for international recognition. Apparently, if the above-mentioned course was followed, the revolution would ultimately remain a primarily domestic event with a modest impact on the international sphere. Yet this would also compromise the Khomeinist revolutionary identity.

Though Khomeini tamed his radical rhetoric somewhat during the key period of the revolutionary struggle, he never really abandoned it and kept attacking particularly the United States as a symbol of global imperialist decadence. This 'reeducation of the Iranian people to the new revolutionary ideology' (Beeman, 1983, p. 191; see also Kamrava, 2014, p. 149) had a tangible impact on the radicalised fringes of the revolting public and the hard-line elements of the nascent movement. Already on 14 February 1979, protesters attacked the American embassy in Tehran but were subsequently forced to leave for the time being (see Guerrero, 2016, pp. 168–88).

It was only the second takeover that entered popular history. Khomeini's explicit endorsement and sanctification of it set off far-reaching consequences. The most immediate one was the resignation of Bazargan's government and a *de facto*– in many ways decisive – Khomeinist coup (see Moin, 2000, pp. 234–7; Bowden, 2007, p. 30; Arjomand, 1988, p. 139). That this coup occurred in the international context, however, cannot be seen as wholly arbitrary. The seizure of the embassy represented the Khomeinists' first major international action. Being characteristically executed by 'activists', it cut right into the vein of interstate politics. It terminated the contingent normalisation of the revolutionary polity's foreign relations and catalysed a major international conflict. Whereas, during its antecedent stage, the revolution remained – despite the bravado regarding its international significance – still largely a domestic event, it was this act, possessing a dimension of theatricality and being televised around the world, that rendered it more tangibly global and universal. The Khomeinists reasserted their universalist subjectivity through the 'revolution bigger than the first revolution' (Khomeini, 1999, p. 489). Importantly, all this was enabled by the relative seriousness of the incident, consisting especially of the 444-day-long detention of fifty-two diplomats with, needless to say, grave political, economic and security repercussions for Iran as a state. As must be remembered, though, it was these repercussions which redeemed the veracity of the event and rendered it a real confrontation.

On the other hand, the costs seemed still to be carefully modulated. Despite the fact that the United States was confronted with all the consequences, the 'attack' was eventually seen only as a breach of the Vienna Convention, one step short of a breach of Westphalian sovereignty itself. When the Soviet embassy in Tehran fell victim to an incursion of protesters in December 1980, this was dispersed, and despite many mutual contentious issues and Khomeini's inflammatory rhetoric, the Khomeinists showed restraint in their relations to the second, more immediately neighbouring superpower (see Chubin, 1983; Yodfat, 2011, pp. 103, 106; Rubinstein, 1981, pp. 604–9). Neither did the Khomeinists use the state overtly to attack and invade other countries and abstained from unleashing its *machine de guerre* in a pan-Islamic revolutionary struggle.

As will be further discussed, this pattern repeated itself over the following years. While continuing to perpetuate revolutionary action, the Khomeinists modulated it, so it would not comprise an unequivocal attack on another country's sovereignty, thus avoiding putting their state in an untenable position. Despite this policy leading Iran into isolation, it did not give rise to any pretext for direct action. This can be further illustrated by the phenomenon of the 'export of the revolution'.

The Revolution Beyond State Boundaries

The 'export of the revolution' came to represent the epitome of the Khomeinist effort to enhance the revolutionary change in the Iranian exterior by subversive political and military means. The phrase can be considered especially apposite.

In fact, it was coined only after the revolution and cannot be found anywhere in Khomeini's discourse before it – probably having never been uttered. This stems from the fact that the original Khomeinist vision of international politics was much more forthright in its universalism and worked directly with the notion of the unstriated space of the *umma*. It was only after the revolutionary change had been confined by national boundaries that speaking about 'export' gained its proper meaning. I will briefly survey two distinct cases of this policy, demonstrating certain traits which can be further generalised.

The Gulf Case

The first case concerns the three Gulf states with larger proportions of Shi'i *Ithnā'asharī'a* populations: Saudi Arabia, Bahrain and Kuwait. Despite now being largely forgotten, the Islamic Revolution reverberated in these areas from 1979 onwards and political tensions surfaced, especially in the first two states. In November 1979, crowded demonstrations (subsequently known as the *Intifada* of Muharram 1400) counting tens of thousands erupted in the Saudi Qatif and al-Hasa regions, resulting in tens of casualties, followed by a continuous cycle of protests and repression. A similar protest, though lesser in scale, took place in Bahrain, culminating in April 1980 (Louër, 2008, pp. 160, 161–2; Matthiesen, 2010, p. 181; Marschall, 2003, p. 35). These minor uprisings, organised by already politicised local Shi'i activists, were quelled relatively quickly and successfully.

Nevertheless, revolutionary mobilisation did not immediately cease and continued by means of the agency of local 'vanguard' organisations. Among these were the Islamic Front for the Liberation of Bahrain and the Organisation for Islamic Revolution in the Arabian Peninsula, as well as several other lower-profile groups (see Louër, 2008, pp. 159, 164–6). Tied to Iran or based directly there, these groups attempted to follow up on the initial popular uprisings and promote what was basically the political programme and interests of the Khomeinists in the Gulf countries. They engaged in propaganda, as well as occasional violent actions which, despite never reaching large proportions, included some serious incidents. In December 1981, the Bahraini government thwarted an attempted coup to overthrow it in a violent uprising. In Saudi Arabia, a similar coup attempt was alleged to have occurred in February 1983, resulting in mass arrests. In December 1983, a series of explosions hit Kuwait, targeting – besides public infrastructure – the American and French embassies, followed over the next two years by other bombings and the attempted assassination of the Kuwaiti Amir (Marschall, 2003, pp. 36–8). It was only in the late 1980s that this violence receded.

To assess in this particular case the meaning of 'export of the revolution', it must be stressed that the relation between the Khomeinist leadership and the events occurring on the territories of the three mentioned states was not straightforward. With the advent of the Islamic Revolution, the Khomeinists attracted some of the pre-existing Shi'i political movements and organisations, as was the case with the followers of Muhammad al-Shirazi or the Da'wa Party. These movements, operating in Iraq and other Gulf states, subsequently adopted the Khomeinist political project or got very close to it (Louër, 2008, p. 177ff.), like, for instance, the chief instigator of the Shi'i political mobilisation in Bahrain, Hadi al-Mudarrisi, who designated himself the official representative of Khomeini (Louër, 2008, p. 158).

This does not mean, however, that these movements would simply succumb to Khomeinist quasi-sovereignty. While activists and groups in the Gulf drew both material and organisational support from the Iranian territory (facilitated mainly by the Office of Liberation Movements, initially working as a branch of the IRGC; see Marschall, 2003, p. 30), at least some of their actions were probably autonomous and led to conflicts with the Khomeinist establishment, itself divided and notoriously hesitant, with frequent feuds occurring between the Foreign Ministry (which, together with people such as President Khamene'i, methodically denied the Islamic Republic of Iran's complicity; see Marschall, 2003, pp. 31, 37) and more 'freelance' radicals (see Matthiesen, 2010, p. 183; Marschall, 2003, p. 32). Members and leaders of foreign oppositional groups frequently migrated and often ultimately ended up in Iran, expelled by their own governments as well (Louër, 2008, p. 170) and possibly taking positions in the Islamic Republic's official structures (Marschall, 2003, p. 31). Meanwhile, the bombing of political and public infrastructure in Kuwait most likely involved the participation of Lebanese Hizbullah cadres, including Imad Mughniyya (Louër, 2008, pp. 173–6), and were coordinated with the attacks on the Saudi and Kuwaiti embassies in Beirut (Marschall, 2003, pp. 35–6).

This all points to the occurrence of a rather dispersed agency, distinct from the agency of a state, which can be attributed to a transnational network – an assemblage of radicals emerging in a brief Khomeinist upsurge in the Gulf Shi'i regions after the revolution, inspired by the very character of the Khomeinist political project which, by way of its universalist agenda, allowed for a deterritorialised, transnational belonging. The spread of the revolution depended upon these 'nomadic' actors and was, strictly speaking, not only an export. The Khomeinist agenda was simultaneously 'imported' (Marschall, 2003, p. 28) across state boundaries by the locals – or maybe even more precisely, an attempt was made to create an enterprise which would effectively ignore these boundaries. The Islamic Republic related to these networks largely as a territorially separate and organisationally limited entity and as more of a safe haven than headquarters.

In any case, these attempts did not succeed. Neither public unrest nor 'vanguard' action was able to shake the stability of the local political structures, and at the end of the day the Iranian Khomeinist leadership showed restraint in mobilising the means of state power to their advantage. The pattern already described surfaced: the revolutionary activities occurred on the territory of legitimate neighbouring states, and such support could trigger serious conflict. The Khomeinists, already isolated and strained by interstate conflict with Iraq, could hardly afford that. The established and stable Westphalian boundaries eventually proved resistant to the revolutionary agency of a movement with limited scope.

Hizbullah and the Cases of Weakened Statehood

Efforts to facilitate the spread of the revolution eventually did bring some measure of success. In this regard, a paradigmatic case is the establishment and agency of the Lebanese Hizbullah. What was the principal difference that distinguished this case from the previous ones?

Definitely, in the Lebanese case as well, the emergence of revolutionary activity consisted in the making of local activists who became politicised and engaged in transnational activities well before the revolution (De Vore and Stähli, 2015, pp. 340–1; Ostovar, 2016, pp. 113–15). Hizbullah emerged through the differentiation of these activists from the broader Shiʻi community and its political structures on the grounds of their acceptance of the Khomeinist doctrine (Azani, 2011, pp. 47–59). In contrast to previous cases, the movement quickly evolved into an effective and powerful organisation possessing its own *war machine* and the capacity to act independently – not only on the subnational level of Lebanon, but also internationally. As is known, Hizbullah has retained this position until the present day.

Two differences conditioned this development: first, Hizbullah was able to project its power within the Lebanese territory more freely; and second, it received incomparably greater support from the Iranian territory. This included the direct intervention of the IRGC and investments estimated as about US$140 million annually over the following years (De Vore and Stähli, 2015, p. 337). The early Hizbullah got close to the Iranian Khomeinists to the point that it explicitly adopted the doctrine of *vilāyat-i faqīh* and virtually the religious and political authority of Khomeini as well. By creating a semblance of transnational belonging, the Khomeinist dream of establishing a broader Islamic polity perhaps came closest to its realisation (see Wimberly, 2015, p. 694). Arguably, these differences can then be attributed to the state of civil war in Lebanon. The successes of the Khomeinist agency and the movement's 'proxy' activities have virtually been limited to analogous cases: the Afghan Hazara *mujahidin* (the Soviet intervention in Afghanistan and civil war), Palestinian militias in the West Bank and Gaza (the long-term conflict over contested Palestinian statehood), Iraqi Shi'i armed groups (the civil war after the US intervention in 2003), or more recently, the Houthis in Yemen (the civil war from 2014 onwards). From where did this correlation stem?

The space, which had already been politically 'open' and where statehood was contested by different local groups and interventionist forces, was clearly more opportune. It is necessary to realise, however, that the spread of revolution occurred only thanks to its facilitation by means which can be called 'hybrid'. While, like Hizbullah, other groups (e.g. the Afghani Hazara Hizb-i Vahdat and the Iraqi SCIRI umbrella) virtually identified with the Khomeinists by accepting the *vilāyat-i faqīh* doctrine and the authority of the Iranian Khomeinist leadership, this relationship never gained a dimension of a real unification with IRI's territorial sovereignty and waned, or was relegated to a largely symbolic domain, in the long run (see Wimberly, 2015, pp. 698–707; Ostovar, 2018, p. 1239). This points to the fact that local Khomeinist groups also preferred a strategic and opportunistic attitude to the local statehoods.

The example of Hizbullah is, again, illustrative. Despite its identification with the Khomeinist programme, the movement never lost the character of its 'locality'. With the effective end of the civil war in October 1990, this locality was further accentuated within the movement's identity. Hizbullah progressively integrated itself into the renewed domestic political process in the country (see Azani, 2011, p. 75ff.), and despite retaining both Khomeinist ties and a great measure of autonomy from the state (even including the capacity to conduct an independent international agency), it began to present itself consistently as a defender of Lebanese statehood rather than its subverter (see, for example, Nasrallah, 2006) – despite the situation being viewed in quite the opposite way by its critics. This pattern has appeared in more or less the same manner in other Khomeinist factions which posed as legitimate contenders for statehood and progressively adjusted their political attitudes in line with changing local circumstances, including modulating their Khomeinist loyalties or even severing them (see Ostovar, 2018). Arguably, this ambiguity was conducive to preserving the continued existence of the Khomeinist assemblage over the long run.

Perhaps the most vivid example of this strategic flexibility came after 2011, when the Khomeinists (with the Lebanese Hizbullah and the Afghani-manned

Fatimid Brigades playing key roles; see Karataş, 2021) rushed to the rescue of Bashar al-Assad's regime in Syria, representing the only allied traditional nation state in the region. A similar mobilisation occurred against the threat posed to the Iraqi Republic by the ISIS insurgency after 2014. Both of these campaigns eventually enhanced the Khomeinist presence and relevance across the region (Friedman, 2018). This all points to the fact that statehood played an ambiguous role in the Khomeinist 'export' of the revolution, or perhaps more precisely, in the effort to build a transnational enterprise comprising mutually aligned subjects partaking in coordinated political agency and aiming to gain regional influence in defiance of other hegemonic powers. As its *sine qua non*, this effort was clearly conditioned by the Khomeinist success in seizing the Iranian nation state, which became the source of the movement's prestige and material power. This success facilitated local mobilisation driven by the quasi-universalist message (if eventually limited largely to Shiʻi communities) in other places as the second necessary precondition for the actor's entrenchment as a transnational movement. As it emerged, however, the local offshoots of Khomeinism became susceptible to falling prey relatively easily to counterrevolutionary action by local governments, apart from specific cases – where no effective centralised state power was present. Coordinated support provided to these groups by the Iranian Khomeinists eventually concentrated on this limited number of cases. And even there, the support and mutual cooperation were progressively adjusted according to the changing political conditions – the most marked shift being from an inclination towards a shared subjectivity and belonging in the 1980s to looser ties and a peculiar *modus vivendi* with the state system from the 1990s onwards.

Conclusion

The Iranian Islamic Revolution of 1979 left a lasting legacy in the Middle Eastern region. This legacy is most often viewed in terms of further signifying the crisis of the postwar nationalist and secularist political and social ideologies, ushering in the rise of the Islamic ones, inspiring the political activisation and emancipation of the indigenous Shiʻa, and – from a more recent perspective – also triggering the ascent of Iran to the position of a major regional revisionist power.

In contrast to the prevailing perspective which situates the revolution mainly in just the one state and assesses it through the 'nation statist' prism (with its basic dichotomy of exterior / interior and state / non-state embedded in the 'Westphalian myth'; Osiander, 2001), this chapter has attempted to highlight a different facet – that of an event which precipitated an occurrence of what is conceptualised in this volume as a *hybrid revolutionary agency*.

As has been shown, this agency stemmed directly from the aspirations of the Khomeinist movement to overcome the limiting framework of the nation state in the name of broader Islamic universalism. In fact, the Khomeinist assemblage emerged as the first significant example of an Islamic-inspired actor to attempt such a thing in direct confrontation with the local nation statehoods on a large scale and the first one with which both overseas and regional forces interested in preserving the *status quo* had to contend. As such, and despite all the conceivable differences, it can also be regarded as a predecessor of similar later attempts on the part of the radical Sunni movements (including ISIS).

Notably, the Khomeinist revolution, despite both its self-imposed limitations and the counterrevolutionary action taken against it, did not remain without any effect. Both the lasting Hizbullah presence in Lebanon and the post-2003 situation in Iraq can be stated as examples of the ongoing deterritorialisation (and, in fact, heteronomy; see Ruggie, 1993, pp. 150–1) in the regional Westphalian order, sustained largely by the repertoire of strategies developed by the Khomeinist leadership after the revolution. Incidents as recent as the January 2019 assassination of the IRGC Quds Force commander Qasim Suleimani (a self-styled nomadic organiser of the Khomeinist 'resistance front' across the region) on Iraqi soil by a US drone as a 'terrorist' also attest to the ongoing relevance of the hybrid conflict over the limits of this order, which is now usually attributed to a mere clash of national interests. Whether the universalist and revolutionary Khomeinist subjectivity will play any further significant role in this conflict is yet to be seen.

Notes

1. Especially in its classical definition of a national community possessing the right to self-determination. This was also the vision against which Khomeini initiated his protest in 1963.
2. Notably, Khomeini personally added to this outcome by his strict refusal to accept any organised transition of power (Arjomand, 1988, p. 102).
3. It is worth mentioning that the phenomenon of parastatism became ingrained in the Iranian domestic political system (see Buchta, 2000, pp. 1–77) and can thus be seen as a kind of protracted *deterritorialisation* of the post-revolutionary state – a phenomenon also observed by Arendt (1973, p. 257) in Nazi and Bolshevik movements.
4. Bazargan even met with US ambassador W. Sullivan as early as 21 February (see Hovey, 1979).

References

Abrahamian, E. 1993. *Khomeinism: Essays on the Islamic Republic*. Berkeley: University of California Press.

Arendt, H. 1973. *The Origins of Totalitarianism*. New York: Harcourt Brace Jovanovich.

Arjomand, S. A. 1988. *The Turban for the Crown: The Islamic Revolution in Iran*. Oxford: Oxford University Press.

Azani, E. 2011. *Hezbullah, The Story of the Party of God: From Revolution to Institutionalization*. New York: Palgrave and Macmillan.

Beeman, W. O. 1983. 'Images of the Great Satan: Representations of the United States in the Iranian Revolution'. In Keddie, N. R. (ed.). *Religion and Politics in Iran: Shi'ism from Quietism to Revolution*. New Haven, CT: Yale University Press.

Boroujerdi, M. and Rahimkhani, K. 2018. *Postrevolutionary Iran: A Political Handbook*. New York: Syracuse University Press.

Bowden, M. 2007. *Guests of the Ayatollah: The First Battle in America's War with Militant Islam*. New York: Grove Press.

Buchta, W. 2000. *Who Rules Iran: The Structure of Power in the Islamic Republic*. Washington, D.C.: Washington Institute for Near East Policy and the Konrad Adenauer Stiftung.

Chubin, S. 1983. 'The Soviet Union and Iran'. *Foreign Affairs* 64 (1): 921–49.

Dabashi, H. 1993. *Theology of Discontent: The Ideological Foundations of the Islamic Revolution in Iran*. New York: New York University Press.

DeLanda, M. 2016. *Assemblage Theory*. Edinburgh: Edinburgh University Press.

Deleuze, G. and Guattari, F. 1987. *Thousand Plateaus: Capitalism and Schizophrenia*. Minneapolis: University of Minnesota Press.

DeVore, M. R. and Stähli, A. B. 2015. 'Explaining Hezbollah's Effectiveness: Internal and External Determinants of the Rise of Violent Non-State Actors'. *Terrorism and Political Violence* 27 (2): 331–57.

Enayat, H. 2001. *Modern Islamic Political Thought*. London: I. B. Tauris.

Esposito, J. L., and Voll, J. O. 1996. *Islam and Democracy*. New York: Oxford University Press.

Friedman, B. 2018. 'Iran's Hezbollah Model in Iraq and Syria: Fait Accompli?'. *Orbis* 62 (3): 438–53.

Ghamari-Tabrizi, B. 2008. *Islam and Dissent in Post-Revolutionary Iran: Abdolkarim Soroush, Religious Politics and Democratic Reform*. London: I. B. Tauris.

Gillespie, K. 1990. 'US Corporations and Iran at the Hague'. *Middle East Journal* 44 (1): 18–36.

Guerrero, J. G. 2016. *The Carter Administration and the Fall of Iran's Pahlavi Dynasty: US–Iran Relations on the Brink of the 1979 Revolution.* London: Palgrave Macmillan.

Harris, K. 2017. *Social Revolution: Politics and Welfare State in Iran.* Oakland: University of California Press.

Hovey, G. 1979. 'New Iranian Prime Minister Holds His First Meeting with U.S. Envoy'. *The New York Times,* 21 February.

Hunter, S. T. 2010. *Iran's Foreign Policy in the Post-Soviet Era.* Santa Barbara: Praeger.

Kamrava, M. 2014. 'Khomeini and the West'. In Moghaddam, A. A. (ed.). *A Critical Introduction to Khomeini.* Cambridge: Cambridge University Press.

Karataş, I. 2021. 'Iran's Use of Afghan Shiite Migrants as Proxies: The Case of Liwa Fatemiyoun'. *The Journal of Iranian Studies* 5 (1): 31–53.

Khomeini, R. 1981. *Islam and Revolution: Writings and Declarations of Imam Khomeini,* translated by Hamid Algar. Berkeley, CA: Mizan Press.

Khomeini, R. 1999. *Sahife-ye Emam, Vol. X.* Tehran: Markaz-e Nashr-e Asar-e Emam Khomeini.

Louër, L. 2008. *Transnational Shi'a Politics: Religious and Political Networks in the Gulf.* New York: Columbia University Press.

Marschall, C. 2003. *Iran's Persian Gulf Policy: From Khomeini to Khatami.* London: Routledge.

Matthiesen, T. 2010. 'Hizbullah al-Hijaz: A History of the Most Radical Saudi Shi'a Opposition Group'. *Middle East Journal* 64 (2): 179–97.

Moin, B. 2000. *Khomeini: Life of the Ayatollah.* New York: Thomas Dune.

Murray, D. 2010. *US Foreign Policy and Iran: American–Iranian Relations Since the Islamic Revolution.* London: Routledge.

Nasrallah, H. 2006. Speech on 22 September at the Divine Victory Rally in Beirut. Available at: <https://blogs.mediapart.fr/le-cri-des-peuples/blog/240218/hassan-nasrallahs-speech-after-july-2006-war-divine-victory-rally> (last accessed 14 June 2022).

Osiander, A. 2001. 'Sovereignty, International Relations, and the Westphalian Myth'. *International Organization* 55 (2): 251–87.

Osman, T. 2016. *Islamism: What It Means for the Middle East and the World.* New Haven, CT: Yale University Press.

Ostovar, A. 2016. *Vanguard of the Imam: Religion, Politics and Iran's Revolutionary Guards.* Oxford: Oxford University Press.

Ostovar, A. 2018. 'Iran, its Clients, and the Future of the Middle East: The Limits of Religion'. *International Affairs* 94 (6): 1237–55.

Panah, M. 2007. *The Islamic Republic and the World: Global Dimensions of the Iranian Revolution.* London: Pluto Press.

Randjbar-Daemi, S. 2013. 'Building the Islamic State: The Draft Constitution of 1979 Reconsidered'. *Iranian Studies* 46 (4): 641–63.

Roy, O. 1994. *The Failure of Political Islam*, translated by Carol Volk. Cambridge, MA: Harvard University Press.

Rubinstein, A. Z. 1981. 'The Soviet Union and Iran under Khomeini'. *International Affairs* 57 (4): 599–617.

Ruggie, J. G. 1993. 'Territoriality and Beyond: Problematizing Modernity in International Relations'. *International Organization* 47 (1): 139–74.

Sabet, A. G. E. 2013. 'Wilayat al-Faqih and the Meaning of Islamic Government'. In Moghaddam, A. A. (ed.). *A Critical Introduction to Khomeini*. Cambridge: Cambridge University Press.

Sidahmed, A. S. and Ehteshami, A. (eds). 2018. *Islamic Fundamentalism*. London: Routledge.

Wimberly, Jason. 2015. '*Wilayat al-Faqih* in Hizballah's Web of Concepts: A Perspective on Ideology'. *Middle Eastern Studies* 51 (5): 687–710.

Yodfat, A. 2011. *The Soviet Union and Revolutionary Iran*. Abingdon: Routledge.

10

Sealed with a Thumbprint: The Hybrid Politics of a Martyrdom Contract

Arran Robert Walshe

Introduction: A Dispirited *Mujahid* in a Dreary, Peculiar Desert

As Iraq descended deeper into the chaos of sectarian violence and civil strife that defined the post-2003 invasion years, the militant outfit Islamic State of Iraq (ISI)[1] faced a profound human resource challenge. Would-be volunteer suicide bombers, the vast majority of whom were non-Iraqi and were brought into Iraq surreptitiously by the organisation, would suffer a change of heart when confronted with the practical reality of their charge. An ISI strategy document written by an anonymous, but assumed to be leading, militant speaks to the profound isolation and mental fatigue that would accompany the martyr's early days, often leading them to renege on their pledge. Entering Iraq, the strategist writes, the *mujahid* arrives first in al-Anbar from Syria, a 'dreary, peculiar desert', and spends months moving from safe house to safe house, often left idle in camps, cut off from their handlers and other fighters (Unknown Author, 2008a). When the local Emir finally determines the martyr's mission, his morale deteriorates when he learns that the mission is not as spectacular as they might have hoped, perhaps only against a few Iraqi security or coalition outposts. Or, the author of the document notes, the increasingly demoralised fighter hears of a prior brother's unsuccessful operation, where the *mujahid* triggered their explosives too early, or too late, or just as often as not were stopped by security forces before they could carry out the operation. 'Depression', the author writes, 'crawls into his heart [. . .] the brother decides to transfer from suicide bomber to fighter, but his request will be rejected by the Emirs, as it is considered the state's decision' (Unknown Author, 2008a, p. 6). Although the precise process is unclear, it would seem from other documents recovered in US military raids that the dispirited jihadist

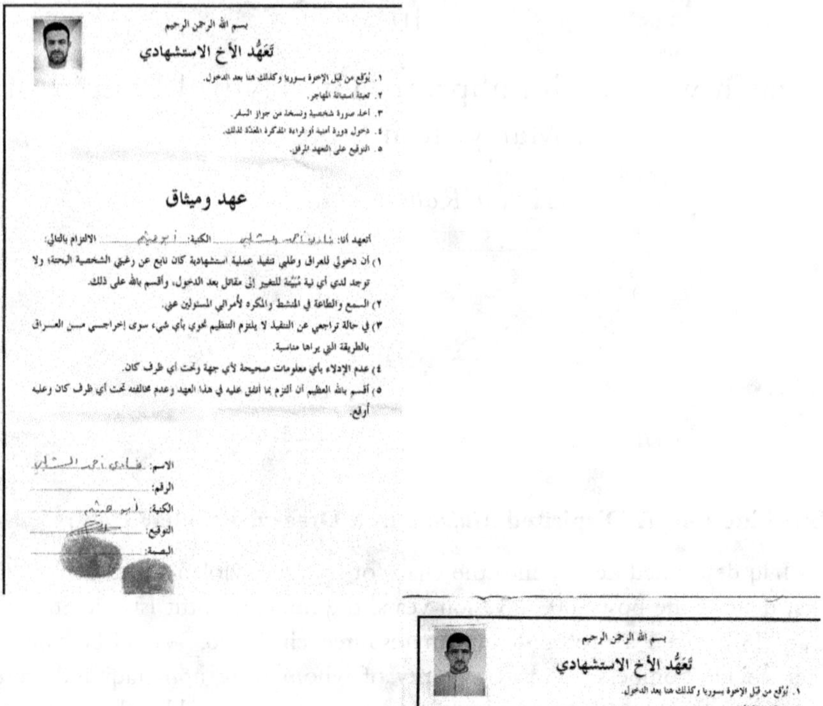

بسم الله الرحمن الرحيم

تَعَهُّد الأخ الاستشهادي

١. يُوَقّع من قبل الإخوة بسوريا وكذلك هنا بعد الدخول.
٢. تعبئة استبانة المهاجر.
٣. أخذ صورة شخصية ونسخة من جواز السفر.
٤. دخول دورة أمنية أو قراءة المذكرة المعدّة لذلك.
٥. التوقيع على التعهد المرفق.

عهد وميثاق

أتعهد أنا: .... الكنية: .... الالتزام بالتالي:

١) أن دخولي للعراق وطلبي تنفيذ عملية استشهادية كان نابع عن رغبتي الشخصية البحتة؛ ولا توجد لدي أي نية مُبَيّتة للتغيير إلى مقاتل بعد الدخول، وأقسم بالله على ذلك.
٢) السمع والطاعة في المنشط والمكره لأمرائي المسئولين عني.
٣) في حالة تراجعي عن التنفيذ لا يلتزم التنظيم نحوي بأي شيء سوى إخراجي من العراق بالطريقة التي يراها مناسبة.
٤) عدم الإدلاء بأي معلومات صحيحة لأي جهة وتحت أي ظرف كان.
٥) أقسم بالله العظيم أن ألتزم بما أتفق عليه في هذا العهد وعدم مخالفته تحت أي ظرف كان وعليه أوقع.

الاسم: ....
الرقم: ....
الكنية: ....
التوقيع: ....
البصمة: ....

بسم الله الرحمن الرحيم

تَعَهُّد الأخ الاستشهادي

١. يُوَقّع من قبل الإخوة بسوريا وكذلك هنا بعد الدخول.
٢. تعبئة استبانة المهاجر.
٣. أخذ صورة شخصية ونسخة من جواز السفر.
٤. دخول دورة أمنية أو قراءة المذكرة المعدّة لذلك.
٥. التوقيع على التعهد المرفق.

عهد وميثاق

أتعهد أنا: .... الكنية: .... الالتزام بالتالي:

١) أن دخولي للعراق وطلبي تنفيذ عملية استشهادية كان نابع عن رغبتي الشخصية البحتة؛ ولا توجد لدي أي نية مُبَيّتة للتغيير إلى مقاتل بعد الدخول، وأقسم بالله على ذلك.
٢) السمع والطاعة في المنشط والمكره لأمرائي المسئولين عني.
٣) في حالة تراجعي عن التنفيذ لا يلتزم التنظيم نحوي بأي شيء سوى إخراجي من العراق بالطريقة التي يراها مناسبة.
٤) عدم الإدلاء بأي معلومات صحيحة لأي جهة وتحت أي ظرف كان.
٥) أقسم بالله العظيم أن ألتزم بما أتفق عليه في هذا العهد وعدم مخالفته تحت أي ظرف كان وعليه أوقع.

الاسم: ....
الرقم: ....
الكنية: ....
التوقيع: ....
البصمة: ....

Figure 10.1 A martyrdom contract. © Harmony Program, Combating Terrorism Center, West Point.

would be forced to return to their home country before being recruited again as a fighter, a time-consuming, costly and inefficient practice.

To combat this change of heart, the Islamic State of Iraq instituted a set of martyrdom contracts whose stipulations were set out in such a way as to mitigate the managerial problems that arose from the organisation's bureaucratisation of jihad and encourage the jihadist to follow through on his violent charge. This chapter takes the figure of the dispirited jihadi, and the contracts and bureaucratic structures that the organisation instituted to manage his frustrated desire for self-destruction, as emblematic of the process that this book has been tracing.

The Islamic State of Iraq, a political–religious utopian movement, produced hybrid forms of contractual authority in a period of intense territorialisation, sedentarisation, bureaucratisation and hierarchisation (Bunzel, 2016; Dodwell et al., 2016; Johnston et al., 2016). What is interesting about the group at this time is that while it rejected, and actively sought to undermine, the sovereignty of the new Iraqi state, its structural, institutional form mirrored that of its enemy. The process of shifting from a deterritorialised jihad to a territorial militancy created basic organisational and managerial problems that the managers, a newly self-declared class of jihadist bureaucrats, struggled to address. The group's internal documents from this time highlight the fraught nature of this process, creating fissures and disconnects between a managerial class whose goal it was to rationalise and bureaucratise the jihad, and fighters whose practical experience of this rationalisation, as described above, was profoundly dehumanising.

This contrast, the epistemic fissure between the incipient bureaucratic logics enacted by the state, and the utopian visions of jihad that these drew these fighters to the Islamic State, produced what Gilles Deleuze specifies as a 'problem', a fundamental concept that forms the very basis of his ontology. Deleuze explains his understanding of problems as 'singularities deployed in a problematic field', defined by its proximity to 'which the solutions are organized' (Deleuze and Boundas, 1990, p. 56). Deleuze's interlocutors have worked to unpack this characteristically opaque definition (Voss, 2013), highlighting how Deleuze's framework skirts a resolution by being what John Brady (2020) glosses as '*progressively determined*'. Put another way, problems may have solutions, but the process, the act of 'becoming', by which the solution is found will create alternate methodologies for approaching the problem, which then will only shift the sands under which the problem was created in the first place. As Ditrych et al. argue in this volume, revolutions such as those carried out within the jihad are a process: 'not something simply *done*', they write, 'but rather dynamically *becoming*'. The case of the disenchanted suicide bomber, and the ambient ambivalence of the organisation's fighters more generally, suggest that this becoming is a highly contingent affair, subject to a continuous process of creative management of, critically, sets of *problems* that the organisation must address.

Deleuze and Guattari's (2013) concept of the 'war machine' (*machine de guerre*) is helpful for exploring these tensions, as the Islamic State's managerial and ideational practices were produced through a constant tension between its dispersed, deterritorialised, rhizomic incarnations and the effects of state-making. The Islamic State of Iraq negotiated the challenges produced by this sedentarisation and bureaucratisation, and by its territorial expansion, by pulling on, borrowing from and syncretising an array of authoritative forms of knowledge and practice as an exigency to manage the essential problem that its fighters' ambivalence made visible. In this sense, the development of the Islamic State was not simply an unpacking of an already stable set of principles, concepts and traditional forms of knowledge and practice, but rather the enactment of what the editors of this volume describe as a 'set of intensities that can be *activated*'. What was activated ranged from contract law to conceptions of noble sacrifice, martyrdom and, as noted above, tools of bureaucratic human resource management.

The ambivalence of the suicide bombers and fighters described in the internal documents of the Islamic State of Iraq, and the contracts produced to manage them, are a result of an epistemic, moral and ethical breakdown (Zignon, 2007) between the *mujahid*'s dream of self-cultivation through militancy and self-destruction, on the one hand, and the seemingly banal institutional and bureaucratic environment that they find themselves in on the other. The practical exigencies of revolutionary jihad produced a need to formalise, hierarchise and bureaucratise the social, economic and political relationships within the jihad, which in turn resulted in profound demoralisation among at least some of the organisation's workforce. This produced what David Scott (2004) proposed as a 'problem-space', which the group then responded to, notably by further formalising these ambiguous, unregulated and amorphous relationships in juridical terms through the contract form. This chapter charts the contingent and hybrid politics that spring from this ambivalence. Whether in popular or scholarly accounts, the politics of the Islamic State, and the jihad more broadly, are often presented as an effect of power, as an appropriation by these actors of a set of structural, if structurally diverse, resources. However, what is often lost in these accounts is the necessary, and critically consequential, role of contingency in the reformation of these structural resources. The case of the dispirited *mujahid* allows us to orient our analysis towards that ambivalence and contingency.

Stipulations and Hierarchies: The Dispirited *Mujahid* as a Free Agent of Labour

Although the pre-eminent militant group fighting in Iraq during this period, retaining that stature demanded careful management of ISI's production of violence as it grew, and careful management of the fighters, managerial staff and suicide bombers that came into its service. As one set of scholars (Johnston et al., 2016, p. xvi) has described, this balancing act was one between attracting talent, motivating employees, maintaining morale and equity, and managing the time of human capital. ISI's internal documents paint a picture of a group obsessed with bookkeeping, a liability in the context of asymmetrical anti-state insurgency, but a necessary one to achieve a level of scale in the organisational economics of ISI's jihad in Iraq. This production of violence necessitated a steady and consistent flow of *mujahidin* to carry out the organisation's managerial goals, and who also managed a complex set of bureaucratic practices which made their insurgency possible on a day-to-day basis. Documents seized in a set of US military raids paint a picture of an organisation concerned not only with jihad, but with founding a state, exerting a form of sovereignty over the territory it came to control, regulating and keeping tabs on its variegated labour force to discourage graft, and standardising the various rights, responsibilities and obligations between the *mujahidin* and the incipient militant state.

Counterterrorism scholars describe ISI at this period in its history as a 'vertically integrated organization with a central management structure and functional bureaus', which they sought to replicate at multiple lower geographical levels across the territories that it was operational in at that time (Johnston et al., 2016, p. 7). From this vantage point, ISI was little different from any other centralised bureaucratic organisation; it self-consciously borrowed from technologies and cultures of human resource and bureaucratic management that are commonplace in global and local capital-intensive economies. Human capital was allocated in this system rationally: salaries and compensation were carefully managed, and 'designed for an environment where labor was plentiful, and the organization needed to recruit loyal members and screen out opportunists' (Johnston et al., 2016, p. xvii). The adoption of these formal administrative structures was in response to basic managerial problems as the organisation grew, and more so when it began to think of itself and act 'like' a state. 'The first issue which our economy suffers from', complains the ISI strategist, 'is because of a lack of centralization' (Unknown Author, 2008a, p. 23) in comparison with other groups, such as the Lebanese *Hizbal-llat* and the Islamic Army in Iraq.[2] Notably, the strategist also complains that not only do these groups enjoy the patronage of political and religious figures, some-

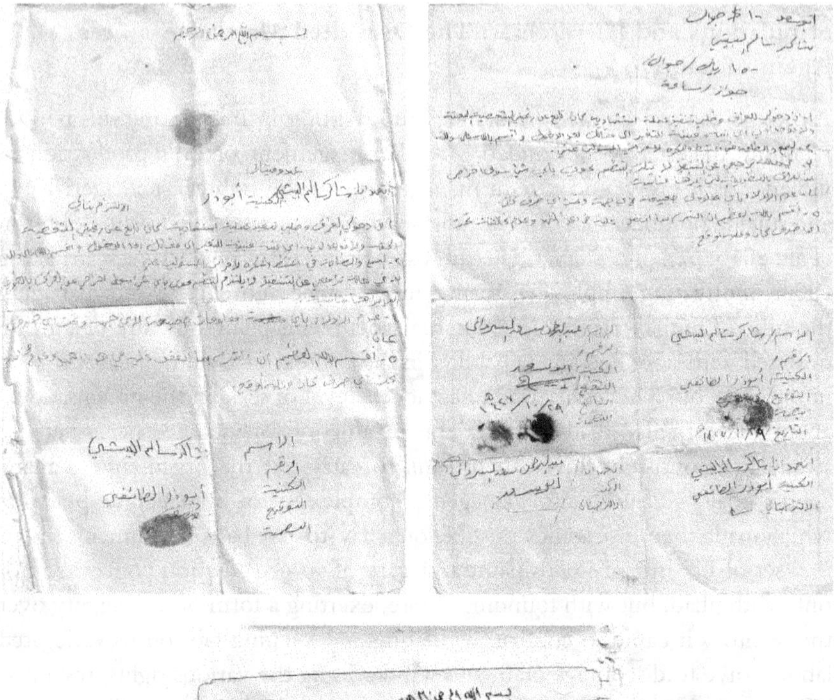

Figure 10.2 A martyrdom contract. © Harmony Program, Combating Terrorism Center, West Point.

thing that the Islamic State of Iraq complained that they lacked, but moreover that they were often given logistical and technical support by the intelligence services of the countries they operated in (Unknown Author, 2008a, p. 23).

The stipulations of the martyrdom contracts produced by the Islamic State rhetorically produce and present the martyr as an agentive labourer, free, within the logics of the contract, to offer up his services to an organisation – in this case, the Islamic State of Iraq – who are conversely duty-bound through the contract to supply the martyr with the means to carry out his operation. Labour functions here as more than an analytical metaphor, but rather as a set of assumptions, logics and rationalities that underwrote the authority that the Islamic State was actively seeking to cultivate. The first stipulation of the martyrdom contract attests that the martyr's

> Entry into Iraq and request to carry out a martyrdom operation emanates (*naba'a*) entirely from my pure own personal desire; and furthermore, I have no premeditated intention of changing over to be a combatant following my entry, upon which I swear to god. (Unknown Author, 2008b)

The martyr-in-waiting, as with a contracted labourer, is expected to carry out his duties, whether they are vocational or not, and if he does not, then the organisation is free to 'fire' him and put him back on to the market. *Mujahidin* would often join other organisations after they found the Islamic State too restrictive and bureaucratic. The strategist tells of the 'painful reality' represented in the story of Abu-Mujhan al-Masri, an Arab national of Italy who, after repeated requests for transfer to a more active *wilayat*, left for Lebanon to join the Fatah al-Islam Group (Unknown Author, 2008a, p. 7). The logic of this primary stipulation rests on an assumption of voluntary exchange, for if a life, a soul or labour is not freely given, the very relationship between the contractor and the broker is made coercive, undermining the logic of a contract that it is self-consciously produced as an act of agentive freedom. It also makes clear that the contractor – in this case, the would-be suicide bomber – is engaging in a marketplace which he has complete agency to partake in or eschew at leisure.

Writing from a normative position, legal scholar Patrick Atiyah (1985, p. 18) argues that, in market conditions, 'all that the law can do is to police the bargaining process, to try and ensure that the contracts are indeed the result of free, voluntary, [. . .] and informed process [. . .] there is simply no basis for saying that a free and voluntary exchange is unfair'. Voluntary, or fair, exchange is ostensibly a cornerstone of contractual authority in the vision of social relationships and a set of rationalities that a normative free market position offers. By borrowing from this vision of market rationality, the contractual stipulations produce the figure of the martyr as agentive not only in the ritual sense of sacrificing himself through martyrdom, but as an individual selling their labour power on an open marketplace of which al-Qaʻida holds the means of production: the suicide vests, logistical knowledge and cars to carry out the operation. As a document, the contract frames an ethics of desire alongside self-destruction, producing and performing market-based notions of contractual authority by fusing desire, agency and an ethic of self-destruction within it.

The pledge's second stipulation sets out that the martyr must 'listen and obey commanders appointed over me in both cases when carrying out actions I am eager to perform or in those done under duress' (Unknown Author, 2008c). Internal correspondence between the Islamic State's managers in this period often complain of foreign fighters acting in problematic and imperious ways. According to one scholar (Fishman, 2009, p. 5), 'many foreign fighters had unrealistic expectations of the Iraqi jihad and a sense of moral superiority relative to their Iraqi counterparts, who tended to be less ideologically moti-vated. The differences created deep tensions with local fighters frustrated by the imperious foreigners.' Internal documents admit to a broad and ongoing struggle within the organisation to manage its human capital, notably grappling with the unreliability of Syrian human smugglers, the unrealistic and romantic expectations of jihad created by the organisation's propaganda, managerial mis-communication, tension between foreign and local fighters, an unclear com-mand structure and poor use of financial resources. These struggles resulted in what one internal analyst (Unknown Author, 2008a) referred to as a mental, or internal, paralysis (*shalal nafsi*) in the *mujahid*.[3] With the organisation claim-ing it would be wasteful, suicide *mujahidin* were not even given basic training, nor trained to use a weapon or other militant skills, as other *mujahidin* would be. They were thus left to solitary contemplation of a fate that had, once enmeshed in ISI's bureaucracy, become fully divorced from their own sense of agency (Gergen, 2008, pp. 58–9).

Although physically sequestered from the ISI body politic, these would-be martyrs existed within an emergent sacrificial economy designed by its manag-ers to balance tasks and practices in such a way as to advance its political goals: that is, to carry out insurgency. As such, this was what normative economists would consider a 'thick' labour market: defined by a high level of labour supply, and demand for that labour from multiple employers (Johnston et al., 2016, p. 51). The commanders here function as a managerial class over the martyr-worker to which he owes his fealty, moving his act outside of the forms of agentive, interior sacrifice that animated much of the critical schol-arship on martyrdom. The martyr, once contracted, is curiously agentive in entering into the contract under market conditions – as noted above, a 'thick' market – but once contracted, he is bound by the responsibilities of his charge so long as he continues in the job. However, just as with any other market condition, the labourer is thought to be free to leave his job if the conditions or 'duress' prove to be intolerable or for any other reason. Documents suggest that over half of the individuals who entered Iraq to fight were designated to carry out a suicide operation (*'amaliyyat al-istishhadiyya*), while the remainder were designated fighters or clerical workers. The documents are unclear about whether these categories represented the preference of the *mujahid*, or were a designation given by officials once they arrived – or, as is most likely, were a mix of both. Over three-quarters of the 390 suicide bombers between August 2006 to August 2007 were brought into the country this way, out of a total 600 *mujahidin* who are listed (Gergen, 2008, pp. 58–9). Insurgents carried out 394 suicide attacks in Iraq within this period, which resulted in over 16,000 casualties, although given the uneven nature of the source material, from these numbers it is possible to imagine that hundreds of would-be martyrs reneged on their pledge over the course of the insurgency.

Just so, the third stipulation of the martyrdom contract binds the signatory thus: 'in the event that I renege on the execution [of the operation], the organization shall have no obligation towards me other than to send me out of Iraq in the manner that we deem appropriate' (Unknown Author, 2008d). The organisation is engaging in due diligence, ensuring that it is not responsible for an individual for whom, by virtue of that individual having broken the contract between them, it refuses responsibility. And, potentially, the cycle may begin again as the labourer seeks yet another organisation to offer his labour up to – which, as noted above, was not an unheard-of happening.

The fourth stipulation figures primarily as a non-disclosure agreement, that the signee 'not divulge any factual information to any entity under any circumstance whatsoever'.

Finally, the fifth stipulation notes that the candidate must 'swear by God Almighty that I shall adhere to that which I have agreed in this covenant and not to violate it under any circumstances whatsoever, to which I hereby sign' (Unknown Author, 2008d). For the contract to be complete, it includes a passport photo. The name is then given, alongside a number specific to the individual, a record of his alias, signature and, finally, an inkblot thumbprint. The inclusion of the thumbprint is a curious biopolitical touch, since the martyr, if he carries out his operation, will have no more thumbprint with which to verify the validity of the document. In the thumbprint the agency of the *mujahid* is performed, certified and displayed, advancing and bolstering the conceptual edifice of the contract's bureaucratic authority.

This relation is not necessarily novel, but is intrinsic to the functioning of labour within which value is exchanged within a market determined by a set of political and material relationships; suicide bombing becomes abstracted, alienated, a means to a greater end rather than an act whose goods are internal to itself. 'External labor', Marx wrote in his 1844 manuscripts, 'labor in which man alienates himself, is a labor of self-sacrifice, of mortification' (Marx and Engels, 1987, p. 74). Capitalist production disguises, through juridical mechanisms such as a contract, relations of domination and servitude, making us appear, writes Allen. W Wood (1972, p. 36), as 'independent owners of commodities [who] exchange their goods as free individuals [. . .] thus giving rise to the illusion that these relations themselves are entirely the result of a voluntary contract between independent persons'. Yet this more classical Marxist approach fails to address precisely what forms of material or symbolic capital are being negotiated in a sacrificial economy in which the body of the labourer is completely obliterated, and what new forms of social relationships might be produced, exploited or alienated in the act.

Magical Potential: the Dispirited *Mujahid* Between Enchantments

Max Weber's (Weber and Eisenstadt, 1968) claim of revolutionary charismatic power declining into the mundane, predictable and bureaucratic forms of sovereign authority has provided the dominant scholarly frame for understanding the interpenetrations of contemporary institutions, power and religion. Conversely, scholars of terrorism and Islamist politics more generally have tended to assume that the rise of Islamic militancy attends to, and is enacted as a rejection of, a broader 'disenchantment' (Maznah, 2020), which is itself taken as a given. The case of al-Qaʻida and the development of the Islamic State give us cause to rethink Weber's rigid break between an enchanted, spiritual past and a more rationalised, juridical modern free of kinds of magic that filled the world with potential (Eneborg, 2014). The Islamic State offered its followers a vision of sovereignty, revolutionary action, forms of Islamic militancy and cultures of sacrifice that integrated with corporate logics and the bureaucratic power of global capital apparatuses. Indeed, the case of the Islamic State, in all its iterations, suggests that, rather than a *re-enchantment*, the project of *disenchantment* was never complete, that the secular rationalities and 'functional differentiation' (Casanova, 1994) that attend to advancing capitalist logics only unevenly mobilised certain rationalities. Thinking of the practices of the Islamic State of Iraq enacting a war machine activates a sensibility towards the ways in which Islamic militancy in this period – not as an effect of global power, or a mere reflection, but through its constitution – provoked shifts and changes within the dominant structure in which it became embedded. This was not done solely through armed resistance, but in and through embedding itself within and in opposition to the formal bureaucratic governance structures.

Unlike the abject figures of bare life that function within a protracted period or state of exception, ISI's would-be martyrs were political actors caught in the reanimation of a specific vision of sovereignty that the Islamic State of Iraq self-consciously sought to construct in this period. This period is one where the jihadist was, in practice, being domesticated by internal and external forces, rationalising the Islamic State's governing and management structures to function on an economy of scale that could resist and withstand US and Iraqi government attacks against it. Just as the Islamic State's later manifestations utilised the dominant sociopolitical infrastructure of the time, the memes and mediatised violence that were so central in its semiotic ideology (Keane, 2007, p. 16), in this earlier period the organisation incorporated the practical managerial ideology of the world it inhabited. Creating state structures was central to ISI's practical management strategy and its politics of legitimacy (Belanger-McMurdo, 2015), not only creating bureaucracies and rational modes of territorial governance, but in fact governing much like latter-day twentieth-century Euro-American liberal-left reformists who sought to advance social justice through the liberational potential of state bureaucracies (Graeber, 2015). Attendant on this bureaucratic vision are the golems of efficiency, rationalisation, hierarchy and a whole set of ideas which, even to jihadists who have set themselves the goal of destroying a global system ostensibly predicated on these rationalities, are so commonplace and naturalised that even they could not help but replicate them in their political and social project.

For Achille Mbembe (2003, p. 16) the figure of the martyr exists within, subverts and retools what he terms a 'relation of enmity', a condition of liberal democracy – potentially of all existing political systems – to find within and without enemies that must be controlled, disciplined and have violence inflicted upon them, and, through the mechanisms of racism, be excluded from the body politic. For Mbembe, concerned as he is with the 'generalized instrumentation of human existence and the material destruction of human bodies and populations' (Mbembe, 2003, p. 14), the martyr – and here he speaks specifically of the suicide martyr – confronts the logic of survival in its biopolitical mode through its own logic of self-destruction. This logic is one of objectification, where the suicide martyr, in choosing to destroy its own body, takes itself out of the traditional categories of sovereignty and becomes animal, with life no longer the object of politics but an abstracted desire for eternity, and in doing so, collapses the future into the present. Yet Mbembe's martyr is a profoundly abstracted figure, its relationship to life and death conceptual, divorced from the bureaucratic conditions which this chapter is sketching. Mbembe seems to be working from the principle that political meaning and its challenge to our understanding of sovereignty stem from its agentive decision, its rejection of the corporeality of sovereign control in a biopolitical apparatus. 'The terrorist project', he writes, 'aims to effect the collapse of a society of rights, whose deepest foundations it objectively threatens' (Mbembe, 2019, p. 33) and is thus a corollary of the state of exception embodied in anti-terrorist mobilisation, state violence and the collapse of systems of rights that are the ostensible justification for the entrenchment of liberal democratic modes of governmentality. Yet the contracted suicide bomber that is produced in the contracts discussed in this chapter strikingly exists in a memetic relationship to 'state' power. The suicide martyr is curiously reversed in its relationship to sovereignty, not existing autonomously, but dialectically with that power.

Utopia, Territory, Sovereignty: the Dispirited *Mujahid* and Breaks in the Code

This complex, shifting and potentially contradictory dialogism is a central component of what Ditrych et al. (in this volume) consider the fundamental *recoding* and *repurposing* of sovereignty by the hybrid revolutionary actor. However, my analysis here privileges certain tones of revolutionary theory that are more muted or only left suggested in what Mohamedou (2017, p. 2) refers to as literature rooted in 'policy-oriented security expertise'. First, that Abu Musab al-Zarqawi's revolutionary utopian dream of the Islamic State of Iraq was an institutional break from the more cautious policy of bin Ladin and other al-Qaʿida is well established in the counterterrorism literature and other genres of academic writing on the Salafi-Jihadist movement. However, what has received less attention is how the explicit aim – indeed, what made it distinctly utopian – was not only the production or performance and enunciation of sovereignty against or oriented dialogically toward established state structures, but the territorialisation of a space of ethical self-cultivation within and through a specific set of logics specific to the globalised jihad. The Islamic State, both in this period and in its later iteration, was not solely a *political* space where the *mujahid* enacted a set of instrumental acts in support, or as a component, of a revolutionary political–religious movement. Rather, this territorialisation was profoundly ethical; the *mujahid* cultivated themselves and underwent a self-conscious process of subjectification towards themselves as a specific type of Muslim subject, and it was the duty of the Islamic State's managers to manage, enact and protect this nascent space of Islamic immanence.

Enacting a utopian vision, particularly in the crucible of a profoundly violent anti-state insurgency, necessitates the development of structures which, I am arguing, produces breaks, disjuncture and rips and tears, and which must be closed, accorded and sutured. The symbolic and material resources that structure this relationship may themselves be pulled from heterogeneous sets of knowledge that, once inserted into the smooth space of the war machine's utopian vision, produce new potentialities, new inconsistencies and new challenges to the smoothness of that *war machine*. The revolutionary process of recoding sovereignty may be in places agentive or purposeful, or at least appear so, but in other environments the creative process of recoding opens cracks and breaks in the syntax of the code, which must, through exigency, be filled with what is at hand. To elaborate on the editors' position, not only is sovereignty a set of historically situation practices, but also it is performed and produced through enactment and creative struggle; hybridisation refers not only to the revolutionaries' structural resources, but to the complex set of responses that the exigencies of militancy, among other factors, demand.

Faisal Devji (2008) argues that contemporary Islamist militancy such as that enacted by al-Qa'ida Islamic State can be referenced only against the broader development of globalist conceptions of humanity as political object. This modern, all-encompassing conception of humanity, which developed in relation to postwar economic, social and political shifts, not least of which was the advent of nuclear weapons, was novel in that it reterritorialised humanity as a subject both everywhere and, conversely, nowhere in particular. It was al-Qa'ida's humanism, their claim to work against, but within the logics of, global human rights discourses – indeed, in many ways to fulfil their promise – which allowed it to reformulate its dispersed, deterritorialised jihad as one of cultural and religious *intimacy* within an incipient territorialised Caliphate (Herzfelt, 2015). The epistemic break that is described in their internal documents is not only an effect of bureaucratisation, but a tension brought on by forms of territorialisation which produced a spatial shift. The Islamic State was not simply an organisation with instrumental aims – that is, the taking of territory, the destruction of a government, the founding of a Caliphate and so on – although it certainly advanced these goals, but it also critically justified and offered itself as a *territory* in and through which one could cultivate a pious self as a *mujahid* through and within the disciplining effects of militancy and sacrifice. Scholars concerned with the spatialisation of piety in Islamic movements have suggested that part of our difficulty in understanding these movements stems from our unwillingness to consider political movements as having, at least in part, non-instrumental aims such as the cultivation of a pious subjectivity (Hirschkind, 2006). This non-instrumental aspect of its political project is critical to making sense of the organisation and the internal tensions, conflicts and struggles that defined its self-making.

As Richards notes in this volume, jihadist militants often drew on spatial tropes from early Islam, notably framing the contemporary geopolitical struggle as one reflecting the Ummayad framing of its own imperial territory as *dar al-islam* (the abode of peace), in contrast to the Byzantine *dar al-harb* (abode of war). This eighth-century concept, originating from theologian and jurist Abu Hanifa, did not refer simply to geographical territory as an abstracted space of political or social relationships, but critically to a space in which Muslims could, or could not, fully enact the material and social practices that made them a Muslim. ISI's semantic de- and reterritorializing across an axis of peace / war not only is an assertion of the legitimacy of carrying out militancy against an enemy, such as the taking of territory, but also carries a doctrinal assertion that one can truly *be* a Muslim *inside* of *dar al-islam* (Albrecht, 2016). The Islamic State's enunciation and manifestation of the war machine's potentialities involve the dual formation of an insurgency on the one hand – which, in the face of state and imperial military power, must remain at least party diffuse and deterritorialised – and on the other its *raison d'être* centred on the *spatialisation* of its Islamic State as an entity within which one is given the opportunity to cultivate oneself as a pious self through militant jihad.

Scholars interrogating forms of Muslim subjectivity that have developed in the last half-century have offered alternative readings of social domination that tend to assume that late-modern, secular and capitalistic forms of knowledge, institutions and practices work in tandem to discipline otherwise unruly or ungovernable forms of social life. However, this characterisation of power elides political movements, subjectivities, and collective projects whose aim, curiously from a liberal sensibility, is to cultivate forms of self-discipline that do not, or seem to not, accord with established and popularly enacted notions of social and political freedom. I argue that this perspective is critical to understanding a group like the Islamic State and Salafi-Jihadism more broadly as a political, social and religious movement in that it opens up an understanding of the group's analeptic utopianism as not simply one where social and political relationships were arbitrarily ideal, or because it was then that Muslims enjoyed military and institutional hegemony, or because of a rigid originalist textualism; rather, I want to suggest that many who engaged in jihad believed the historical Caliphate provided the means for a Muslim truly to enact their vision of Islamic subjectivity (Huq, 2009). And it is this spatiopolitical relationship which, in part, made the whole project of contemporary jihadism so compelling for many.

Conclusion: the Dispirited *Mujahid*'s Rage and Self-pity

Shortly after the 9/11 attacks, Bernard Lewis (2002) suggested that the suicide bomber was fast becoming emblematic of the long, slow decline of Islam, and the Arab world more broadly. It is two decades since he wrote this piece, but perhaps there is truth in his words, only to suggest that the suicide bomber more fittingly stands as a metonym for the condition of an ascendent neo-liberal global order, along which we descend 'a downward spiral of hate and spite, rage and self-pity, poverty and oppression'. In the chapter above I have suggested that the hybridity of the Islamic State of Iraq's practices is a product of conceptual and practical problems that it faced through, and because of, the development and territorialisation of its jihad. Empirical approaches often pose the Islamic State of Iraq as an aberration, or challenge to the contemporary global order, rather than exploring the entanglements and interpenetrations around it, something to which this chapter has sought to offer a corrective. More than providing a window on to the quotidian bureaucracy of a clandes-tine militant operation, the account of the contracted suicide bomber, and his ambivalence in the face of its logics, display the shifting and hybrid forms of authority that underwrite the 'managed savagery' of the Islamic State, and of state forms more broadly.

The critical fault in many security studies and political science approaches to the Islamic State is an assumption of the group's radical alterity, its aberrative status in the otherwise smooth functioning of a global hegemonic system of rational state and substate actors. Conversely, a pernicious cultural relativism running through the models that scholars employ may obscure ways in which these actors live very much in the same 'world' as everyone else, even if they may declare an aim not to. More than offering a limited answer to *why* and *how* the Islamic State draws on market-based managerial and legal practices and authority, I have also suggested, tentatively, that to understand this process it is important to consider that *territorialisation* is often linked to a spatialisation of subjectification – in this case, of jihadist virtue.

These institutional, bureaucratic and cultural accords should not be taken simply as a statement that there is any moral equivalency between an organ-isation like al-Qa'ida, the Islamic State and other corporate entities, whether states or otherwise, but rather I do want to propose a form of intimacy. I am suggesting that this intimacy stems from a set of shared resources, employ-ing shared schemas in a conceptual universe which assumes set terms, pro-cesses and structures, for how the law that governs it can be authorised: for example, in contract. More than accord, the violence of al-Qa'ida and other corporate entities are wrapped in an embrace that inculcates and justifies these violent schemas within and through each other, although darkly, and in complex ways. That a bureaucrat of the Islamic State of Iraq should find the labour contract form the most efficient and comprehensible way to embody the kind of authority that the circumstances demanded, I am suggesting, speaks to this mutuality and towards a recognition that struggle is always process of *becoming*.

Notes

1. Led by Aby Musab al-Zarqawi until his death in 2006, the organisation referred to itself as Jama'at al-Tawhid wal-Jihad until 2004, when it pledged allegiance to Osama bin Ladin's network and rebranded as Tanzim Qaidat al-Jihad fi Bilad al-Rafidayn. After briefly joining with the Mujiahideen Shura Council, an umbrella of militant jihadist organisations in Iraq, the group declared itself in September 2006 the Islamic State of Iraq. Internal documents from the Islamic State of Iraq and al-Shām, later simply the Islamic State, which is the primary object of the issue's focus, demonstrate the institutional continuity between this earlier period and its later manifestations in terms of leadership, organisational structure and, indeed, in practice.
2. The moniker *Hizballat* is often used in place of *Hizballah* by jihadist groups, a sectarian rejection of their spiritual claims to jihad as a Shi'i group, suggesting they are, rather, the party of the pre-Islamic God Lat. The Islamic Army in Iraq, conversely, was an anti-state militant group founded after the invasion and made up largely of ex-Ba'ath party members. al-Qa'ida and the Islamic Army competed for dominance and manpower within the insurgency, eventually spilling over to armed conflict in 2006, around the time these documents were published.
3. The original military translator of the document for the Harmony project rendered this in a somewhat prurient fashion as *mental impotency*.

References

Albrecht, S. 2016. 'Dār al-Islām and Dār al-Harb'. In Fleet, K., Kramer, G., Matring, D., Nawas, J. and Rowson, E. (eds). *Encyclopaedia of Islam*. Boston: Brill.

Atiyah, P. S. 1985. 'Contract and Fair Exchange'. *The University of Toronto Law Journal* 35 (1): 1–24.

Belanger-McMurdo, A. 2015. 'A Fight for Statehood? ISIS and Its Quest for Political Domination'. *E-IR*. Available at: <https://www.e-ir.info/20

15/10/05/a-fight-for-statehood-isis-and-its-quest-for-political-domin ation/> (last accessed 14 June 2022).

Brady, J. C. 2020. 'Deleuze on Problems, Singularities, and Events'. *Epoche Magazine* 34.

Bunzel, C. 2016. 'From Paper State to Caliphate: The Ideology of the Islamic State'. Washington, D.C.: Brookings Institution.

Casanova, J. 1994. *Public Religions in the Modern World*. Chicago: University of Chicago Press.

Deleuze, G. and Boundas, C. V. 1990. *The Logic of Sense*. London: Athlone Press.

Deleuze, G. and Guattari, F. 2013. *A Thousand Plateaus: Capitalism and Schizophrenia*. London: Bloomsbury Academic.

Devji, F. 2008. *The Terrorist in Search of Humanity: Militant Islam and Global Politics*. London: Hurst.

Dodwell, B., Milton, D. and Rassler, D. 2016. 'Then and Now: Comparing the Flow of Foreign Fighters to AQI and the Islamic State'. West Point: Harmony Project / Combatting Terrorism Center.

Eneborg, Y. M. 2014. 'The Quest for "Disenchantment" and the Modernization of Magic'. *Islam and Christian–Muslim Relations* 25: 419–32.

Fishman, B. 2009. 'Dysfunction and Decline: Lessons Learned from Inside al-Qa'ida in Iraq'. West Point: Harmony Project / Combatting Terrorism Center.

Gergen, P. 2008. 'Bombers, Bank Accounts, and Bleedout: al-Qa'ida's Road in and Out of Iraq'. West Point: Harmony Project / Combatting Terrorism Center.

Graeber, D. 2015. *The Utopia of Rules: On Technology, Stupidity, and the Secret Joys of Bureaucracy*. New York: Melville House.

Herzfelt, M. 2015. 'Practical Piety: Intimate Devotions in Urban Space'. *Journal of Religious and Political Practice* 1 (1): 22–38.

Hirschkind, C. 2006. *The Ethical Soundscape: Cassette Sermons and Islamic Counterpublics*. New York: Columbia University Press.

Huq, M. 2009. 'Talking Jihad and Piety: Reformist Exertions among Islamist Women in Bangladesh'. *The Journal of the Royal Anthropological Institute* 15 (1): 163–82.

Johnston, P. B., Shapiro, J. N., Shatz, H. J., Bagney, B., Jung, D. F., Ryan, P. and Wallace, J. 2016. *Foundations of the Islamic State: Management, Money, and Terror in Iraq, 2005–2010*. Santa Monica: RAND Corporation.

Keane, W. 2007. *Christian Moderns: Freedom and Fetish in the Mission Encounter*. Berkeley: University of California Press.

Lewis, B. 2002. 'What Went Wrong?'. *The Atlantic*. Available at: <https://

www.theatlantic.com/magazine/archive/2002/01/what-went-wrong/302 387/> (last accessed 14 June 2022).

Marx, K. and Engels, F. 1987. *Economic and Philosophic Manuscripts of 1844*. Buffalo, NY: Prometheus Books.

Maznah, M. 2020. *The Divine Bureaucracy and Disenchantment of Social Life: A Study of Bureaucratic Islam in Malaysia*. London: Palgrave Macmillan.

Mbembe, A. 2003. 'Necropolitics'. *Public Culture* 15: 11–40.

Mbembe, A. 2019. *Necropolitics*. Durham, NC: Duke University Press.

Mohamedou, M. 2017. *A Theory of ISIS: Political Violence and the Global Order*. London: Pluto Press.

Scott, D. 2004. *Conscripts of Modernity: The Tragedy of Colonial Enlightenment*. Durham, NC: Duke University Press.

Unknown Author. 2008a. 'Analysis of the State of the ISI'. Harmony Database. West Point: Combatting Terrorism Center.

Unknown Author. 2008b. 'Fadi Ahmad al-Shalabi Martyrdom Pledge'. Harmony Database. West Point: Combatting Terrorism Center.

Unknown Author. 2008c. 'Khalaf Ahmad Nawfal al-Rashdan Martyrdom Pledge'. Harmony Database. West Point: Combatting Terrorism Center.

Unknown Author. 2008d. 'ISI Template for Suicide Operation Pledge'. Harmony Database. West Point: Combatting Terrorism Center.

Voss, D. 2013. 'Releuze's Rethinking of the Notion of Sense'. *Deleuze Studies* 7: 1–25.

Weber, M. and Eisenstadt, S. N. 1968. *On Charisma and Institution Building: Selected Papers*. Chicago: University of Chicago Press.

Wood, A. W. 1972. 'The Marxian Critique of Justice'. *Philosophy and Public Affairs* 1: 244–82.

Zignon, J. 2007. 'Moral Breakdown and the Ethical Demand: A Theoretical Framework for an Anthropology of Moralities'. *Anthropological Theory* 7 (2): 131–50.

11

Iran, Proxy Warfare and the Tradition of State Sovereignty

deRaismes Combes

Introduction

On 2 January 2020, the United States launched a drone strike near Iraq's Baghdad airport, killing Iranian General Qasim Suleimani under the pretext of preventing an imminent attack on US troops in the region. As head of the Quds Force, the military wing of Iran's Islamic Revolutionary Guard Corps (IRGC), Suleimani was held in high esteem throughout Iran, a revered figure whom many considered more powerful than the President, Hassan Rouhani. Imagine, for a moment, that Iran sent a drone to assassinate Chairman of the Joint Chiefs of Staff Mark Milley as he arrived in Baghdad to meet with an Iraqi potentate. The United States would have surely considered such an attack an unprovoked act of war, responding in kind. Or, what if a Russian general was about to launch an attack against US allies in Syria, one that would also endanger American lives? Would the US government consider a pre-emptive drone strike? Probably not.

Such thought experiments are compounded by myriad other factors, of course. Still, that the United States openly killed a top government official of a sovereign state on another sovereign state's territory seems shocking. That many American pundits did not question the legitimacy of assassinating a state official and instead focused on the strategic implications of the assassination is equally telling (for example, Ward, 2020; Goldenberg, 2020). What makes Iran more deserving than other state actors of treatment that has been prohibited – at least normatively – between states for decades?

One answer, and certainly one that the Trump administration proffered at the time, was that Suleimani and his Quds Force were terrorists. Since 9/11, the terrorist moniker has come with a host of legal 'permissions' that basically

equate such actors to cancers in need of excision: too irrational, too ideological, too fanatical for the rule of law.[1] In truth, the Islamic Republic of Iran has
carried some form of this mantle – if not in practice, then in perception – since
the 1979 revolution and the subsequent US embassy hostage crisis. At first
glance, many American officials appear to have equated these historical acts to
a sort of abdication of legitimate state-ness. In such a light, Iran's subsequent
interference in the region through proxies is like a malignant tumour seeking
to metastasise across the Levant, destroying the sanctity of other states' territorial wholeness and eroding the very doctrine of sovereignty in the process.
Yet Washington has also often expressed the hope that Tehran might return
to the Westphalian fold. On balance, Iran seems to inhabit a unique discursive
space in the United States, somewhere between (il)legitimate sovereign state
and nefarious transnational (Islamist) malefactor.

Two empirical questions follow from this observation. First, how does a
state position itself as 'sovereign' in the international arena? Second, given
different modes of power projection, how is that same state positioned by
others? For its part, the Islamic Republic considers itself a sovereign entity
as legitimate as any other. How, then, might we understand the disconnect
between Iran's performance of its state-ness and the United States' interpretation and response? More specifically, how does Iran's use of proxies contribute to its image in the West of sovereign-state delinquent? And what role
does that purported delinquency play in contesting or shoring up the existing
world order?

As others do in this volume, I answer by adopting the concept of the
hybrid revolutionary actor to provide a framework for understanding the current global system and its malcontents. I centre this hybridity on poststruc-
turalism's use of the 'exception' to argue that Iran embodies sovereignty at
the very borderline of its theoretical expression. In this liminal space, Iran's
performance of state-ness both disrupts and reinforces the 'traditional' notion
of what it means to be a state.[2] As a result, Iran becomes intrinsic to and constitutive of the very existence and understanding of traditional sovereignty
held in the West. Expressed differently, Iran's assertion of its sovereignty via
extraterritorial proxies concomitantly reinforces the United States' own legitimacy as it polices the 'correct' boundaries of state-ness. Consequently, the goal
of this chapter is to 'illuminate the generative structures of meaning through
which the resistance to the dominant order is made intelligible' (Ditrych et al.,
Introduction to this volume) – made intelligible to the revolutionaries themselves, but just as importantly, to those defending the existing system.

I organise my argument in three sections. First, I explore the connection between sovereignty and the exceptional. While other chapters draw on

Deleuze and Guattari's notion of the war machine, I borrow from Derrida, Lacan and Foucault to highlight the complementary relationship between the two regimes – imperial (existing order) and nomadic (revolutionary reorder). I next detail the push and pull of official US discourse on Iran's place in the world, a discourse that vacillates between outright condemnation and subtle coaxing. Finally, I explore the dynamics of this characterisation, particularly how the theoretical framing of hybridity reveals an ontologically necessary role for the nomadic in defining and delimiting the contemporary international system – but a role that is nonetheless not intrinsic to the state of Iran.

Sovereignty: Schmitt and Poststructuralism

I argue that Iran's current function in the international system is as the marker of sovereignty's undecidability; Iran bolsters Westphalian sovereignty by paradoxically enacting what Westphalian sovereignty is perceived not to be. The paradox of being and not being is best articulated by the German political theorist Carl Schmitt (2006, p. 5), who defines the sovereign as 'he who decides on the exception'. Similar to Hobbes, Schmitt (2006, p. 120) characterises the exception as 'principally unlimited authority, which means the suspension of the entire existing order'. The exception proves the rule. Consequently, the definition of sovereignty is not necessarily Weber's monopoly on legitimate force. Rather, sovereignty is more aptly a 'monopoly to decide' on what is legitimate and what is not (Schmitt, 2006, p. 13). Returning to Hobbes, the power of the Leviathan is absolute only if it exists outside the rules.

Schmitt's conceptualisation of sovereignty as inherently exceptional fits with a poststructuralist reading, particularly in the vein of Derrida and Foucault, wherein order is made possible and meaningful only by its rupture, a moment of heterogeneity and violence. The exception is therefore the 'constitutive principle' of sovereignty as a means of order and a norm of international organisation (Prozorov, 2016, p. 82). Andrew Norris (2000) writes: 'If sovereignty decides upon its own limits, its decision cannot be bound by those limits. The sovereign is the unlimited power that makes limits, or in other words, the ungrounded ground of the law.' The 'ungrounded-ness' is at once constitutive yet heterogeneous: within and without. The exception, as Derrida notes, is already built into the very notion of sovereignty, like a secret back door. Or, as Sergei Prozorov (2016, p. 18) writes, sovereignty 'is permanently contaminated by the exception'. This 'other within'-ness of the exception is both the condition of possibility of sovereignty (Westphalian or otherwise) and at the same time, in the Derridean sense, the 'condition of *impossibility* of its completeness or closure' (Prozorov, 2016, p. 85; Derrida, 1998, p. 144).

How does this relate to Iran? Broadly speaking, Iran positions itself as 'sovereign' in the international arena and gets positioned by others in that arena as the embodiment of Schmitt's exception, which in this case centres on Iran's 'rupture' of the (perceived) foundational norm of sovereignty by meddling in other states' affairs via proxy. In Derridean terms, Iran performs sovereignty by choosing to selectively ignore it. Still, by contesting or disrupting its meaning, Iran also generates or reinforces that very meaning. It does so in at least two respects: the first simply because the Iranian government conceives of itself as legitimately sovereign; and the second because the international community's censure reinforces that there is a 'right' way to do sovereignty, *but this is not it*. Regarding the latter, Iran's choice of action is not made in a vacuum but on a world stage of other actors also performing their own versions of sovereignty. And although sovereign states are by (traditional) definition equal, some are more 'equal' than others. Some performances are perceived as more legitimate; Power differentials matter.

Here, I turn to Foucault's interest in how power disciplines particular populations, not just by being imposed, but across the breadth of instruments of social control otherwise perceived as benign. Foucault argued that those instruments produce a particular form of knowledge about what appropriate behaviour looks like, a process he called governmentality (Foucault, 1991, pp. 102–3). Drawing on this line of thinking, Tanja Aalberts (2012) offers insight into how sovereignty is performed and regulated on the international stage. She concentrates on how states collectively bound what is appropriate or responsible sovereign behaviour not only through juridical (top-down) power, but through the productive disciplinary power associated with governmentality.[3]

In the latter's calculus, sovereignty stems from the ability of an institution to successfully limit collective understanding of the imaginable, the knowable, the possible. Aalberts (2012, p. 137) asserts that the Westphalian notion of statehood is a governmental project of spatially and strategically organising or structuring the international environment to produce a certain order and understanding of statehood. As such, sovereignty and state-ness are co-constituted and contingent on one another. Crucial to that process, 'the very principle of sovereign equality paradoxically becomes the ground for making distinctions between sovereigns' (Aalberts, 2012, p. 127). That is to say, most states mirror one another by following certain behaviours, projecting power within a similar standard of practice (Derrida's homogeneity). But a few states do not. The former are comparatively 'good' stewards of the global world order, acting 'appropriately', *because* the later scofflaws of the system are not. Once again, the exception defines the rule.

International protocols, tacit rules, international law and international organisational procedures continually police a set of standards for what the norm of sovereignty is or should be (Dillon, 1995, p. 341; Weber, 1946). Those states unwilling to abide by the norm are securitised – especially after 9/11 – as dangerous to the wellbeing of the system itself. Aalberts (2012, p. 153) continues, 'these states are identified as irresponsible precisely because they are constituted and governed by the (social) laws of international society, because they wear the "legal persona of sovereignty"' but do not act accordingly. Interventions against such rogue states are therefore legitimised by the necessity to bring them back into the fold. Namely, a state can be (acceptably and responsibly) sovereign only in a certain way, even if a literal definition of sovereignty implies that states as Leviathans can behave as they want.

In line with Aalberts, I argue that Iran's use of proxies outside its territorial borders is a specific performance of sovereignty that both reifies the norms ascribed to the word (having absolute power within a recognised space and respecting others' absolute power in their recognised spaces) and rebels against those self-same norms as a form of productive power. Iran (re)affirms its sovereignty by generating the ire of other state actors (in this case, the United States) for not enacting sovereignty in the 'right' way. At the same time, breaching 'sovereignty etiquette' also produces a particular subjectivity that gives Iran licence to rebel against the norm. As such, using proxies as a form of productive power might be construed as a means of changing the boundaries of acceptable sovereign behaviour altogether – in other words, being revolutionary.

The United States and Iran's Proxy Warriors

Three major challenges beset revolutionary Iran from the outset and ultimately helped shape the Islamic Republic's broader outlook on the world and its place in it (for a detailed analysis of this time period, see Koláček in this volume). First, governance in the fledgling regime was a fluid affair in the months following the Shah's departure, as the country flirted with economic collapse (Abram, 2011, pp. 107–12; Axworthy, 2008, pp. 261–5). *Āyatollāh* Rohullah Khomeini responded to the growing lawlessness by establishing the Islamic Revolutionary Guard Corps in May 1979 to consolidate his power and preserve the Islamic spirit of the state.[4] Second, during this fragile period, Iranian students stormed the US embassy in Tehran on 4 November 1979, taking American diplomats captive and prompting a US-led arms embargo. Third, deciding to capitalise on Iran's fragility, Iraq launched an air and ground assault on 22 September 1980 to reclaim the contested waterway of Shatt al-Arab.

The Iranian military (Artesh) was incapable of repelling Iraq's superior military forces, and the IRGC quickly found itself on the front lines, engaging in guerrilla warfare. Adding insult to injury, almost all the Middle East sided with Saddam Hussein.[5]

The IRGC's and the *Āyatollāh*'s take-away from the crucible of these events was a particularly pessimistic, zero-sum view of the international system (Akbarzadeh, 2019, p. 324; Wehrey et al., 2009, pp. 49–55). Iran was on its own; self-preservation had to be won largely outside the bounds of 'normal' geopolitics. In short, Iran's ideology of seeing itself as the bannerman of the Islamic oppressed, coupled with the logistical constraints of the arms embargo, left Iran turning to alternative means of power projection.[6] The IRGC relied on what it was good at: asymmetrical warfare, which meant creating substate allies and leverage in the hostile backyard of the Middle East.

Great powers, including the United States, have long utilised such groups abroad for political ends in lieu of paying the costs of direct confrontation. Why, then, is Iran's use of proxies so vilified? The standard line on Iran in the West is that it 'breaks the rules' by exporting its particular brand of Shi'i extremism across the region as a means of gaining influence and power (for instance, Kia, 2017; Tabatabai and Clarke, 2019). At the farthest end of the spectrum of American fearmongering, Iran seeks to take over the region entirely (for example, Muñoz, 2017; Trofimov, 2016; Benjamin and Simon, 2019). One explanation for these perceptions (official or otherwise) centres on the rhetorical coupling of Iran to 'terrorism', beginning with the 1979 US embassy hostage crisis. Played out nightly on the evening news, the hostage crisis calcified public enmity towards the nascent Islamic Republic (Feuerherd, 2017).[7] Indeed, President Carter began his 1980 State of the Union address by acknowledging the hostages as 'innocent victims of terrorism and anarchy', whose shocking and violent capture and ongoing imprisonment 'violate[d] the moral and the legal standards of a civilized world'. Nonetheless, officials in Washington tempered their condemnation with back-channel efforts to engage with the *Āyatollāh* (Fattahi, 2016). This push and pull between delegitimisation (for example, not 'civilised') and diplomacy has characterised the US–Iranian relationship ever since, particularly regarding Tehran's extraterritorial activities.

Although Khomeini envisioned the Republic as a bastion for all Muslim oppressed, Iran's efforts to win support abroad have resonated most strongly with other followers of Twelver Shi'ism (Ostovar, 2018, p. 1238). Iran's first such relationship began shortly after Israel invaded Lebanon on 6 June 1982, when the *Āyatollāh* saw an opportunity to create common cause with the beleaguered Lebanese Shi'a. Members of the Quds Force set up camp in the

Bekaa Valley outside Beirut to train Lebanese fighters, ultimately establishing a new militant organisation known as Hizbullah.[8] Hizbullah adopted the same Islamist jurisprudence as Iran, pledged allegiance to the *Āyatollāh*, and took up the role of revolutionary warrior defending the underdog and combatting social injustice anywhere (Chehabi, 2006, p. 227).

The shared religious affinity between Iran and its proxies has often informed adversaries' claims that Tehran is a revisionist power attempting to take control of a broad swath of the Levant known as the Shi'i Crescent (for example, Trofimov, 2016). Hizbullah plays an outsized role in these perceptions of Iran as an expansionist power abrogating international norms. Through force and / or political machinations, Hizbullah has served Iran as a powerful obstacle to Israel and the United States and is openly cited by Iranian officials as 'a significant pillar of . . . Iran's military doctrine of deterrence' (Akbarzadeh, 2019, p. 325; Juneau, 2016, p. 649). Tehran sees Hizbullah as a necessary projection of power to ensure the Republic's vital interests in the region. In other words, for them it is a legitimate component of Iranian statecraft. However, the tactics employed by the Lebanese proxy, prime among them hostage-taking, immediately delegitimised it and Iran in the eyes of the West.

The first incident took place in July 1982 when David Dodge, the acting president of the American University of Beirut, was taken hostage in response to the Israeli kidnapping of four Iranian embassy officials. As the Lebanese Civil War drew on, Hizbullah abducted a total of twenty-four additional Americans and a host of foreign nationals (Ranstorp, 1997, p. 108; Kepel, 2021, pp. 116–17). President Reagan quickly tied the kidnappings to the Islamic Republic and vowed to uphold his predecessor's arms embargo against a state that supported terrorism.[9] He also pressed American allies and others not to sell weapons to Iran. However, like Carter before him, the President struggled between condemning and isolating Iran from the global community, and the political and moral imperative to rescue American citizens (Hijazi, 1991, p. 18).[10] Indeed, Reagan found himself mired in scandal when it was revealed that his administration had attempted to address the ongoing hostage crisis in Lebanon by selling weapons to Iran in what came to be known as the Iran-Contra Affair.[11]

The Reagan administration initially justified its actions to Congress and the American public by claiming that they were making overtures to the Iranian moderates (headed by parliamentarian Akbar Hashemi Rafsanjani), who had indicated that they could persuade Hizbullah to release their captives (Butterfield, 1988, sec. 7, p. 10; New York Times, 1987, p. 12; Reagan, 1990, p. 506; Kornbluh and Byrne, 1993, p. 215; Tower et al., 1987, p. B-100). In an address to the nation on 13 November 1986, Reagan admitted to a secret diplomatic initiative to Iran, in part 'to eliminate state-sponsored terrorism and subversion'. He continued, 'At the heart of our quarrel has been Iran's past sponsorship of international terrorism . . . We made clear that Iran must oppose all forms of international terrorism as a condition of progress in our relationship.' The first step towards renouncing its past transgressions, Reagan said, was for Iran to compel Hizbullah to free the hostages. He concluded, 'The Iranian revolution is a fact of history, but between American and Iranian basic national interests there need be no permanent conflict.' Statements like these reflect a tacit acknowledgement of Iranian sovereignty and an effort to bring the republic into the international 'fold' (of proper state actors who do not sponsor proxy militias). However, Reagan's attempt to balance his condemnation of terrorism and those who sponsor it with acknowledgement of Iran's geostrategic position and potential did not go over well domestically (Saad, 2016). The resulting political scandal in many ways reflected the depth of antipathy felt by the American public towards Iran, eclipsing the potential utility of state-to-state diplomacy (Meislin, 1987, sec. 1, p. 1).

Being marked a 'state sponsor of terrorism' left the Islamic Republic in a tenuous position vis-à-vis the United States for the remainder of the twentieth century.[12] But the tone of the terrorist sobriquet changed in intensity and meaning after 9/11. The George W. Bush administration's Manichean division of the world into 'with us' or 'with the terrorists' left little discursive room for Iran to play both sides. With the reformist Mohammed Khatami in power, Iran briefly considered some form of reconciliation with the United States (Axworthy, 2013, pp. 359–61; Kessler, 2007; Parsi, 2007). In this spirit, Tehran initially aided the Bush administration with intelligence and other assets in their efforts to capture or kill al-Qaʻida operatives in neighbouring Afghanistan. However, that partnership ended abruptly when, five months after the attacks, Bush famously branded the country part of the 'Axis of Evil' in his 2002 State of the Union address (along with Iraq and North Korea).[13]

Still, after the United States invaded Iraq and toppled Hussein, Washington took steps to reassure Tehran that they had no plans for further regime change (Weisman, 2003). Under Khatami's influence, Iran kept a low profile and supported its longtime Iraqi proxy, the Supreme Council for Islamic Revolution in Iraq (SCIRI), and its military wing, the Badr Brigade, as it participated in the US-led democratising process next door (Pollack, 2004, pp. 343–55).[14]

The situation changed when Mahmud Ahmadinejad won the presidential election in 2005, representing the opposite end of the political spectrum. Ahmadinejad's provocative rhetoric, Holocaust denial and nuclear weapons posturing reconfirmed for Washington that Iran was a bad apple and could not be trusted to play by the rules (Pollack, 2004, pp. 373–4). The republic's litany of transgressions reappeared with more frequency in US discourse: Iran did not recognise the sovereignty of other states; Iran flouted international laws and conventions; Iran was bent on destroying Israel and harming the United States, maybe with nuclear weapons; and Iran believed any form of engagement with the 'imperialist' West was tantamount to capitulation (Priest, 2006; Lieberman, 2006). In his speech to the United Nations General Assembly on 19 September 2006, Bush upbraided the regime once again, linking Tehran and its proxies with the perpetrators of 9/11 as 'enemies of humanity'. Carrying over his distinction between extremists and 'the community of nations [defending] civilization', he extended an olive branch to the Iranian people and their 'many contributions to civilization', which their leaders squander by 'fund[ing] terrorism and fuel[ing] extremism'.

Ahmadinejad's election coincided with an exponential rise in sectarian violence in Iraq, as the country flirted with civil war. Even as Tehran was overtly encouraging SCIRI to work with the United States, the Quds Force began covertly arming, training and funding various other Shi'i militias, including Muqtada al-Sadr's Mahdi army (Eisenstadt et al., 2011, pp. ix–x, 8–11). Iran's strategy, Janus in nature, was 'to provide its political allies with the means to undermine or eliminate political rivals, and to bring about a humiliating and chastening defeat for the United States that would deter future U.S. military interventions in the region' (Eisenstadt et al., 2011, p. 8). Known collectively by the US-led coalition as 'special groups', Iran's proxies are estimated to be responsible for up to half of all attacks on coalition forces during the occupation (Kagan, 2006–7; Horton, 2020). In his address to the nation announcing the Iraqi surge on 10 January 2007, Bush castigated Iran for supporting Shi'i 'death squads' and 'providing material support for attacks on American troops'. His administration also made moves to classify the IRGC a 'specially designated global terrorist' (Wright, 2007), as American public opinion soured further amidst a rising US death toll in Iraq (Washington Post, 2007). Indeed, Bush voiced increasing concern over Iran at the end of his presidency, referring to the nation as a 'tyrannical regime' (24 July 2008) that represented one of the most pressing threats to regional security as 'the world's leading state sponsor of terror' (11 January 2008).

Pledging to reset relations in the broader Middle East, the Obama administration ultimately took a more conciliatory approach to Iran, culminating in the 2015 Joint Comprehensive Plan of Action (JCPOA). However, violence and instability continued in Iraq, erupted in Syria, threw Lebanon into bouts of chaos, and ended with the rise of ISIS.[15] Iranian proxies had a hand in all of it.[16] At a speech announcing the nuclear deal on 5 August 2015, Barack Obama praised diplomacy as the answer to the immediate threat of a nuclear Iran while still cautioning that the JCPOA did not resolve all the problems between the two states. He continued,

> We have no illusions about the Iranian government, or the significance of the Revolutionary Guard and the Quds Force. Iran supports terrorist organizations like Hezbollah. It supports proxy groups that threaten our interests and the interests of our allies – including proxy groups who killed our troops in Iraq.

However, he reasoned, since Tehran had thus far never successfully been compelled to cut off support for its proxies, he was not willing to hold out for a tougher deal when the stakes were so high (Obama, 2016). Obama's rhetoric is yet another example where political expediency moderated total vilification. Still, his efforts faced stringent opposition domestically from both political parties. By September, 49% of Americans disapproved of the deal.[17] House Speaker John Boehner warned that the JCPOA would 'embolden Iran – the world's largest sponsor of terror – by helping stabilize and legitimize its regime as it spreads even more violence and instability in the region' (Torres, 2015).

The election of Donald J. Trump brought about another sea change in US foreign policy. Trump withdrew from the nuclear deal in May 2018 and followed through on designating the IRGC a terrorist organisation. According to the President, Iran did not deserve any carrots like the JCPOA because of its meddling and arms smuggling across the region. He asserted,

> The Iranian regime is the leading state sponsor of terror. It exports dangerous missiles, fuels conflicts across the Middle East, and supports terrorist proxies and militias such as Hezbollah, Hamas, the Taliban and Al Qaeda. Over the years, Iran and its proxies have bombed American embassies and military installations, murdered hundreds of American service members, and kidnapped, imprisoned, and tortured American citizens. The Iranian regime has funded its long reign of chaos and terror by plundering the wealth of its own people . . . the deal does nothing to constrain Iran's destabilizing activities, including its support for terrorism.

Secretary of State Mike Pompeo defended the pull-out in a speech to the Heritage Foundation on 21 May 2018, also concentrating on Iran's use of terrorist proxy groups that 'jeopardize[d] Iraq's sovereignty' and that of other states, murdered innocent civilians and even threatened Europe: 'Iran has . . . displaced more than six million Syrians and caused over five million to seek refuge outside of its borders. These refugees include foreign fighters who have crossed into Europe and threaten terrorist attacks in those countries.' Finally, amid heightened tensions at the end of 2019, Trump gave the order to assassinate Suleimani, justifying his decision to kill the 'number-one terrorist' in the world because 'Suleimani made the death of innocent people his sick passion' (Trump, 2020). 'He was a monster' (BBC, 2020).

As the above interventions indicate, Iran's use of proxies over the last four decades has, according to the United States, run roughshod over its neighbours' territorial and political independence. Some in Washington and elsewhere argue that such meddling is really a more nefarious intimation of Iran's desire for regional hegemony, a claim that helped earn the country its axis-of-evil membership. Regardless, by ignoring other states' sovereign rights as a 'state sponsor of terror', Iran seems to rebel against the normative world order, a delinquency that, for many US experts and officials alike, positions the Islamic Republic outside the bounds of legitimate state-ness. That is, Iran's misconduct gives other states permission to treat it exceptionally, as a security threat not just to specific states but to the very concept and practice of contemporary international affairs. At the same time, an ambiguity remains, as suggested by the epithet itself. On the one hand, '*state* sponsor' connotes a certain degree of legitimacy as a sovereign political actor. On the other hand, 'sponsor of *terrorism*', particularly after 9/11, negates that authority, relegating the republic to a dangerous pariah in need of disciplining. In the next section, I deconstruct this logic and illustrate how 'Iran as pariah' paradoxically sustains the very system it purportedly calls into question.

Hybrid Sovereignty?

With reference to the broader argument of the book, contemporary Iran *enacts* its version of state-ness as an attempted (revolutionary) break from existing patterns of governance even as it (perhaps inadvertently) adopts and recodes some of those very patterns.[18] At the same time, the United States has responded to such attempts with diplomatic overtures meant to discipline Tehran back towards the 'righteous path' of Westphalian political practice, as well as with castigating rhetoric connotatively stripping Tehran of its legitimacy. Ditrych et al. describe this parallel subjectivity construction process as an 'entanglement with the international order' that invariably affects *both* the 'dominant sociopolitical order and its discontents' (Ditrych et al., this volume). Drawing on Deleuze and Guattari's concept of the *war machine*, they characterise this entanglement between the nomadic – or smooth – spaces of revolution and the imperial – or striated – spaces of Westphalian sovereignty as constitutively hybrid in nature.

I approach the political concept of hybridity from the field of postcolonial studies, beginning with the work of literary critic Homi Bhabha. The term 'hybrid' connotes mixture, the product of mixing disparate parts together. However, Bhabha cautions: 'hybridity is never simply a question of the admixture of pre-given identities or essences'; it is not the syncretising of two to make one. Rather, as Aletta Norval explains, 'Hybridity is that which allows for the contestation of the coincidence of colonial discourse with itself, that which subverts the discourse's presumed unitary nature and thus questions its assumed authority' (Norval, 1999, p. 104). That is to say, the colonial encounter mutates the identities of both the coloniser and the colonised, but it also presents the colonised with a mode of intervention and resistance against the very same colonizers' 'consensual sense of cultural community' (that is, 'all Algerians are now French') (Norval 1999, p. 105). This leads Bhabha to insist that 'cultural and political identity are constructed through a process of alterity' (1994, p. 251), a notion that resonates with Schmitt's and Derrida's concept of the exception.

While alterity is implicit in the war machine's 'power of protean metamorphosis' (Ditrych et al., this volume), I underscore alterity's ongoing and underlying existential and political need to differentiate nomad from imperialist – 'Self' from 'not Self' – even as that differentiation nonetheless results in hybridisation. Applied here, Iran's enactment of state-ness is a political practice of establishing the state's 'truth' of the world and its place in it vis-à-vis others (Walker, 1993; Adler and Pouliot, 2011). That worldview facilitates Iran's performance of sovereignty through exception, which translates into being both Self and not Self. Hybrid. A space between. Viewed from the other side, the push and pull between the United States' disciplining attempts and denunciation are both practices meant to reassert 'correct' participation in the extant liberal world order. The former seeks to cajole Iran into membership, while the latter in many ways dismisses the very premise of Iranian sovereignty as forfeit. In both cases, Iran's positioning as hybrid revolutionary actor reconfirms for Washington the moral and political validity of the existing Westphalian system.

Bhabha (1994, p. 2) writes that 'the intersubjective and collective experiences of *nationness*, community interest, or cultural value' are negotiated in 'the overlap and displacement of domains of difference'. From the interstices of difference, from that point of hybridity, actors assert 'the 'right' to signify from the periphery of authorized power and privilege', instead of from its centre. Gokhan Bacik has explored the concept in relation to the Arab world. To Bacik (2008, p. 33), hybrid sovereignty is neither fully Western nor fully traditional, but a product of the two, inhabiting an 'in-between space in no-man's land'. For him, that production is born of the violence of identity *de*struction, which takes place when the West imposes different values, rules and norms on others. The result is not totally belonging to the one, and no longer being allowed to belong fully to the other (Norval, 1999, pp. 104–5). In this case, Iran is not fully sovereign in the conventional sense but is no longer free to enact statehood as its rulers deem fit.

While Bhabha concerned himself almost exclusively with the marginalised identities of the postcolonial world, Norval divorces alterity from a singular connection to postcolonialism. The hybrid space is then one of *potential* intervention, *potential* political contestation, across some sort of difference that is nonetheless indeterminate, 'undecidable' in the Derridean sense, prior to articulation (Norval, 1999, p. 110). Extrapolating from this, Norval posits that hybridity should be thought of 'as an experience of thinking the in-between, the borderline itself. Rather than a celebration of impurity, hybridity would imply a difficult, never-ending negotiation between purity and impurity' (Norval, 1999, p. 111).

Iran's exceptional enacting of sovereignty by employing proxies can be construed as exactly this negotiation process, the right to legitimacy from the periphery. Periphery here goes beyond Bhabha's focus on the geographical Global South and returns to the idea that the exception, which is necessary for sovereignty to be understood as it is, nonetheless is located at the margins. Part of Iran's attempt at radical restructuring acknowledges a kin community beyond national boundaries, which thereby permits the state to aid and engage with these extraterritorial bodies, even as such engagement flies in the face of the norm of 'traditional' state sovereignty. Using proxies, Iran operates (or intervenes, to follow Bhabha and Norval) in the interstices between belonging and not-belonging. As such, while the 1979 revolution ostensibly sought to radically reorder a particular national and regional landscape away from the Western concept of the political, it has resulted in a continuous practice of revolutionary hybridity that nonetheless adopts and interacts with certain scripts from that pre-existing political order (best encapsulated in the epithet '*state* sponsor of *terror*'). Deterritorialisation is therefore both a facet of Iran's hybrid subjectivity, but also perversely an acknowledgement of the existing Westphalian system.

For instance, the relationship Iran has with Hizbullah allows Tehran to be an integral (though ostensibly invisible or deniable) player in the domestic and foreign policies of Lebanon (Juneau, 2016, pp. 649–50). While the United States and its allies constantly decry Iran's perfidy and illegitimacy whenever Hizbullah does something the international community does not like, opposition to Tehran within the confessional country has been successfully muted

194 DERAISMES COMBES

over the years by redirecting dissent instead into a shared antipathy towards Western and Israeli meddling. Hizbullah draws on its social activism and militancy to present itself through the pall of nationalism. In this light, they are a needed layer of defence to preserve Lebanon's territorial integrity, especially given Israel's frequent border predations, made manifest in 2006 when Hizbullah successfully repelled the Israeli Defense Force's (IDF's) invasion of southern Lebanon. Lebanese support for Hizbullah ebbs and flows, but Iran-as-hybrid has been able to project power successfully beyond its borders using proxies, despite vacillating proxy nation support and despite pressure from the United States and its allies. As Obama noted on 5 August 2015 when justifying the nuclear deal,

> Iran has been engaged in these activities for decades. They engaged in them before sanctions and while sanctions were in place. In fact, Iran even engaged in these activities in the middle of the Iran–Iraq War – a war that cost them nearly a million lives and hundreds of billions of dollars. The truth is that Iran has always found a way to fund these efforts.

Like *war machine*, the postcolonial lens for understanding hybridity also focuses on the tension between convention and revolution. Yet in some ways, this lens is more subtle. It explores how that tension manifests across time and geographical space, what Deleuze and Guattari refer to as the war machine's assemblage, but it is less interested in where the tension ultimately leads than the role of the tension in the interim.

Conclusion

The theoretical implications of my analysis bear directly on the mutability of the Westphalian system. As illustrated above, the sovereign state system is not a fixed reality of the global world order. The deconstruction of sovereignty as a perpetual performance marked by the exception means that a non-conforming actor must be present perversely to reinforce others' conventional enactments. The notion of hybridity further clarifies the role of the non-conformer as neither fully belonging nor fully not belonging. As such, the hybrid actor remains within the bounds of sovereignty but abuts the edges of its meaning through that actor's exceptional practices. Two inferences follow.

First, the hybrid space marking the margins of common understanding also introduces a direct normative and ontological challenge. Here, Iran's behaviour forces policy-makers and scholars alike to confront the disciplining nature of the liminal structure of Westphalian sovereignty and how or why so many are interested in preserving it. Seen in this light, Iran's disruption or 'bad' behaviour is a potential mode of productive power[19] that offers an ontologically meaningful opportunity to change the system itself, or to change the ingrained belief in the necessity of a particular system. That rupture may, over time, shift what is considered common.

The second inference follows from the first. Derrida's notion of the surplus of language suggests that complete homogeneity of meaning or practice is impossible, but the remaining exception does not have any specific or endogenous characteristic. It does not need to be always defined by the same thing, which, in this case, has been Iran's use of proxy forces. Consequently, shifts in the 'proper' meaning of sovereignty are not rooted in some putative 'truth' or essence of state-ness, but rather in the negotiation between the discourses and practices of the actors themselves. Contemporary definitions of the state system – Westphalian or otherwise – cannot spotlight 'appropriate' state-ness, whatever that may mean, without a foil to illustrate 'inappropriate' state-ness. Therefore, even if Iran were to act appropriately, whether by changing its own practices or as a result of a change in perception over what is appropriate in the first place, another actor would inevitably be assigned or take up the revolutionary mantle.[20]

Iran plays a particular and necessary part in today's world order that sustains the sense of that order as it rebels against it. By using proxies to project power in the Middle East, the Islamic Republic has eschewed the supposedly foundational edict of non-interference in the internal affairs of others. In so doing, Iran has shined a spotlight on what contemporary sovereignty means, disrupting common assumptions and provoking a backlash from the United States, which then attempts to reaffirm the propriety of the original meaning (even as it uses its own proxies or interferes abroad itself). On the surface, the imbalance of power between the two suggests that the traditional conceptualisation of sovereignty will retain dominance. However, as American overtures to the Islamic Republic over the years indicate, the fact that Iran still uses 'terrorist' proxies while also engaging in international statecraft implies that the tolerated practice of Iranian sovereignty has, indeed, subtly shifted away from the mythical Westphalian mould, despite lip service to the contrary.

In effect, the very notion of sovereignty has the potential to migrate towards a new understanding that is neither Westphalian nor Iranian, but some form of shared space. This, indeed, is what Deleuze and Guattari's *war machine* is meant to illustrate. However, even here, even in this 'neutral' territory, there will be a new periphery, inhabited by a new revolutionary. While the resulting exception is ineluctable, Iran's casting is not.

Notes

1. The Obama administration, for instance, used such arguments to justify the extraterritorial killing of American cleric Anwar al-Awlaki without due process in 2011.
2. The conventional understanding of sovereignty has calcified around three premises: states have the right to govern themselves without outside interference; states are presumably equal political units; and no higher authority exists to constrain them (for example, Gilpin, 1981, p. 17; Krasner, 1999, p. 88). This invocation has not been without its own paradoxes (for example, Lyons and Mastanduno, 1995; Glanville, 2013, p. 79).
3. Foucault defines governmentality in contradistinction to the hierarchical power of a Leviathan to be a lateral process of social control fostered through disciplinary institutions and particular ways of knowing. The power of governmentality is therefore its ability to direct actors to govern themselves.
4. The IRGC was designed to be an independent militia. They refused any outside oversight from the existing Iranian military.
5. As well as the United States, even after Iraq used (banned) chemical and biological weapons (Sabet and Safshekan, 2019, pp. 102–3; Hiltermann, 2007, pp. 151–67).
6. The Iranian military did rebuild its missile programme after the war as a 'conventional deterrent umbrella' that allowed the IRGC to recruit and train proxies more confidently outside of Iran's territorial boundaries, short of provoking the proxy state's retaliation. See Sabet and Safshekan, 2019, p.104.
7. Carter notes this mood in his 1980 State of the Union address: 'In response to the abhorrent act in Iran, our Nation has never been aroused and unified so greatly in peacetime.'
8. The IRGC successfully siphoned off members of the secular Amal Party by drawing on religious symbolism, which provided a source of hope to the Lebanese militants at a time when it was in short supply. See Axworthy, 2013, pp. 222–3; Norton, 1987, pp. 63–4, 167–87; Qassem, 2005, p. 235.
9. The designation 'State Sponsor of Terrorism' was not made official until 19 January 1984.
10. This was further confirmed by the George H. W. Bush administration in January 1992.
11. Still, the first sale of weapons to Tehran took place in 1981, a year before Dodge was taken hostage in Lebanon.
12. For instance, Bill Clinton, in his nomination acceptance speech on

29 August 1996, reminded Americans that 'as long as Iran trains, supports, and protects terrorists . . . they will pay a price from the United States'.

13. According to Bush administration officials, including Iran in the speech was less calculation and more rhetorical device / prop, given the need for 'three' to make up an axis. See Pollack, 2004, p. 352. For more on the repercussions of the speech, see Heradstveit and Bonham, 2007.

14. For a broader look at the relationship between the United States and the Khatami regime, see: Crist, 2012, pp. 416–39. Iran originally formed SCIRI in November 1982, recruiting Iraqi refugees from the Shi'i Islamist Da'wa Party and other exiled Iraqi dissidents to aid in the war against Saddam. See Ostovar, 2018, pp. 1244–6.

15. Numerous Iranian-backed militias were incorporated into the Iraqi government's umbrella Popular Mobilization Forces (PMF), formed by *Āyatollāh* Ali al-Sistani in a 2014 *fatwa* to defeat the Islamic State. See Kirmanj and Sadq, 2018, p. 158; IFP, 6 August 2016.

16. Both as instigator and, in the case of ISIS, opponent.

17. Approval numbers decreased between July and September 2015 from 33% to 21%. See Pew Research, 8 September 2015.

18. For instance, Iran's participation in international organisations like the United Nations.

19. Productive not in the conative sense of 'useful, or better', but in the agnostic sense as 'produces change', regardless of whether it should or not.

20. Of course, there could be more than one set of revolutionary actors at any given time, as this book suggests vis-à-vis ISIS.

References

Aalberts, T. E. 2012. *Constructing Sovereignty Between Politics and Law*. London: Routledge.

Adler, E. and Pouliot, V. 2011. 'International Practices'. *International Theory* 3 (1): 1–36.

Ahram, A. 2011. *Proxy Warriors: The Rise and Fall of State-Sponsored Militias*. Stanford: Stanford University Press.

Akbarzadeh, S. 2019. 'Proxy Relations: Iran and Hezbollah'. In Akbarzadeh, S. (ed.). *The Routledge Handbook of International Relations in the Middle East*, 321–9. London: Routledge.

Axworthy, M. 2008. *A History of Iran: Empire of the Mind*. New York: Basic Books.

Axworthy, M. 2013. *Revolutionary Iran: A History of the Islamic Republic*. Oxford: Oxford University Press.

Bacik, G. 2008. *Hybrid Sovereignty in the Arab Middle East: The Cases of Kuwait, Jordan, and Iraq.* New York: Palgrave Macmillan.

BBC. 2020. 'Qasem Soleimani: Trump Says US Killed "a Monster"'. *BBC News*, 7 January. Available at: <https://www.bbc.com/news/world-middle-east-51027619> (last accessed 14 September 2021).

Benjamin, D. and Simon, S. 2019. 'America's Great Satan', *Foreign Affairs* 98 (6). Available at: <https://www.foreignaffairs.com/articles/middle-east/2019-10-15/americas-great-satan> (last accessed 30 March 2020).

Bhabha, H. K. 1994. *The Location of Culture.* London: Routledge.

Butterfield, F. 1988. 'Arms for Hostages – Plain and Simple', *New York Times*, 27 November, sec. 7, p. 10.

Carter, J. 1980. 'State of the Union Address'. 23 January. Jimmy Carter Library. Available at: <https://www.jimmycarterlibrary.gov/assets/documents/speeches/su80jec.phtml> (last accessed 5 August 2022).

Chehabi, H. 2006. 'Iran and Lebanon in the Revolutionary Decade'. In Chehabi, H. (ed.). *Distant Relations: Iran and Lebanon in the Last 500 Years.* New York: I. B. Tauris.

Crist, D. 2012. *The Twilight War: The Secret History of America's Thirty-Year Conflict with Iran.* New York: Penguin Press.

Derrida, J. 1998. *Of Grammatology.* Baltimore: Johns Hopkins University Press.

Dillon, M. 1995. 'Sovereignty and Governmentality: From the Problematics of the "New World Order" to the Ethical Problematic of the World Order'. *Alternatives* 20 (3): 332–3.

Eisenstadt, M., Knights, M., and Ali A. 2011. 'Iran's Influence in Iraq: Countering Tehran's Whole-of-Government Approach'. Policy Focus #111, April. Washington, D.C.: Washington Institute for Near East Policy.

Fattahi, K. 2016. 'Two Weeks in January: America's Secret Engagement with Khomeini'. *BBC News*, 3 June. Available at: <https://www.bbc.com/news/world-us-canada-36431160> (last accessed 2 September 2021).

Feuerherd, P. 2017. 'How the Iran Hostage Crisis Changed International Journalism'. *JSTOR*, 4 November. Available at: <https://daily.jstor.org/how-the-iran-hostage-crisis-changed-international-journalism/> (last accessed 23 June 2021).

Foucault, M. 1978. *The History of Sexuality, Volume 1: An Introduction.* New York: Pantheon.

Foucault, M. 1991. *Discipline and Punish: The Birth of a Prison.* London: Penguin.

Gilpin, R. 1981. *War and Change in World Politics.* Cambridge: Cambridge University Press.

Glanville, L. 2013. 'The Myth of "Traditional" Sovereignty'. *International Studies Quarterly* 57 (1): 79–90.

Goldenberg, I. 2020. 'Will Iran's Response to the Soleimani Strike Lead to War?'. *Foreign Affairs*, 2 January. Available at: <https://www.foreignaffai rs.com/articles/iran/2020-01-03/will-irans-response-soleimani-strike-lead -war> (last accessed 29 February 2020).

Heradstveit, D. and Bonham, G. M. 2007. 'What the Axis of Evil Metaphor Did to Iran'. *Middle East Journal* 61 (3): 421–40.

Hijazi, I. A. 1991. 'Talks in Iran Seek to Free Hostages'. *New York Times*, 17 March, 18.

Hiltermann, J. R. 2007. 'Outsiders as Enablers: Consequences and Lessons from International Silence on Iraq's Use of Chemical Weapons during the Iran–Iraq War'. In Potter, L. G. and Sick, G. G. (eds). *Iran, Iraq, and Legacies of War*, 151–67. London: Palgrave Macmillan.

Horton, A. 2020. 'Soleimani's Legacy: The Gruesome, Advanced IEDs that Haunted U.S. Troops in Iraq', *Washington Post*, 3 January. Available at: <https://www.washingtonpost.com/national-security/2020/01/03/sole imanis-legacy-gruesome-high-tech-ieds-that-haunted-us-troops-iraq/> (last accessed 10 September 2021).

IFP Editorial Staff. 2016. 'General Soleimani to Play Major Role in Mosul Operation: Iraqi Spokesman', *IFP News*, 6 August. Available at: <https://if pnews.com/general-soleimani-play-major-role-mosul-operation-iraqi-spo kesman> (last accessed 30 March 2020).

Juneau, T. 2016. 'Iran's Policy Towards the Houthis in Yemen: A Limited Return on a Modest Investment'. *International Affairs* 92 (3): 647–63.

Kagan, K. 2006–7. 'Iran's Proxy War against the United States and the Iraqi Government'. *Iraqi Report*. Washington, D.C.: Institute for the Study of War.

Kepel, G. 2021. *Jihad: The Trail of Political Islam*. London: Bloomsbury Academic.

Kessler, G. 2007. '2003 Memo Says Iranian Leaders Backed Talks'. *Washington Post*, 14 February. Available at: <https://www.washingtonpost.com/wp-dyn/content/article/2007/02/13/AR2007021301363.html> (last accessed 14 September 2021).

Kia, S. 2017. 'Iran: The Story of Proxy Militias'. *The Hill*, 6 March. Available at: <https://thehill.com/blogs/congress-blog/foreign-policy/322443-iran -the-story-of-proxy-militias> (last accessed 30 March 2020).

Kirmanj, S. and Sadq, A. K. 2018. 'Iran's Foreign Policy towards Iraq and Syria: Strategic Significance and Regional Power Balance'. *The Journal of Social, Political, and Economic Studies* 43 (1&2): 152–72.

Kornbluh, P. and Byrne, M. 1993. *The Iran-Contra Scandal: The Declassified History*. New York: New Press.

Krasner, S. 1999. *Sovereignty: Organized Hypocrisy.* Princeton: Princeton University Press.

Lieberman, J. 2006. 'Why We Need More Troops in Iraq'. *Washington Post,* 29 October. Available at: <https://www.washingtonpost.com/wp-dyn /content/article/2006/12/28/AR2006122801055.html> (last accessed 16 September 2021).

Lyons, G. M. and Mastanduno, M. (eds). 1995. *Beyond Westphalia? State Sovereignty and International Intervention.* Baltimore: Johns Hopkins University Press.

Meislin, R. J. 1987. 'Iran-Contra Hearings'. *New York Times,* 18 July, sec. 1, 1.

Muñoz, C. 2017. 'Iran Nears Completion of "Shiite Crescent" Across Middle East'. *The Washington Times,* 5 December.

New York Times. 1987. 'Arms, Hostages, and Contras: How a Secret Foreign Policy Unraveled'. 19 November, 12.

Norris, A. 2000. 'Carl Schmitt's Political Metaphysics: On the Secularization of "the Outermost Sphere"'. *Theory & Event* 4 (1).

Norton, A. 1987. *Amal and the Shia: The Struggle for the Soul of Lebanon.* Austin: University of Texas Press.

Norval, A. J. 1999. 'Hybridization: The Im/Purity of the Political'. In Edkins, J., Persram, N. and Pin-Fat, V. (eds). *Sovereignty and Subjectivity,* 99–114. Boulder, CO: Lynne Rienner.

Obama, B. 2015. 'Remarks by the President on the Iran Nuclear Deal'. 5 August. American University, Washington, D.C. Obama White House Archives. Available at: <https://obamawhitehouse.archives.gov/the-pre ss-office/2015/08/05/remarks-president-iran-nuclear-deal> (last accessed 5 August 2022).

Obama, B. 2016. 'Statement by the President on Iran', 17 January.

Ostovar, A. 2018. 'Iran, Its Clients, and the Future of the Middle East: The Limits of Religion'. *International Affairs* 94 (6): 1237–55.

Parsi, T. 2007. *Treacherous Alliance: The Secret Dealings of Israel, Iran, and the United States.* New Haven, CT: Yale University Press.

Pew Research. 2015. 'Support for Iran Nuclear Agreement Falls'. 8 September. Available at: <https://www.pewresearch.org/politics/2015/09/08/support -for-iran-nuclear-agreement-falls/> (last accessed 14 August 2021).

Pollack, K.M. 2004. *The Persian Puzzle: The Conflict between Iran and America.* New York: Random House.

Priest, D. 2006. 'Attacking Iran May Trigger Terrorism', *Washington Post,* 2 April. Available at: <https://www.washingtonpost.com/archive/politics /2006/04/02/attacking-iran-may-trigger-terrorism-span-classbankheadus

-experts-wary-of-military-action-over-nuclear-programspan/23cf71d9-d2
cc-4f38-864e-da1f626107e0/> (last accessed 16 September 2021).

Prozorov, S. 2016. *Foucault, Freedom and Sovereignty*. London: Routledge.

Qassem, N. 2005. *Hizbullah: The Story from Within*. London: Saqi.

Ranstorp, M. 1997. *Hizb'allah in Lebanon: The Politics of the Western Hostage Crisis*. New York: St Martins Press.

Reagan, R. 1990. *An American Life*. New York: Simon & Schuster.

Saad, L. 2016. 'Gallup Vault: Reaction to Iran-Contra 30 Years Ago'. *Gallup*, 25 November. Available at: <https://news.gallup.com/vault/198164/gal lup-vault-reaction-iran-contra-years-ago.aspx> (last accessed 16 September 2021).

Sabet, F. and Safshekan, R. 2019. 'The Revolutionary Guard in Iranian Domestic and Foreign Power Politics'. In Akbarzadeh, S. (ed.). *The Routledge Handbook of International Relations in the Middle East*, 96–109. London: Routledge.

Schmitt C. 2006. *Political Theology: Four Chapters on the Concept of Sovereignty*. Chicago: University of Chicago Press.

Tabatabai, A. M. and Clarke, C. P. 2019. 'Iran's Proxies Are More Powerful than Ever'. RAND Corporation, 16 October. Available at: <https://www.rand.org/blog/2019/10/irans-proxies-are-more-powerful-than-ever.html> (last accessed 30 March 2020).

Torres, J. 2015. 'McConnell: Iran Deal a Result of "Flawed Perspective"'. *ABC News Radio*, 14 July. Available at: <http://abcnewsradioonline.com /politics-news/mcconnell-iran-deal-a-result-of-flawed-perspective.html> (last accessed 14 August 2021).

Tower, J., Muskie, E. and Scowcroft, B. 1987. *Report of the President's Special Review Board*, 26 February. Washington, D.C.: U.S. Government Printing Office.

Trofimov, Y. 2016. 'After Islamic State, Fears of a "Shiite Crescent" in Mideast'. *Wall Street Journal*, 29 September.

Trump, D. J. 2020. 'President Trump Statement on Death of Iranian Commander'. *C-Span*, 3 January. Available at: <https://www.c-span.org /video/?467859-1/president-trump-speaks-air-strike-killed-iranian-com mander> (last accessed 14 September 2021).

Walker, R. B. J. 1993. *Inside/Outside: International Relations as Political Theory*. Cambridge: Cambridge University Press.

Ward, A. 2020. 'The Case for Killing Qassem Soleimani'. *Vox*, 8 January. Available at: <https://www.vox.com/world/2020/1/8/21055785/trump -iran-case-for-kill-qassem-soleimani> (last accessed 29 February 2020).

Washington Post. 2007 'Tougher on Iran'. Editorial, 21 August. Available at:

<https://www.washingtonpost.com/wp-dyn/content/article/2007/08/20
/AR2007082001581.html> (last accessed 12 September 2021).

Weber, M. 1946 [1921]. 'Politics as a Vocation'. *Wikisource*. Available at:
<http://fs2.american.edu/dfagel/www/class%20readings/weber/politicsa
savocation.pdf> (last accessed 20 March 2020).

Wehrey, F. Thaler, D. E., Bensahel, N., Cragin, K., Green, J. D., Kaye, D. D.,
Oweidat, N. and Li, J. J. 2009. *Dangerous but not Omnipotent: Exploring
the Reach and Limitations of Iranian Power in the Middle East*. Santa Monica:
RAND Corporation.

Weisman, S. R. 2003. 'U.S. Takes Softer Tone on Iran, Once in the "Axis of
Evil"'. *New York Times*, 29 October. Available at: <https://www.nytimes
.com/2003/10/29/world/us-takes-softer-tone-on-iran-once-in-the-axis
-of-evil.html> (last accessed 14 September 2021).

Wright, R. 2007. 'Iranian Unit to Be Labeled "Terrorist"'. *Washington Post*,
15 August. Available at: <https://www.washingtonpost.com/wp-dyn
/content/article/2007/08/14/AR2007081401662.html>   (last   accessed
11 September 2021).

12

Conclusion: Recalling the Hybrid Revolutionary

Ondrej Ditrych, Jan Daniel and Jakub Záhora

Latour (1999) famously engaged in 'recalling' Actor–Network Theory (ANT) years after it was introduced to social theory – using but then also characteristically subverting a metaphor borrowed from the automotive industry in relation to faulty cars. Ideas cannot really be recalled like cars once they are out in the world, and they start to act in and on the world. Therefore, Latour argued, the best one can do is not to abandon the creature one has created but 'continue all the way in developing its strange potential' (Latour, 1999, p. 24). At the end of this book, we are at a different situation – we *can*, for now, recall the notion of the hybrid revolutionary developed at the outset of this project and then confronted with a variety of empirical matter. What does this recalling suggest about its future potential for enquiring how political orders are subverted – and maintained on diverse scales, from local to global? How does our car perform after driving some strange ways, and what it can do in the world?

The notion of the hybrid revolutionary employed in this volume seeks to illuminate the paradox of movements that aim to reorder the political order radically by means of revolutionary practice, yet do so by recoding and repurposing, rather than rejecting the constitutive norms and everyday management practices of this order. The fundamental assumption underlying analysis of the political dynamics investigated in this volume, not particularly revolutionary in itself within the realm of philosophy and social theory, is that there are no pure forms. The basic perspective, inspired by the work of Deleuze and Guattari, and dialogical encounters with it, enables us to unpack this impurity ('hybridity') and theorise revolutionary processes in global politics today.

Revolutionaries in the modern epochal time frame are, we propose, nomadic war machines occupying the milieu of exteriority outside the enclosed space of the state. They are *bodies without organs*, resisting the interiorisation function of the state which encloses, measures and regulates. Where the state acts to preserve its organs, war machines are after destruction – yet turned into an experimental, creative movement. *Rhizomatic* rather than arboreal in structure, they are, however, also heterogeneous assemblages that are in a constitutive and complementary relationship with the state, appropriating and absorbing, repacking and repurposing parts of the previously existing state structures – as well as neoliberal government routines, snippets of mass popular culture codes or pieces of the (hyper)modern infrastructure of global flows.

It is this relationship that makes them hybrids. The preceding chapters trace how revolutionary actors seek to overhaul particular political constellations, driven by alternative visions of political ordering, and yet their subjectivities and modes of conduct remain inevitably intertwined and embedded in the conditions they contest. In other words, there is constant metamorphosis as war machine and state, two diagrams of power historically taking diverse concrete shapes, act on each other through multiple hybridisation processes, absorbing elements of the power structures they contest into their own practice and subjectivity.

War machine is not a concept, with inevitably essentialising action for the token – such as a particular revolutionary entity – to which it is attributed. It is, rather, a set of intensities that can be activated in the world and its understanding. In this book, we forced it to dialogical, and sometimes critical encounters. Perhaps we did not – not yet, at least – manage to *deconceptualise* it, and our particular recoding of the movements treated in this book betrays not an entirely severed relationship with the epistemology that seeks to render, in a manner echoing the efforts of the state form, social and political dynamics legible, classifiable and manageable. What we hope to have achieved, on the other hand, is an illumination of the various forms and scales of entanglement of (hybrid) revolutionaries and the political orders they seek to upend – so staking out a new space for thinking global order, violence and revolution as not a single dramatic and spectacular event, but rather a process in which hybrid assemblages of revolt and counterrevolt *become* and interact.

This is the intended relationship of this book to the revolutionary war machine and the state – rendering visible features and intensities in the process of their entangled becoming, the hybrid *constitution* of the revolutionary subjectivity (and the state's) and the subject *effects* of revolutionary practice in the normative order which hybrid revolutionaries seek to remake. Even if they fail, hybrid revolutionaries leave their trace on the order – engendering counterrevolutionary practices that change this order in non-intended ways, at times also appropriating ('innovative') features of revolutionary war machines by the state apparatuses.

What does this entangled becoming, as investigated in this book, mean for advancing the scholarship on revolutionary actors and political violence subversive to the present political orders? In the remainder of this concluding chapter, we propose three broad insights relevant for making sense of revolutionary processes and their effects that are illuminated by employing the concept of the hybrid revolutionary actor: the notion of entanglements between state form and war machine throughout the revolutionary processes; translocality of the revolutionary dynamics; and overcoming the agency / structure binaries in understanding the subjectivity and practices of these actors.

Revolutionaries Between the State and the War Machine

Following Deleuze and Guattari's own work on the matter, the cases in this book explore the unstable and fluid boundaries between the war machine, the irreducible element of war and revolutionary change that has resisted sedentarisation and interiorisation by the state apparatus, and the state forms, and various entanglements of the two in the political life. The previous chapters thus highlight how revolution is always seeking to enact some radically new reality, imagined in utopian terms, but also how revolutionary vision and practice are heterogenous multiplicities – alloys that combine and collapse old and new, disrupt as well as stabilise. The Deleuzian perspective here allows us to unpack this heterogeneity and point out the hybridity of political utopias and a range of violent and non-violent practices that are intended to bring them about.

ISIS, the core focus of our explorations, is exemplary of these recombinations and appropriations across various registers. Indeed, as the authors of this volume repeatedly stress, ISIS cannot – in spite of various attempts of state apparatuses – be reduced to a singular entity which would capture and encapsulate its project. In Iraq and Syria, its militants quickly repurposed organs of the state and its bureaucratic infrastructures and *modus operandi*. In fact, as one of the chapters in this book points out, their direct predecessors, al-Qaʻida in Iraq, had been already developing their own forms of state-making before capturing those of their opponents.

Indeed, ISIS's transformative vision of utopian revolution was to be enacted through mundane bureaucratic governance that was, in its form, not that different from the one practised by many authoritarian governments around the region. At the same time, the vision of a global Caliphate was being enacted through practices that drew on various ideological and technological infrastructures, whether those of neoliberal self-improvement, previous revolutionary utopias or global communication networks. These were vastly different from the political practice of territorial rule by the entity in the Middle East and its justifications, as well as from the particular use of religious codes which were purportedly animating the global political vision. However, they have been inseparable from the enactment of the group as a whole. While ISIS's technological savvy has been repeatedly acknowledged as one of the key reasons behind the movement's rise to prominence on the global stage, the analysis in this volume makes it clear that the Islamists' use of modern communication technologies or managerial methods was not simply a tactical means. It rather goes to the heart of the constitution of a modern revolutionary subject that is composed of hybrid assemblages of various rationalities, conduct and (not only political) technologies. Although this is certainly true of every movement examined in this book (and others), the example of ISIS with its restorative political project makes this hybrid constitution of subjectivity clearly visible.

This is further highlighted by the fact that, in spite of ISIS's apparent rejection of practices associated with the dominant societal and political framework, its communication relied on mainstream pop culture tropes and visions of 'good life' recognisable to anybody consuming 'Western' cultural artefacts. Similarly, ISIS's operations were further closely related to and, as traced in this book, *reliant* on, routines of neoliberal government which are, indeed, one of the key constitutive features of the world that we – and ISIS – inhabit. While – as observed repeatedly in the preceding pages – the jihadist is portrayed as a figure alien to the modern self, and his or her *modus operandi* is constructed as an exemplarily abhorrent form of political violence, the infrastructure that enables and facilitates enactment of such subjectivity and practices is not strange to anybody familiar with the (neo)liberal market environment. Jihadi groups might be embroiled in a struggle against the state apparatus and imperial policies, but this very struggle is predicated on elements which constitute the modern political forms that underpin those of their adversaries. All of this shows that ISIS and other movements studied in this book are not so much the ultimate Other of the hegemonic order, or anachronistic machines seeking to reconstitute an idealised version of a political past; they are, rather, entities that materialise and signify how the revolutionary process is always composed of both hegemonic and counterhegemonic registers of thought and action.

ISIS is illuminating, rather than exceptional, in terms of these combinations – as other cases in the volume demonstrate. Echoing ISIS's appropriation of Baathist state structures and cadres to form what some predicated would in time become yet another 'normal state', Iran's revolutionaries underwent a swift sedentarisation that provided for lasting tensions between the state form and war machine in the Khomeinists' governmental assemblage resulting from different modes of conduct and thinking the movement and the state's place and role in the global political architecture. The complex relationship between the Iranian state and the Khomeinist revolutionary *avant-garde* thus again shows that the revolutionary subject is never just that. Not only does the existing order exercise normalising pressure on the revolutionary subjectivity, but the would-be transformative political vision is not impervious to the constellations to which it appears to be radically opposed. Similar dynamics have also been traced in the Bolshevik project, whose global anti-systemic ambitions were soon curtailed when faced with the pressures exercised by the established order. Still, in a manner similar to the ambiguous relationship of the Iranian state with revolutionary groups, the Bolshevik war machine retained some traces of its presence within the bureaucratised authoritarian state form.

These cases suggest that there are no pure forms and neat divisions. Even in the modern epochal time frame, we have never been modern (Latour, 1993). This book's reading of revolutionary forms sensitises us to the new forms of the well-known entanglement between the revolutionary desire for dissolution of all boundaries and the rapid establishment of new ones – encapsulated in the relations between the Deleuzian war machine and state form. The perspective put forward here builds on the perennial tensions between the two to illuminate that not only can the revolutionaries not escape the straitjacket of the political conditions which they contest; they are their embodiments to an extent situated at the border of the norm, expressions of the war machine that, however, appropriates, recodes and repurposes elements of the state form and sometimes colonises the latter's body organs.

Such an understanding challenges the mechanisms of radical othering of the revolutionary as the pest, *hostis humani generis*. ISIS, and the others, are of this world. This is not to condone their violence – nor any other practice that may be framed as emancipatory by the revolutionaries but turns out to be a product of the despotic war machine. Rather, it shows how revolutionary practice is embedded in and draws on the established repertoires of the normative order against which it stands in radical opposition – from horrifically violent performances of sovereignty to mundane disciplinary and biopolitical practices of modern liberal government intended to make the individual and population visible, actable – and ultimately docile. Revolutionary subjectivity is always relational and becoming – what matters are relations, compositions and flows, and durability is a contingent production. It features tensions between revolutionary desires, their capture and institutionalisation or stratification – not in linear succession, but at times with internally controversial simultaneity.

While the focus in this volume is on revolutionaries, by pointing out that there are no pure forms in global politics, it also opens up space to reflect on how the state form is never pure either, devoid of elements of war machine logic and dynamics. It is always a contingent hybrid, too – something that the stabilising practices of the state seek to conceal, together with its infamous origin, while rendering the revolutionary war machine as the radical Other and so (re)producing the normative order by illuminating the revolutionaries' practices of transgression. This has been showcased in this volume by tracing US strategies of representing Iran's revolutionary movement (and the state) as a pariah with significant effects on reinforcing the foundations of the *status quo* global political order – such as the sovereignty norm. The (relative) symmetry between the revolutionaries and the established powers in terms of adopting, appropriating and repurposing war machine and state elements, and their contingent complementarity, is something that we believe can also guide further research into global politics and prove to be a fertile ground for future theorising of both revolution and political order.

Translocality of the Revolutionary Practice

Developing the notion of the inherent hybridity of revolutionary thought and action, the volume further demonstrates that the relations, flows and disruptions generated by revolutionary practices in global politics tend to be translocal. They transcend the Westphalian grid of enclosure of the state system – and, as cases such as the Palestinian revolutionary projects show, this applies even to those efforts which appear to be centred around a vision of the normative nation state. Their practice and even strategy may be territorially bounded; their political utopias are not. The studies in this volume show the complex of highly localised, territorialising practices but also the deterritorialising, translocal ones affixed in the same heterogenous assemblage – and how the nomadological perspective is useful in dissolving these lines and transcending the nation state as a category of thought. They also show how the impurity of revolutionary ideals relates simultaneously to a variety of ideational structures in what perhaps is somewhat reductively termed 'order' here, hybridising and producing emergent effects of their own, and problematising the very notion of revolution's locale in space and time.

While the political horizon of these revolutionary projects might revolve around territorially bounded states, their practices reach out to multiple locales and to multiple registers. Even in the case of the Palestinian revolutionary groups seeking to reclaim their national homeland, not only did the revolutionaries engage in spatially dispersed practices, which, moreover, exploited aircraft technologies that at the time were marking the international and ignored national boundaries; their revolutionary visions were embedded in the local politics in camps, as well as the decolonisation movement seeking to overturn the global distribution of power – Palestinian political subjectivity could not be pinned down to one locale.

The Palestinian case further shows, importantly, that the translocality of revolutionary agency is related not only to the actual carrying out of revolutionary projects. The ideas which animate these projects are inherently translocal, ignoring state boundaries and circulating across various spaces in which they are (re)appropriated, modified and further transmitted (Selbin, 2010). While this has been accelerated by modern technologies and the emergence of cyberspace, the anti-colonial dynamics – which the Palestinian groups and the Iranian revolutionary state were both part of, although in different ways – demonstrate that even if material practices might in some cases be relegated to discrete physical spaces, the revolutionary movements are not comprehensible without ideational exchanges which transcend multiple, diverse boundaries. This is not meant to separate thought and action radically in a Cartesian manner, but rather to highlight that, as observed in the studies in this volume, revolutionary subjectivity cannot be reduced to one demarcated space nor, as the detected continuities between different revolutionary movements manifest, to a singular temporal frame.

To return to ISIS, this movement too betrays this translocality with considerable intensity. The localised everyday governance in the Middle East with its capital and local offices was in stark contrast not only to its globe-encompassing ambitions, but also to how these were translated into an array of globally dispersed practices. 'Lone-wolf attacks' and other personal acts of violence and resistance towards the existing constellations of power and their ordering mechanisms might appear as merely individual incidents but together they constitute the revolutionary subject that cannot be pinned down territorially. The ISIS project thus shows how contestations of the normative order take place across a variety of spaces, yet remain subjected to the same underlying logic.

But the translocality of revolutionary processes does not pertain only to revolutionary subject formation and the subject's transformatory (and simultaneously reconstructive) practices. The interplay and interaction between the (revolutionary) war machine and state forms lead to enactment of counter-practices seeking to disrupt the revolutionary projects and restore the existing order. In this regard, there is a link between governmental programmes to contain the Bolshevik threat in interwar Europe and the current countering / preventing violent extremism (C/PVE) policies which seek to mitigate the threat of 'radicalisation' amongst certain demographics. What connects them is not just the novelty of the interventions and ways of problematisation of processes perceived to feed into the revolutionary ethos and conduct, and the scale of resources invested in tackling the threat. Efforts to counteract hybrid revolutionaries are necessarily also located at different sites and at different intensities, encompassing global society.

These cases point out, then, that the drama of the state and war machine conflict is not played out within the confines of the chessboard – Deleuze and Guattari's nomadic war machines instead move in the smooth space represented by the go (Wei Chi) board, open and unconstrained. For hybrid revolutionaries, we propose, these planes intersect, and their movements betray a 'topographical complexity' (cf. Law, 1999) resulting from territorialising and deterritorialising practice, rules that are rejected but also repurposed and followed, scripts and political technologies – including territory itself – that are appropriated, repacked and repurposed, producing creative possibilities but also tensions in their constitution. All of this makes it difficult to *place* revolutionary action – to put it simply, where revolution starts and ends in space. To understand the various movements covered in this book better necessitates releasing our thought of revolution from the territorial trap: to make it *nomadic*, released from the dogmatic confinement (that also has a *security* function) that embraces the total subject (whose centre seeks to hold) in favour of activating our political consciousness to the multiplicity – contravening the conventional understanding of sovereignty – and creative motion of decentred elements affixed in transient and mutating (reassembling) assemblages.

The studies in this book illuminate the translocality of hybrid revolutionary actors. Their practice and even strategy may be territorially bounded; their political utopias are not. The story of their revolutions benefits from erasing state boundary lines within whose confines it is usually told. Like a true rhizome, the hybrid revolutionary has no beginning or end, only the middle – and that is where we propose to focus future, nomadic investigations.

Escaping the Agency / Structure Debates

Attending to entanglements between a revolutionary and the political order, of which the state apparatus is the key building element, advances the overcoming of aspects of the structure / agency binary in the study of the revolution. As we pointed out earlier, hybrid revolutionaries cannot dissociate from the structure of this order. They are not dependent on it either, simply locked in its *epistémé* or the flows of global neoliberal governmentality and unable to escape the straitjacket of the (modern) state and the rationalities and technologies whereby it rules at a distance and polices the economy. This is not to deny that these structural conditions shape revolutionaries' conduct, as the history of the Bolshevik revolutionary *avant-garde* turning into a sedentarised despotic state clearly shows. This and other cases of sedentarisation feed into, and maintain, the *status quo*, as the revolutionary agency is in some form reconciled with the structure that it embarked on disrupting.

Despite their (initial) radical alternative positionality to the Westphalian statescape, hybrid revolutionaries maintain a productive relationship with it – a relationship of constitution and complementarity. This relationship of revolutionary nomads and sedentaries is a dynamic one, producing contingent hybrids recoding elements borrowed from each other. In the case of hybrid revolutionaries, these elements include the constitutive norm of the Westphalian statescape, sovereignty or mechanisms of meaning-making through which resistance to the dominant order can even be made intelligible, communicated and acted upon. For the normative order, the emergence of a hybrid revolutionary who challenges it may lead to asserting its constitutive norms but also innovation to respond to the perceived threat. This innovation may comprise territorialisation and the increased control of previously smooth spaces, but also adapting states' apparatuses by borrowing features from the revolutionary war machine as networked, mobile and 'smoothing out space' (Weizman 2019). It emerges that the borrowing of elements between different modes of political existence ushers in constellations in which the distinction between (normative *status quo*) structure and the (revolutionary) actors is no longer sustainable. The two are intertwined and cannot be conceived without each other.

Thinking revolutionary movements as hybrid illuminates the intensities in the constitution of modern revolutionary subjectivity that result from the complementarity of the war machine and the state form, and generate a potential to understand better the violent pressures in the current order that the hybrid revolutionaries challenge yet also, unintentionally, participate in (re)producing. The hybrid revolutionary does stake out thinking space for detecting the current limits of thinking and practising (radical) alterity, and the conditions for creating new, alternative means of organised social life. Moreover, thinking revolutionary practice as hybrid provokes reassessment of the normative fabric of the current order beyond its daily and periodic contestations (identified by Ruggie (1986) as incremental or conjectural forms of social time) by pointing out its key underlying features that, wilfully or not, are also reproduced by its radical contenders.

What is missing in this nomadological framework, on the other hand, as pointed out by Richards in her chapter, is – at least for now – the emancipatory potential of revolutionary action conceived in these terms, even as such a concept departs from the many strands of extant revolutionary theory. While the role of discursive recourses to emancipation has been foregrounded in many existing studies, it remains to be investigated how it figures within the nomadic constellations of the revolution.

Travels with Hybrid Revolutionaries

The story of the hybrid revolutionary does not end with this book; nor does the story of tensions and sometimes violent ruptures in the global order that can be told using the hybrid vocabulary – indeed a fitting one since hybridity defines the world we inhabit and, despite all stabilising and sanitising practice, is the norm rather than the exception. The book may, we recognise, unintentionally feed into the recent trend of locating the hybrid revolutionary subjectivity in the Middle East, with the effect of reifying the Orientalist notion of the region's exceptionality. Yet, on the contrary, in our rendition the hybrid perspective is meant to destabilise the cartographical and hierarchical understanding of order, (ab)normality and (counter)conduct. It sensitises us to ambivalences and tensions that are part and parcel of the existing political realities and their underpinnings. It proposes a novel perspective on how political order is maintained, challenged and reconstituted, not only in the peripheries, but in the centre too. Having recalled it in this Conclusion, to diagnose some key features of how it operates 'out there', we now release it again, hoping it will be of use.

For existing movements, ISIS and others, or those yet to emerge – including in the centres of liberal normative order – are also likely to feature in the perennial contest (and complementarity) of the war machine and the state in the future. The images showing the storming of the US Capitol in January 2021 are now icons of violent pressures inside Global North societies faced with resistance to the centre and undermining its hegemony. War machines do not just rise in global peripheries. Deleuze and Guattari were already alerting their readers in the 1980s to the fact that not only does the state ('an empty form of appropriation') colonise the people, but the people may also reform themselves into a war machine rising against their state, and even ward off the state form (Deleuze and Guattari, 1987; see also Lambert, 2010). The Trumpist war machine that channelled the desire for a radical break with the present order and temporarily took over the state apparatus is a case in point. It is not to disappear in any sort of healing process ending the 'uncivil war', as Joe Biden seems to think – it is no longer an organ of the state's body politics. So the last words are Donald Trump's: 'We will be back in some form.'

References

Deleuze, G. and Guattari, F. 1987. *A Thousand Plateaus: Capitalism and Schizophrenia*. Minneapolis: Minnesota University Press.

Lambert, G. 2010. 'The War-Machine and "a People Who Revolt"'. *Theory & Event* 13 (3).

Latour, B. 1993. *We Have Never Been Modern*. Cambridge, MA: Harvard University Press.

Latour, B. 1999. 'On Recalling ANT'. *Sociological Review* 47 (1): 15–25.

Law, J. 1999. 'After ANT: Complexity, Naming and Topology'. *Sociological Review* 47 (1): 1–14.

Ruggie, J. G. 1986. 'Social Time and International Policy'. In Karns, M. (ed.). *Persistent Patterns and Emergent Structures in a Waning Century*. New York: Praeger.

Selbin, E. 2010. *Revolution, Rebellion, Resistance: The Power of Story*. London: Zed Books.

Weizman, E. 2019. *Forensic Architecture: Violence at the Threshold of Detectability*. New York: Zone Books.

Index

EU representative:
Easy Access System Europe
Mustamäe tee 50, 10621 Tallinn, Estonia
Gpsr.requests@easproject.com

www.ingramcontent.com/pod-product-compliance
Lightning Source LLC
Chambersburg PA
CBHW070323270326
41926CB00017B/3737